ORGANIZATIONAL CHANGE

Human Resource Management Series Foreword

The two integrating themes of this series are organizational change, and the strategic role of the human resource function.

The 1980s witnessed a fundamental shift in thinking with respect to the organizational role of the personnel function. That shift is typically reflected in the change of title – to human resource management – and revolves around the notion that effective human resource management is a critical dimension of an organization's competitive advantage. Personnel or human resource management is thus now more widely accepted as a strategic business function, in contrast with the traditional image of a routine administrative operation concerned with hiring, training, paying and terminating.

The range of issues with which personnel managers must now deal has widened considerably, as has the complexity and significance of those issues. Conventional texts in this subject area typically have the advantage of comprehensiveness, by offering a broad overview of the function, its responsibilities, and key trends. Such coverage is always bought at the expense of depth. The aim of this series, therefore, is not to replace traditional personnel or human resource texts, but to complement those works by offering in-depth, informed and accessible treatments of important and topical themes, written by specialists in those areas and supported by systematic research.

The series is thus based on a commitment to contemporary changes in the human resource function, and to the direction of those changes. This has involved a steady shift in management attention towards improved employee welfare and rights, genuinely equal opportunity, wider employee involvement in organization management and ownership, changing the nature of work and organization structures through business 'reengineering', and towards personal skills growth and development at all organizational levels. This series documents and explains these trends and developments, indicating the progress that has been achieved, and aims to contribute to best management practice through fresh empirical evidence and practical example.

David Buchanan
Series Editor
Loughborough University Business School

ORGANIZATIONAL CHANGE: A PROCESSUAL APPROACH

Patrick Dawson
The University of Adelaide

In Memory of My Father

Paul Chapman Publishing Ltd
144 Liverpool Road
London
N1 1LA

British Library Cataloguing in Publication Data

Dawson, Patrick
Organizational Change: Processual
Approach. – (Human Resource Mangement
Series)
I. Title II. Series
658.3

ISBN 1 85396 237 6

Typeset by Inforum, Rowlands Castle, Hants
Printed and bound in Great Britain by
Athenaeum Press Ltd, Newcastle-upon-Tyne

A B C D E F G H 9 8 7 6 5 4

CONTENTS

LIST OF FIGURES

ACKNOWLEDGEMENTS

This book is based on a series of case studies carried out in three different countries over a period of twelve years. It draws on material from a range of different research groups, universities and organizations.

Acknowledgment is given to members of the New Technology Research Group at the University of Southampton; participants in the Alvey DHSS Demonstrator Project at the University of Surrey; colleagues in the New Technology and The Firm research programme at the University of Edinburgh; and members of the Collaborative Programme on Total Quality Management at Queensland University of Technology and the University of Wollongong. These programmes, plus The Successful Management of Change Project at the University of Adelaide, provided environments of academic support and intellectual curiosity.

In carrying out the research, I would like to thank all the organizations that supported the study and allowed access to personnel and records over long periods of time. I would also like to thank the managers, union officials and employees who participated in the study and spoke openly about the problems and practice of managing change. In particular, I would like to thank Greg Adams, Bob Arnold, Colin Bale, Bob Brown, Ian Gordon, Raymond Grigg, Robin Lamincraft, Alistair Lucas, Barry Matthews, Percy Reed, Terry Seabrook, Charlie Shears, Wally Shuff, Chris Taylor and Ross Willmot.

Financial support for the research has been provided by a range of institutions, including the Economic and Social Research Council (ESRC); the Alvey Directorate of the Department of Trade and Industry and the Science and Engineering Research Council (SERC); the SERC/ESRC Joint Committee; the Australian Research Council (ARC); the Universities of Edinburgh and Adelaide; the Commonwealth Scientific and Industrial Research Organization (CSIRO); and the Key Centre in Strategic Management at the University of Queensland.

In transcribing cases of taped interviews I would like to thank Paula Hollamby, Trish Lyndon, Lyn Mitchell and Fina Peter. Particular thanks are due to Althea Leonard who worked efficiently and showed great skill and ability in dealing with an array of interview material and accompanying accents. Without this help much of the data would still remain inaccessible. Thanks are also due to the students of the Graduate School of Management at the University of Adelaide, who motivated the writing of the book and showed great enthusiasm for projects that sought to combine theory with practice.

For commenting on the initial book proposal and/or parts of the manuscript, I would like to thank Graham Byrne, Lino Dilernia, Nigel Gilbert, Muayyad Jabri, Liz Kummerow, Arie Lewin, Ian McLoughlin, Juliet Webster, Alan Wells and the anonymous reviewers commissioned by Paul Chapman Publishing. I would also like to acknowledge the academic insights that arose from discussions with David Buchanan, Sarah Buckland, Jon Clark and Jan Webb. Finally, I would like to give special thanks to David Buchanan and Sue Thomson who provided their own critical comments on large sections of the text and have been a constant source of encouragement for the completion of an at times daunting piece of work.

ABBREVIATIONS AND ACRONYMS

AGWU:	Australian Government Workers Union
AI:	Artificial Intelligence
AMWU:	Amalgamated Metal Workers' Union
ARC:	Australian Research Council
ASLEF:	Associated Society of Locomotive Engineers and Firemen
CDC:	Communication Data Control
CEO:	Chief Executive Officer
CLS:	**Central Linen Service**
CSIRO:	**Commonwealth Scientific and Industrial Research Organization**
DHSS:	Department of Health and Social Security
DMT:	**Division of Manufacturing Technology (of CSIRO)**
DSS:	Department of Social Security
EDS:	Electronic Data Systems
ENT:	Electronic News Gathering
GM:	**General Motors**
GMHAL:	**General Motors-Holden's Automotive Limited**
GT:	Group Technology
HP:	**Hewlett Packard**
IBM:	International Business Machines
IKBS:	Intelligent Knowledge-Based Systems
ISO:	International Standards Organization
JIT:	Just-in-Time*
LSOC:	Large-Scale Organizational Change
LST:	Large-Scale Transition
MBWA:	Management by Walking Around Management by Wandering Around

MIS: Management Information System
MNC: Multi-National Corporation

NIES: National Industry Extension Scheme
NUR: National Union of Railwaymen

OD: Organizational Development

PCAL: Pirelli Cables Australia Limited
PFA: Process Flow Analysis

QA: Quality Assurance
QC: Quality Circle
QMD: Queensferry Microwave Division (of HP)
QTD: Queensferry Telecommunications Division (of HP)
QWL: Quality of Work Life

SAHC: South Australia Health Commission
SERC: Science and Engineering Research Council

TMCA: Toyota Motor Corporation Limited
TOPS: Total Operations Processing System
TPP: Total Process Prove-out
TQC: Total Quality Control
TQM: Total Quality Management
TSSA: Transport Salaried Staffs' Association

UAAI: United Australian Automotive Industries Limited

VBU: Vehicle Builders Union

Note: Bold type indicates a company where a case history has been used as illustration.

* The acronym is used to refer to the management strategy itself or to the philosophy and thinking behind it. In the text the phrase 'just-in-time' is used in other cases.

1

ORGANIZATIONS IN TRANSITION

Introduction

The gradual emergence of an integrated economic European Community, the growth and development of industries in the Asia Pacific region, and the decline in the buoyancy of the North American market as Japan replaces the United States as number one in the world economic order, have all influenced the ongoing process of organizational adaptation to rapidly changing global demands. What the outcomes of these changes have meant for organizations and how these processes of transformation have been managed is the central theme of this book. The ever increasing body of management literature in this area relies heavily on anecdotes and metaphors in the formulation of prescriptive solutions to the problems of managing transitions (see, for example, Carlson, 1989; Kanter, 1990) whereas the work presented here sets out to provide the reader with a detailed understanding of organizational change through the systematic analysis of new empirical data. To this end, longitudinal case material is drawn from American, European and Australian corporations and a conceptual framework for explaining the process of transition is developed. The case studies are used to highlight a broad depth and range of change issues and how these are managed in a number of different organizational settings. The integration of theories of change with management practice is central to the objective of providing an innovative book on organizational change that is of academic value and practical worth to students of management and, in particular, to those undergoing postgraduate and post-experience courses on the management of change.

The new bias for organizational action

In the management literature, there is evidence of a growing call for managers to act as leaders of change and to be proactive in the search for strategies that will make organizations more competitive (Ulrich and Lake,

1991:77–92; Vesey, 1991:23–33). This new bias for organizational action is based on the premise that companies which cannot manage ongoing change will cease to exist (Peters, 1987:401; Gray and Smeltzer, 1990:615–16). Typically, what is advocated is a revolution in the world of management, through the adoption of policies which discard traditional hierarchical structures, rigid bureaucratic systems and inflexible work practices (Dunphy and Stace, 1990:11–12). For example, Rosabeth Moss Kanter, in her popular book *When Giants Learn To Dance* (1990:344), claims that competitive corporations of the future must develop a strategic business action agenda towards 'flatter, more focused organizations stressing synergies; entrepreneurial enclaves pushing new stream businesses for the future; and strategic alliances or stakeholder partnerships stretching capacity by combining the strength of several organizations'.

The new bias for organizational action rests with an emergent breed of manager whose job involves successfully managing strategic change in work structures, process and product technologies, employment relations and organizational culture. These managers are expected to compete in the new 'corporate olympics' and balance the apparent contradictions between, first, centralizing resources whilst creating autonomous business units and, secondly, replacing staff through 'lean' restructuring programmes, yet maintaining employee-centred personnel policies (Kanter, 1990:17–31). According to Kanter, the seven managerial skills required of these new business athletes comprise: an ability to achieve results without relying on organizational status; the ability to be self-confident and humble; maintaining high ethical standards; attaining co-operative competitiveness; gaining satisfaction from results rather than financial rewards; to be able to work across functions and find new synergies; and the need to be aware of the process, as well as the outcomes, of change (1990:359–65).

The intention behind the listing of managerial competencies is to help managers become 'masters' rather than 'victims' of change. However, due to an over-reliance on metaphors, Kanter presents little of any real use to the discerning manager. As Gabor and Petersen (1991:98) note: 'Cliches and banalities depicted by chapter headings . . . detract measurably from Ms Kanter's fervent and sincere hope that America's business community will be energised to change direction to compete and succeed in the current and future global business climate'.

Questions concerning the substance of change and how the process can be managed in today's context remain unanswered. Whilst there are numerous academic and practitioner models available that seek to explain various aspects of the process of organizational change (Blake and Mouton, 1964; Doz and Prahalad, 1987; Greiner, 1972; Lawrence and Lorsch, 1969; McWhinney, 1990), the predominant models on the management of change remain rooted to the orthodoxy imposed by Lewin's (1951) seminal work. Almost without exception, contemporary management texts uncritically adopt Lewin's three-phase model of planned change (see, for example,

Aldag and Stearns, 1991:710–29; Vecchio, Hearn and Southey, 1992:590–618). The three-stage model of 'unfreezing', 'changing' and 'refreezing' (Lewin, 1952) is commonly taught on management courses and often applied by practitioners in the field of Organizational Development (see Chapter 2). Although this theory has proven to be useful in understanding planned change under relatively stable conditions, with the continuing and dynamic nature of change in today's business world, it no longer makes sense to implement a planned process for 'freezing' changed behaviours. Implementing stability and reinforcing behaviour which conforms to a rigid set of procedures for new work arrangements does not meet the growing requirements for employee flexibility and structural adaptation to the unfolding and complex nature of ongoing change processes. The inability of this model to deal with the continuing dynamics of change highlights the need for an alternative framework. An approach which is less prescriptive and more analytical would further our understanding of the processes involved, and enable practitioners to adopt a broader perspective on the problems and practice of managing change. To this end, a *processual framework* is developed for explaining the process of transition, from the initial conception of a need to change through to the operation of new organizational arrangements.

Towards a processual framework of change

The processual framework developed in this book adopts the view that change is a complex and dynamic process which should not be solidified or treated as a series of linear events. In Chapter 3, three general timeframes associated with organizational transitions are identified. These comprise:

- Conception of a need to change
- Process of organizational transition
- Operation of new work practices and procedures

This framework incorporates the temporal element of large-scale change by commencing with a period which is defined as the conception of a need to change and ending with a post-transitional period of operation, in which emerging organizational arrangements and patterns of working relationships are further refined and developed during ongoing processes of change. Although it is, in practice, difficult to identify the start or completion of a major change programme, it is useful for analytical purposes to identify periods of initial awareness (conception of the need to change) and periods when organizational resources are withdrawn from the management of particular change programmes and the new organizational arrangements form part of daily work routines (operation of new work practices and procedures). In between these two periods lie the complex non-linear processes of change which may comprise a range of different activities and events. Once again, whilst it may prove analytically useful to identify and group a number of activities, tasks and decision-making processes, such as the search and assessment of options or implementation, these should not be treated as representing a series of sequential stages in the process of change (as with conventional stage models). The approach taken here is that organizations undergoing transition should be studied 'as-it-happens' so that processes associated with change can reveal themselves over time and in context.

This temporal framework of change can also be used to accommodate the existence of a number of competing histories on the process of organizational transition (these organizational histories may be further refined, replaced and developed over time). The dominant or 'official version' of change may often reflect the political positioning of certain key individuals or groups within an organization, rather than serving as a true representation of the practice of transition management. They may also act to shape, constrain and promote the direction and content of future change programmes and as such warrant examination under this approach.

In conjunction with this temporal framework, three main groups of determinants are used to explain the process of organizational transition, namely, the substance, context and politics of change. The substance of change is taken to refer to the type and scale of organizational change. For example, do the changes require a transformation in plant, divisional and/or corporate level operations, and to what extent do the characteristics of the change programme (such as in the case of just-in-time production systems or management information systems) enable or constrain the development of new forms of work organization?

This raises a second major concern, namely, the context in which change takes place. It is claimed that a historical perspective on both the internal and external organizational context is central to understanding the opportunities, constraints, and organizationally defined routes to change (Kelly and Amburgey, 1991:610). As has already been noted, the co-existence of a number of competing histories of change can significantly shape the process and outcomes of ongoing change programmes. In this sense, the contextual and historical dimension can both promote certain options and devalue others during the process of organizational change.

The third element which is central to the development of a processual approach is the need to incorporate an analysis of the politics of managing change. On this count, management writers such as Dunphy and Stace (1990) can be criticized for ignoring the political processes associated with trade union and employee actions in response to management's decision to introduce change, whereas political writers such as Braverman (1974) can be criticized for treating management as a homogeneous political group. The position taken here is that an understanding of organizational politics should be central to any approaches which seek to explain the process of managing transitions. For example, the commitment of middle management to strategy implementation cannot be taken for granted (see Porter, Crampon and Smith, 1976). As shown elsewhere, variations in commitment can significantly influence the successful management of change (Guth and MacMillan, 1989), particularly in cases where differing vested interests between management levels and functions do not align with strategic objectives (Wilkinson, 1983). Following the work of Child (1972:13–14), it is possible to view these strategic choices as being modified and challenged collectively by the workforce, or by individual and groups of managers who are responsible for the implementation of corporate strategy.

This alternative framework for analysing the process and outcomes of organizational change is further elaborated in Chapter 3, where a processual approach is developed. The example of technology is used to identify a number of different tasks between the conception of a need to change and the emergence of new work practices and procedures. These transitional tasks rarely occur in a neat linear fashion but, rather, may overlap, occur simultaneously, stop and start, and be part of the initial and later phases of major change programmes (it should also be noted that the tasks identified may not be appropriate to all examinations of change and, consequently, they should be modified or revised to fit either the research or planning requirements of different change programmes). Nevertheless, the grouping of activities and decisions is useful for locating and sorting data on organizations under transition, and for aiding our understanding of the uncharted and muddy waters of change. Furthermore, the approach is used to analytically ground the case studies which are presented in the remainder of the book. These case studies are largely longitudinal in nature and have been carried out over a period of twelve years in three different countries. A summary of the supporting programme of research is provided below prior to a short overview of the main body of text.

The supporting programme of research

The new empirical material presented in this book is based on longitudinal case study research. The common themes running through the various research programmes comprise: new technology, new techniques and the management of change. This has involved detailed case study examinations of the management of innovation and change in British, American and Australian corporations. These include British Aerospace, British Rail, Hewlett Packard, General Motors, Pirelli Cables, Laubman and Pank, and the State Bank of South Australia.

There are five main programmes of research from which data are drawn. The first major piece of research involved an eighteen-month longitudinal study into the effects of computer technology on freight operations management in British Rail. This study was carried out by the author at the University of Southampton, as a member of the New Technology Research Group (a multi-disciplinary research team made up of engineers and social scientists whose primary aim was to study the introduction of new technology in the workplace). Essentially, the research involved a retrospective study of management strategy and industrial relations issues in the implementation of a Management Information System (MIS) and a more detailed study of the effects of change on railway freight supervisors. A detailed programme of observation was conducted in five high capacity marshalling yards in three British Rail regions, and over eighty employees were interviewed, ranging from members of the British Railways Board through to local supervisory managers and shunting yard staff (Dawson, 1986).

The second major programme of research involved a two-phase longitudinal study of the public requirements of a computerized system of welfare benefit advice. This study formed part of a programme of research being carried out by the Alvey DHSS Large-Scale Demonstrator project (the Surrey University research group comprised computer scientists and quantitative and qualitative social scientists whose aim was to design sociologically informed computer systems). The findings from the research have been used to demonstrate the technical problems associated with building and maintaining large knowledge-based computer systems and the social and political dimensions of designing an expert system for use by non-experts (Dawson, Buckland and Gilbert, 1990).

The third research project was carried out by the author at Edinburgh University as a member of the Business Studies department. The main aim of the project was to collect detailed case study data on the process of organizational change in an electronic instrument corporation. The research comprised interviews with production and operations managers, observation of staff activities, informal discussions, and the use of documentary material (see Dawson and Webb, 1989; and Webb and Dawson, 1991).

The fourth project was stimulated by an absence of Australian material on the organizational implications of introducing Total Quality Management (TQM). The project formed part of a broader programme of research being funded by the Key Centre in Strategic Management at Queensland University of Technology. A series of qualitative longitudinal case studies were conducted in a number of different organizations throughout Australia (see Dawson and Palmer, 1993; and Dawson and Palmer, forthcoming). The case study used in this book is that of Pirelli Cables Australia Limited. Although Pirelli Cables was no different from many other corporations, the coverage of their programme (in being part of Pirelli's global corporate strategy for change), the scale of their investment (in terms of the timeframe and people committed to the project) and the substance of the change (in being part of a more general movement towards TQM across industries) made Pirelli Cables an ideal case to study (see also Dawson, 1994).

The fifth major programme was funded by the Australian Research Council (ARC) and was stimulated by MBA students on a course concerned with the problems and practice of managing organizational transition. In writing this book, two case studies from an ARC-funded research programme have been drawn upon. The first involved a longitudinal case study analysis of the implementation of cellular manufacturing at General Motors automotive component manufacturing plant in Australia. Interviews were conducted with key players involved in the change, including senior management and plant management at General Motors-Holden's Automotive Limited (GMHAL); personnel at the Division of Manufacturing Technology of the

Commonwealth Scientific and Industrial Research Organization (CSIRO); and shop stewards and full-time union officials (Dawson, 1991b). The second study centred on a retrospective analysis of the successful management of change at Central Linen Service. The programme of research involved a series of interviews with senior management, supervisors, operators and trade union officials. The aim of the study was to identify the key factors which facilitated the transition from a conventional laundry facility to one of the most advanced automated laundry processing plants in the world (Dawson, 1991a).

The considerable body of data which has resulted from these research projects is used within the main body of the text to document the dynamic processes associated with the management of organizational change. Methodological considerations and the significance of these types of data for increasing our understanding of the complex process of change are discussed further in the Appendix.

An overview of the main text

The four main objectives of the book are as follows:

1. To write a book on organizational change which summarizes the main contemporary issues and makes them accessible to students of management.
2. To document empirical evidence drawn from an intimate knowledge of case study data which have been collected over a period of twelve years.
3. To provide both a critical analysis of the main debates which surround the introduction of new production and service concepts and a set of practical guidelines on the successful management of change.
4. To develop a coherent conceptual framework for the purpose of explaining the process of organizational transition and the adoption of new organizational arrangements.

The main body of the text is dedicated to the task of trying to accomplish a greater understanding of the dynamic and complex processes associated with the successful management of company-wide and plant-level transitions in the uptake of new organizational arrangements. To this end, the initial chapters focus on theoretical debates and conceptual issues which surround academic discussions on organizational change, with the remaining chapters addressing and illustrating some of the major challenges facing modern organizations through providing detailed case illustrations on the corporate, divisional and local management of change.

Chapter 2 summarizes the most popular and prominent models for understanding organizational change. The dominance of Organizational Development (OD) models among behavioural consultants of change and educationalists at graduate schools of management are criticized and the revival of contingency approaches to managing change are appraised. Some of the major weaknesses which surround current theories on organizational transition are highlighted and the emergence of a more recent 'contextualist perspective' is explained and discussed. In Chapter 3, a brief overview of the major issues which surround the movement towards more flexible and collaborative forms of work organization is presented and a processual approach to managing change is developed.

Chapters 4 to 8 examine different change initiatives, involving different levels of transition, within a range of organizations from a laundry service to an electronic components manufacturer. Chapter 4 sets out to provide a historical reconstruction of the factors which facilitated the successful introduction of a fully operational management information system in British Rail's Freight Division. It demonstrates the importance of both internal and external variables in shaping the process of change, and illustrates the weakness of studies which attempt to explain the dynamic and processual nature of change from single events or incidences. This chapter is also used to demonstrate the utility of a processual approach through applying the framework developed in Chapter 3 to an explanation of the process of computerization of British Rail's freight operations.

In Chapter 5, the issue of quality and, in particular, TQM, is examined in a case study analysis of the introduction of TQM in Pirelli Cables. A key question posed in the chapter is how to design, implement and manage a change programme which makes quality control the responsibility of every member of an organization (and not the responsibility of a discrete specialist group or department). In addressing this question, the chapter concludes by discussing the significance of programmes which encourage employee participation in quality issues, and proposing that it is not simply management techniques which are important to the successful management of change, but the way the substance of change is implemented, used, redefined, maintained and developed. Chapter 6 reports on the introduction of a Just-In-Time (JIT) management system in Hewlett Packard (Scotland). The case examines the process by which production management and JIT has been redefined, and highlights the importance of local site implementation to the successful management of a change initiated by corporate management.

In Chapter 7, the growing interest in cellular manufacture as a modern development of conventional group technology techniques is investigated and, following a discussion of the literature, an account is given of the local management of change at a General Motors automotive manufacturing plant in Australia. The case provides a good example of the issues which surround a change strategy which seeks to link the practical aspects of cellular manufacture with more flexible patterns of work arrangements. Chapter 8 looks at the issues surrounding the large-scale introduction of new technology at Central Linen Service (which at the time of the study was the largest and most highly automated linen service in the world). The various stages in the process of managing change are documented, and the problems of gaining employee involvement and creating and maintaining a culture of change are discussed. Chapter 9 then examines an earlier stage in the process of transition, namely, the period in which new products are developed and designed (it is located at the end of the book because its relevance will be highlighted by the other cases). The focus of the chapter is on industrial collaborative projects and the process by which new computer software is developed for company use. Empirical data is drawn from the Alvey DHSS Demonstrator project in Britain, and the CSIRO's Collaborative PC Scheduler project in Australia. These two examples are used to identify and discuss the process of transferring research innovation into programmes of organizational change.

In Chapter 10, the case study material is drawn together in the formulation of a series of practical guidelines on the management of change. The philosophy of senior management, the concerns of employees and trade unionists, the significance of supervision and the restructuring of work to facilitate the formation of collaborative teams and the importance of maintaining employee commitment to change are all examined. The chapter concludes with a discussion of the longer-term implications of the adoption of new manufacturing and service concepts. It is suggested that, in conjunction with the internationalization of business and the ongoing dynamics of change, there are transitions occurring which signify the more widespread emergence of collaborative organizational networks. These networks involve the development of local collaborative customer–supplier relations for the purpose of developing products and services for national and international markets. In some cases, they are also forming part of a broader organizational network (particularly with multi-national corporations), where a greater devolution of control is combined with closer liaison with corporate management and a movement away from purely localized concerns. In this way, the development of collaborative networks is combined with a more international and global organizational focus, which places a higher premium on flexibility, teamwork, quality, participation, collaboration and change.

2

UNDERSTANDING ORGANIZATIONAL CHANGE

Introduction

A change in an organization can refer to any alteration in activities or tasks. For example, there may be minor changes in procedures and operations or transformational changes brought about by rapid expansion into international markets, merger or major restructuring (Kanter, 1991:154). In a highly competitive and rapidly changing international market, a prominent concern with organizational change – and the focus of this book – is on how to manage large-scale transitions at the operational level. The term Large-Scale Transition (LST) is taken to refer to a fundamental change in the organization and control of work in the production of a good or service. Unlike the definition of Large-Scale Organizational Change (LSOC) proposed by Ledford *et al* (1990), this definition would include major divisional and plant restructuring, and is not limited to strategic LSOC of an entire organization (1990:25). For example, changes in the methods by which organizations produce the goods and services which they sell may not flow directly from strategic change. These large-scale operational transitions often have a different dynamic from strategic change and are consequently characterized by distinctive processes. Nevertheless, this definition does support the notion that LSOC involves changes that are both deep and pervasive, and that these transitions often address issues in the organization's environment which may result in strategic redirection (Mohrman, Ledford and Mohrman, 1990:293–4). Moreover, the controversial and unresolved issues raised by Mohrman *et al* (1990:301–2) on whether there is a logical sequence to a change process, whether change can be planned or whether large-scale change unfolds in unpredictable directions, are issues tackled in this book.

For the student of business studies, answers to these questions have generally been derived from the perspectives adopted by textbooks. The approaches taught at educational institutions have tended to be conservative and particularly pervasive. A reluctance to incorporate contrasting theories of change into introductory textbooks has limited the availability and appeal of alternative models (see, for example, Boeker, 1991; Carroll, 1988; Tushman and Romanelli, 1985). Management texts, as a representation of a current 'accepted' state of knowledge, tend to be conservative and adopt very similar structure and styles (in fact the similarity between texts in America and Australia and, to a lesser extent, Britain, is considerable). This conservatism and rigidity to an accepted framework has resulted in a reluctance for educationalists to take on board many of the ongoing academic debates, and provide students with competing models of change.

For practising managers, who may be actively involved in implementing new techniques and new technologies in an attempt to sustain or improve an organization's market position (Twiss and Goodridge 1989), there has been little of substance available. Although questions concerning the basis of these transformational changes, how they should be managed, and what would be the likely consequences for the organization and control of work, have been highlighted in popularized accounts, they have not been seriously addressed (see Kanter, 1991). The common view deriving from these studies is that change should be treated as the norm rather than a series of one-off exercises (Peters, 1987), and that managers and organizations need to break with tradition (Kantrow, 1987; Morgan, 1988). The need to review and renew organization structures and processes (Waterman, 1988), and to adopt new business techniques of creativity, innovation, leadership and change (Majaro, 1988) are the repeated claims made by the so-called 'new wave writers' (see Chapter 1). This has resulted in the proliferation of popular articles and books on proactive management in the design and implementation of change, which will not only further the needs of the organization but also provide an opportunity for improvements in the work of staff (Wood, 1989a:391).

Within the academic community, this focus has generated a number of debates. For example, are the new production and service concepts being introduced by organizations resulting in a proliferation of management fads (Mitroff and Mohrman, 1987:69), real innovations (Dunphy and Stace, 1990), or simply an increased tendency to imitate other organizations (DiMaggio and Powell, 1983)? On these issues, Eric Abrahamson (1991:609) has argued that 'fads and fashions may constitute vital processes that animate random variations from which increasingly efficient innovation can evolve'. Whilst there may be some truth in this claim, the degree to which these changes are bringing about a radical change in the organization and control of work remains open to debate. For example, Pollert (1988) has suggested that these changes are mainly ideological with no substantive basis, whereas others have been more concerned with the degree to which current transitions in work are generally enhancing or eroding the quality of working life and employee involvement (Badham and Mathews, 1989; Campell, 1989; Dankbaar, 1988). However, many of these claims and counter claims are cast in terms of a general debate and are based on relatively little empirical evidence (Dawson and Webb, 1989). The intention here is to reverse this trend through presenting new case study data on the process and outcomes of managing large-scale operational change (see also Wood, 1989b). Although there is a growing body of literature in the area of strategic change, a gap remains for the development of a new theoretical framework for understanding major organizational transitions at the operational level. However, before embarking on this objective, it is first necessary to summarize the current use of dominant theoretical models from which an alternative approach to managing change can be developed.

Within North America and Australia, a rational model of change has prevailed, based on a situational or contingency framework. The basic theoretical tenet is that, whilst there is no one best way of organizing, it is possible to identify the most appropriate organizational form to fit the context in which a business has to operate (Wood, 1979:335). Regaining strategic fit with the arrival of a new organizational order is the emphasis of a number of modern contingency models of managing change (see, for example, Dunphy and Stace, 1990:40–64). The predominance of a single perspective has resulted in the 'closing off' of insights and options which may otherwise be available to organizational practitioners. Whilst contingency theorists may fear that competing models would lead to a 'disintegration of coherent theory into ad hocery, muddle and mere description' (Donaldson, 1988:32), as Wood indicates:

> The contingency theorist neither ignores nor is unable to deal with change . . . but rather treats it as largely unproblematic . . . In effect the contingency theory places the social scientist above the organization's participants and assumes that he can simply impose the 'correct design' on an organization . . . Thus despite its applied orientation, contingency theory remains abstract and scholastic and, in effect, views organization change as essentially an intellectual and technocratic exercise.
>
> (Wood, 1979:337–8)

In tackling the processual nature of change, a 'contextualist' approach has emerged in Britain which advocates the development of an alternative theoretical framework (Clark *et al*, 1988; Pettigrew, 1987a and 1987b). In moving away from a systems approach to change, this perspective sets a timeframe of reference for explaining the dynamic processes by which change unfolds. The context, content and process of change are central to explanations of organizational transition, and longitudinal qualitative research methodologies are deemed most appropriate to the achievement of this objective (Pettigrew, 1987a:650). This competing perspective not only advocates a different research strategy and methodology but also a non-systems approach to studies which seek to explain the process of managing change.

These three knowledge bases – the dominant textbook approach, the prevalence of contingency theories in North America and Australia, and the alternative contextual perspective emerging in Britain – are the focus of the sections which follow. A critical evaluation and summary of these theories are accomplished by: first, providing a critique of the conventional approaches to planned change and, in particular, the limitations of an OD perspective and Lewin's (1952) three-phase model of planned change; secondly, outlining the debate on the organizational ramifications of operating under turbulent environments, and evaluating the implications of a revival in contingency theories as the dominant perspective; thirdly, examining the growing academic movement towards contextual approaches in the study of organizational change; and, finally, following the work of Child (1972), Whipp, Rosenfeld and Pettigrew (1987) and Pettigrew (1990), a call is made for a new pedagogical approach to the subject of managing change.

Managing organizational change: textbook orthodoxy

There is a range of external and internal factors which may necessitate change within an organization. External forces for change include factors such as government laws and regulations, technology, social and economic change, and changes in international agreements on tariffs and trade. They originate in the organization's environment and include such factors as:

1. Technological obsolescence and the need to introduce new technology. Organizations which specialize in high-technology products are particularly prone to these forms of pressure.
2. Major political and social events (for example, a change in a country's relationship with Middle East or East Asian countries may bring about a change in trading arrangements).
3. An increase in the size and complexity of an organization. This may result in the growth of specialist areas and a need to develop appropriate co-ordinating mechanisms.
4. The internationalization of business. This could necessitate adaptation to changing trends and competitive pressures.
5. Government legislation (for example, policies for environmental/pollution control, equal employment opportunity).
6. Economic climate. Fluctuations in the level of economic activity in the national economy can significantly influence organizations.

Following Leavitt (1964), the internal triggers to change are generally characterized as comprising technology, people, task, and administrative structures (see Vecchio *et al*, 1992:591–3). A change in an organization's technology may involve the installation of a single piece of equipment or the complete redesign of a production process. The option of revising administrative structures involves redesigning the structure of an organization and modifying other aspects, such as lines of communication and reward systems. Changing the human aspect of an organization is a popular change strategy (usually adopted by OD practitioners), and involves modifying attitudes, beliefs, values, technical skills and behaviours. The task of an organization refers to the primary product or service of a firm, whether it is concerned with the manufacture of automobiles or the provision of a financial banking service. Consequently, a change in the task of an organization would generally require a fundamental organizational transformation to produce and market different types of goods or services (in practice, these four areas often overlap and a change in one area will often require change in another).

These internal and external triggers to change are often interdependent. For example, a push for a change in technology may result from competitive pressure or from the exposure of local engineering personnel to the benefits of new developments in capital equipment. Similarly, changing employee attitudes at work may be the result of a complex interplay between a change in management style and a general shift in attitude among the populace. Moreover, it should be stressed that people within organizations and, in particular, those in management and senior management positions are often able to influence environmental factors rather than simply respond to them. Agreements between major competitors, the lobbying of key politicians and the use of the media to influence pubic opinion can all be used to facilitate proactive strategies for change. Furthermore, because a change in one factor is likely to result in significant changes to others, it is often difficult to anticipate and plan for every eventuality. For example, a change in technology may result in significant restructuring and bring about an unintended and/or undesirable reaction from the workforce. In fact, resistance to change is a subject which receives considerable attention in the management literature (Aldag and Stearns, 1991: 716–19; Buchanan and Huczynski, 1985:419–23; Dunford, 1992:300–3). Typically, resistance has been identified as resulting from one, or a combination, of the following factors:

- substantive change in job (skill requirements);
- reduction in economic security or job displacement;
- psychological threats (whether perceived or actual);
- disruption of social arrangements;
- lowering of status (redefines authority relationships).

According to Gray and Starke (1988:575–80), a substantive change in the nature of work and the skills required to perform certain functions is likely to engender distrust and resistance, particularly in situations where employees are not informed of the change prior to implementation. Even if these threats reflect an individual's perception of change rather than an actual threat, employee resistance to change is likely to result. In response to the anticipated conflicts with employees, strategies for overcoming resistance to change have become a central concern of textbook approaches to managing planned change (see, for example, Aldag and Stearns, 1991; Gray and Starke, 1988). The two most dominant and pervasive theories (and the ones which are likely to have been the most influential to the intended readership of this book), are Kert Lewin's (1947) three-phase model of planned change and the OD approach.

The first of these two approaches has been found in recent American (see, for example, Baird, Post and Mahon, 1989:261–74; Hodgetts, 1991:454–67; Robbins, 1988:437–44; Steers, 1991:624–32), and Australian (Bailey *et al*,

1991:495–508; Knowles, 1990:87–8; Vecchio *et al*, 1992:599–609) introductory management texts. Whilst less attention has been given to the OD perspective in Britain (see Child, 1984; Dawson, 1986; Fincham and Rhodes, 1988), Lewin's theory remains evident in recent texts (see, for example, Wilson and Rosenfeld, 1990:245–6). The main elements and weaknesses of these approaches, which are being taught in American, British and Australian business studies and management departments, are summarized below.

Although there are many different OD models, the general approach has been described by Huse (1982:555) as 'the application of behavioural science knowledge in a long-range effort to improve an organization's ability to cope with changes in its external environment and increase its internal problem-solving capabilities'. It is based on a human relations perspective which stresses the importance of collaborative management and, according to French and Bell (1983:15), can be defined as 'a long-range effort to improve an organization's problem-solving and renewal processes . . . with the assistance of a change agent or catalyst and the use of the theory and technology of applied behavioural science, including action research'.

Typically, the OD approach is planned; it attempts to consider and include all members of an organization; the proposed change is supported by top management; the objectives of change are to improve working conditions and organizational effectiveness; and an emphasis is placed on behavioural science techniques which facilitates communication and problem-solving among members (Beckhard, 1969). The most common distinguishing characteristics of modern OD approaches are as follows (French, 1969; French and Bell, 1983):

1. The goal is to improve an organization's health and effectiveness.
2. The focus of the change effort is on the whole system (whether an organization or a divisional department).
3. The change programme involves planned interventions that are introduced systematically.
4. Top-down strategies are applied: that is, change begins at the top of an organization and is gradually applied downward throughout the organization.
5. Employees at all levels of an organization must be committed to the change (in other words, change must never be forced).
6. Change is made slowly, allowing for the continual assessment of change strategies.
7. Specialist change agents should be used to guide OD programmes.
8. The approach should be interdisciplinary, drawing on behavioural science knowledge.
9. OD programmes are based on data, so that choices are made on the basis of objective information rather than on the basis of assumptions about what the real issues are.
10. The objective is to achieve lasting rather than temporary change within an organization.

11. The OD approach can be used with both healthy and unhealthy organizations.

Generally, the OD approach involves a number of steps commencing with the appointment of a change agent (usually an individual outside the organization) who intervenes to start the change process. The six major steps in an OD programme comprise: identifying a need for change; selecting an intervention technique; gaining top management support; planning the change process; overcoming resistance to change; and evaluating the change process (Aldag and Stearns, 1991:724–8). However, the main problem with this approach is that it adopts a normative framework and assumes that there is one best way to manage change that will increase both organizational effectiveness and employee well-being. The professional consultants engaged in OD are generally not concerned with the development of theory or with the design of systematic programmes of research but, rather, with a set of normative prescriptions which guide their practice in managing change (Ledford *et al*, 1990:4–6). The OD camp has also been criticized for failing to account for the increasing incidence of revolutionary change which, according to Dunphy and Stace (1990:67), may more effectively be achieved by coercive top-down strategies of change.

Whilst similar arguments can be levelled against Kert Lewin's three-phase model of change (an earlier theory which set the scene for much of what we know as OD today (Weisbord, 1988:175), it remains an influential theory and a common approach advocated by management educationalists (see, for example, Gray and Starke, 1988; Robbins 1988). The main thrust of Lewin's theory (also referred to as the Lewin-Schien model (Aldag and Stearns, 1991:714–15)) is that an understanding of the critical steps in the change process will increase the likelihood of the successful management of change. The three general steps identified by Lewin (1951) comprise unfreezing, changing, and refreezing. Unfreezing is the stage in which there is a recognized need for change and action is taken to unfreeze existing attitudes and behaviour. This preparatory stage is deemed essential to the generation of employee support and the minimization of employee resistance. According to Lewin's (1947) technique of force-field analysis, there are two sets of forces in operation within any social system; namely, driving forces that operate for change and restraining forces which attempt to maintain the status quo. The example of smoking illustrates this, where, although there may be strong driving forces to stop smoking, such as social pressure, cost, fear of cancer, new laws, disapproval of children and the concern of others, the restraining forces of habit, camaraderie, relief of tension, spouse smoking and the dislike of coercive methods may act to maintain the status quo (Weisbord, 1988:79). If these two opposing forces are equal in strength, then they are in a state of equilibrium. Thus, to bring about change you either need to increase the strength of the driving forces or decrease the strength of the resisting forces. Furthermore, as these two sets of forces are qualitatively different it is possible to modify elements of both sets in the management of change. In practice, however, the emphasis of OD specialists has been on providing data that would unfreeze the system through reducing the resisting forces rather than increasing the driving forces (Gray and Starke, 1988:596–629; Weisbord, 1988:94). Once these negative forces have been reduced through disconfirming information, then the consultant embarks on moving the organization towards the desired state. This is the second general step of changing or moving an organization, and involves the actual implementation of new systems of operation. Once this has been complete, then the final stage of refreezing occurs, which may involve the positive reinforcement of desired outcomes to promote the internalization of new attitudes and behaviours. An appraisal of the effectiveness of the change programme is the final element used in the last step to ensure that the new way of doing things becomes habitualized.

This, then, is the basis of Lewin's three-phase model of change, which is still widely taught in business departments and management schools around the world. Whilst the strength of the model lies in its simple representation (which makes it easier to use and understand), this is also its major weakness as it presents an unidirectional model of change. Moreover, by creating an image of a need to design in stability (refreezing), the model has a tendency to solidify what is a dynamic and complex process. It may also result in the creation of cultures and structures not conducive to continuous change. On this point, Marvin Weisbord has argued that Lewin's concept begins to fall apart as the rate of market and technological change enters a state of perpetual transition, rather than the 'quasi-stationary equilibrium' (1988:94). Whilst Lewin's theory may be inappropriate to organizations operating in rapidly changing environments, there are a number of models which have been developed with the sole purpose of explaining the relationship between an organization and its environment (see, for example, Duncan, 1972:313–27). These organizational theories have tended to use a contingency framework for analysing change. As Daft (1986:22) indicates:

> Most research in organization theory is a search for contingencies. Investigators try to understand the relationships among variables so they can recommend which strategies and structures are appropriate in each situation. Because organizations are open systems, one important contingency is the environment. Organization theorists attempt to determine which organization characteristics allow firms to deal effectively with different kinds and rates of environmental change.

In essence, contingency theorists argue that the best way to organize depends on the circumstances. The contingent factors which are deemed to be of primary significance include either single variables, such as technology (Perrow, 1970; Thompson, 1967; Woodward, 1980) or the environment (Burns and Stalker, 1961; Lawrence and Lorsch, 1967), or range of variables, such as in the ambitious study by Pugh and colleagues (Pugh *et al*, 1969a and 1969b) which examined the relationship between contextual factors and structural variables (see also Pugh and Hickson, 1976; Wood, 1979). In short, contingency theorists reject the search for a universal model and aim to develop useful generalizations about appropriate strategies and structures under different typical conditions.

Adapting organizations to turbulent environments: the dominance of contingency theories

There is nothing novel about the concept of environmental turbulence and the need to adapt organizations to shifting markets (Emery and Trist, 1965). The classic work of Burns and Stalker (1961) indicated the importance of organizational design to a firm's ability to innovate and adapt to a turbulent environment. For example, their study showed how it is possible to construct two ideal types of management system. First, a mechanistic system, deemed appropriate for an organization which uses an unchanging technology and operates in relatively stable markets. It is characterized by clear hierarchical lines of authority, precise definitions of job tasks and control responsibilities, a tendency for vertical interaction, an insistence on loyalty to the concern, and an emphasis on task skills and local knowledge rather than general knowledge and experience (Burns and Stalker, 1961: 119–20). Secondly, an organic form which is appropriate to changing conditions, which gives rise to innovation, and the continual willingness to tackle fresh problems and unforeseen requirements. It is characterized by a network structure of control, authority and communication, a reliance on expert knowledge for decision-making, the continual redefinition of individual tasks through interaction with others, and the spread of commitment to the firm beyond any formal contractual obligation (Burns and Stalker, 1961: 121–2).

Whilst this distinction has proven influential in the development of organization theory, it has tended to be used as a means of classifying and differentiating between opposing types of industries and company organization (for example, between the bureaucratic mechanistic system of British Rail and the loose organic system of Rank Xerox), without investigation of the potential for the two structures to co-exist within a single firm. This is perhaps a point which has been lost in the endless summaries of this classic typology. As Burns and Stalker themselves note, 'a concern may (and frequently does) operate with a management system which includes both types' (Burns and Stalker, 1961:122).

However, Burns and Stalker never fully develop their concept of a combinational structure, nor do they explain how this would fit with their contention that under the organic system it is often difficult and far less feasible to distinguish 'informal' from 'formal' organization (1961:122). To say that the organic organization is stratified rather than hierarchical is not sufficient, as it once again implies a holistic rather than partial model of management structure within an organization. Furthermore, whilst there is some commonality with the more recent managerialist literature on change (see, for example, Kantrow, 1987; Morgan, 1988; Peters, 1987; Waterman, 1988), it is questionable whether large-scale change really occurs as rapidly as many of these studies suggest (see also, Dunphy and Stace, 1990). In the cases reported here, the changes were rarely so rapid or unpredictable that an extreme organic system would have been best suited to successful adaptation; rather, these substantive changes generally occurred over a number of years. Secondly, the theory suggests that an organic management system is a necessary condition for accommodating substantial change. However, whilst neither General Motors nor British Rail could be regarded as an organic organization, both successfully managed the process of large-scale organizational change (see Chapters 5 and 7).

Although the present issues which surround environmental change are not new, many commentators advocate that the current climate of change is quantitatively and qualitatively different from those experienced in the 60s and early 70s (Mitroff, 1987; Mohrman and Mohrman, 1990:35–40; Tichy, 1983:388–93). For example, Peter Vail (1989:1–32) likens the rapidity of change within modern business environments to permanent white water and states that: 'The present environment of chaotic change requires a response so different from the traditional managerial approach of diagnose–plan–implement–evaluate that perhaps I should not even use the simple word change to refer to the kinds of events contemporary managers are facing' (Vail, 1989:xiv).

The need to adapt to environmental trends and jolts has stimulated considerable research (see, for example, Aldrich, 1979; Lang and Lockhart, 1990; Meyer, 1982). The break-up of the old Soviet Union and the transformation of Eastern Europe, the attempts to create a unified European Community, the growth in trade in the Asia Pacific region, wars, technological advances, world recessions, and changes in international trade agreements are all part of the current world in which many corporations find themselves. It therefore makes sense to argue that, if organizations are operating in increasingly unpredictable global and national markets, then their ability to manage change becomes increasingly central to their competitive position and ultimate survival. However, according to Schenk (1982:116), this line of reasoning has led to a resurgence in organization theory of unidirectional causal models which focus attention on the relationship between an organization and the environment. In particular, the dominance of contingency theories which have resurfaced following the seminal work of Thompson (1967), Lawrence and Lorsch (1967) and Burns and Stalker (1961) have served to reinforce the conventional orthodoxy on organizational adaptation (Schenk, 1982:115). Moreover, many of the current contingency models of change have not resolved the problems identified in earlier studies. This is perhaps best illustrated in the work of Lex Donaldson (1985) who, building on the Aston research, sets out to develop a model in which the structural characteristics of organizations are linked to a number of contingent variables (see Donaldson, 1986; Pugh and Hickson, 1976). Emphasis is placed on strategies for gaining an effective fit between organizational structure and functional performance (Donaldson, 1987). It is argued that organizational effectiveness can be achieved through adopting one of thirteen different structural designs, the choice of appropriate design being determined by the prevailing strategic conditions. In short, structural adjustment is contingency driven: that is, a change in organizational circumstance resulting in disequilibrium will reduce performance and signal the need for an adjustment of organizational form in order to restore effectiveness (Donaldson, 1987:2–3).

The contingency–design–framework advocated by Donaldson views the organization as a system which needs to adapt to its environment in order to survive. This perspective is closely aligned to the structural functionalist approach which dominates organization theory in North America. For example, American management textbooks are generally based on the assumption that organizational design is the heart of organization theory (see Daft, 1986). As Hinings states in his appraisal of Donaldson: 'Organization theory in North America . . . generally accepts the theoretical and methodological programme espoused by Lex. North America is positivistic and geared to a general organization design framework' (Hinings, 1988:6).

Consequently, Donaldson's claim for the need to reassert contingency theory as the dominant approach to the study of organizations is somewhat lost in the American context. In Britain, however, strong criticisms have been levelled against the view that organization theory should focus on issues surrounding the design of organizations for the purpose of solving practical problems (Donaldson, 1985:155). Child (1988), for example, argues that whilst organizations have to satisfy certain functional requirements, it is questionable whether Donaldson adequately conceptualizes the environment and its role in the development of determining organizational forms. Furthermore, he suggests that this 'gives rise to a non-sociological view of environment which oversimplifies the process of organizational design and transformation' (Child, 1988:13). In other words, through adopting a social scientific approach to change, Donaldson fails to incorporate a processual analysis, and largely ignores the significance of patterns of negotiation and interpretation on organizational outcomes. The rational world of the contingency theorist leads to a restrictive view of the routes and choices open to organizational practitioners. On this point, Wood (1979:339) has indicated that: 'there is evidence to suggest that within given situations an important degree of choice is available between different modes of organization, without serious diseconomies being incurred'. Therefore, in addition to underplaying choice, contingency theories generally fail to account for differences between participants through their focus on the technical problem of matching situations to organizational form (see also Aldrich, 1988; Child, 1988; Clegg, 1988; and Karpik).

A recent rational model of organizational change which adopts this technocratic approach has been developed by Dunphy and Stace (1990) at the Centre for Corporate Change in Sydney. The two dimensions of their model are: first, the scale of change and, secondly, the style of leadership required to bring about change. With regard to the former, the authors identify four types. 'Fine tuning' and 'incremental adjustment' refer to small-scale changes ranging from the refining and clarification of existing procedures through to the actual adjustment of organizational structures. 'Modular transformation' and 'corporate transformation' refer to large-scale changes from divisional restructuring to revolutionary changes throughout the whole organization. On the second dimension, the appropriate style of leadership is seen to range along a continuum from participative to autocratic, namely: 'collaborative', 'consultative', 'directive' and 'coercive'. By using these dimensions, Dunphy and Stace identify four types of change strategies. 'Participative evolution' and 'forced evolution' refer to incremental change through collaborating and directive change respectively. 'Charismatic transformation' is described as large-scale discontinuous change achieved by collaborating means; and, finally, 'dictatorial transformation', which describes major coercive change programmes (see Figure 4.1 in Dunphy and Stace, 1990:82).

Dunphy and Stace argue that the model provides a framework for planned change strategies which challenges the personal value preference of managers and consultants. They suggest that 'appropriate' change strategies are generally determined by the change agent and not by the needs of the organization. For example, they point out that OD practitioners have tended to focus on collaborative models, whereas corporate strategy consultants have tended to select dictatorial transformation as the appropriate strategy for managing large-scale discontinuous change. The authors argue that, whilst there is a place for each strategy, selection should be made on the basis of dominant contingencies.

The prevailing circumstance under which Australian businesses are competing is seen to comprise an age of discontinuity in which the service sector (which accounts for 65% of GDP and employs 68% of the civilian workforce) and the Pacific Basin (which accounts for 60% of Australia's trade) are central to Australia's economic future. The service sector is therefore seen to be crucial to the future of Australia and in need of major renewal and change. Dunphy and Stace (1990:36) view the 1983 deregulation of the financial services sector as an important macroeconomic development, but assert that: 'the ultimate vehicle for change must be the enterprise'(1990:36) and conclude that successful implementation may require a 'predominance of consultative practices' (1990:92).

The two major weaknesses of this contingency approach are: first, that the model does not tackle the political dimensions of change and, secondly, no attempt is made to provide a typology of change strategies and conditions for their use during the actual process of organizational change. In short, the models suggest that there is an appropriate strategy, given that you can identify the context and purpose of change, and that this strategy will see you through the entire process of regaining internal fit with the external environment. Furthermore, whilst they are at pains to point out that appropriate strategies are situationally dependent, they argue that fine tuning is not a viable change strategy in the current environment, and that the most common change strategy of high performers was corporate transformation. However, there are two problems with this strategy. First, as Dunphy and Stace (1990:89) note: 'the conditions needed for making change by charismatic transformation alone are infrequent', indicating that it is rarely appropriate to use such a strategy. Secondly, that the strategy as described does not fit easily along the collaborative dimension. For example, the strategy described does not involve actual participation but, rather, a general acceptance of the direction of change under charismatic leadership (their example of the transformation of Westpac under Bob White supports this). The authors assume that transformative change must occur quickly, and hence that there is little time for consultation or collaboration. The view that *all* organizations which have to undergo large-scale change to meet the changing demands of a discontinuous and dynamic external environment will have little or no time for participation is not supported by the empirical evidence (see, for example, McLoughlin, Rose and Clark, 1985). Hence, the model does not provide a participative transformational change strategy as a viable option. This brings us back to our original criticisms: namely, that little if any attention is paid to either the political processes or the timeframe associated with managing major change. As Wood (1979:341–2) argues, the approach to organizational change should be issue-centred as 'in this way it will hopefully avoid the danger of defining the situation in terms of given solutions (and hence operating with panaceas) and will treat the development and modification of objectives as an integral part of the process of organizational change and not something that can be provided once and for all, ahead and in abstract of the process'. In short, the main problem of contingency approaches to managing change is their tendency to impose unidirectional rational models on what is a complex and dynamic process. The need to contextualize research in examining the content and process of change is demonstrated in the work of Child and Smith (1987), Clark *et al* (1988) and Pettigrew (1987a). The importance of these findings in redirecting attention to the processes of change is briefly summarized in the section which follows.

Beyond the rational model: a contextualist approach

Stuart Clegg, in his book on organizations in the post modern world, argues that:

> Although there are many directions and competing fields of force in organization studies it would be fair to say that its present centre of gravity is as an empirical science premised on quantitative data. There is a research ethos which the culture fosters. It is macho, where theoretical mastery can only ever be ceded to those who control their numbers.
> (Clegg, 1990:105)

Whilst this may explain the attraction and dominance of contingency theories (and a quantitative research bias) in management schools, there is a small but growing group of academics in Britain and to a lesser extent in America, Australia and New Zealand, who are embracing the value and use of qualitative longitudinal research in developing a 'contextualist' approach to managing change.

The term contextualist is used here to refer to the growing number of academic studies which seek to examine processes of change within a historical and organizational context (Johnson, 1987:58). The approach is often multi-disciplinary (Clark *et al*, 1988), drawing on a range of perspectives and methods such as the business historian, the corporate strategist and organization theorist (Whipp *et al*, 1987), and is concerned with a detailed examination of the process of organizational transition (Child and Smith, 1987). For example, in a study of strategic change and competitiveness Whipp *et al* (1987:18) argue that it is important to examine the content of a chosen strategy, the process of change, and the context in which it occurs. They identify two contextual levels in which strategic change occurs: first, those aspects associated with the culture, structure and politics of an organization (what they term the inner context) and, secondly, those linked to the business, economic, political and societal context in which organizations operate (what they term the outer context). This contextualization of change relates back to, and overlaps with, the external and internal triggers to change outlined earlier in the chapter. However, rather than focus on one element to the exclusion of others, this perspective seeks to encompass a knowledge of the whole in order to explain the process by which managers mobilize and reconstruct contexts in order to legitimize the decision to change (Whipp *et al*, 1987:19). Thus, it is the relationship between the content of a specific change strategy, the context in which the change takes place and the process by which it occurs which is the basic analytical framework adopted by the contextualist approach.

In the process of change at Peugot-Talbot, Whipp and his colleagues examine the content, contexts and process involved and conclude that: 'The analytical importance of the context, content and process framework, plus its managerial corollary that formulating the content of a strategic change crucially entails managing its context and process, suggests that managerial processes of assessment, choice and change are at the heart of the strategic development of firms' (Whipp *et al*, 1987:50).

Through examining the context and content of processes of change, advocates of this perspective generally focus on a particular type of research strategy and methodology (Pettigrew, 1990). In contrast to the dominant approach in organization theory which emphasizes the importance of sophisticated quantitative analyses (Ledford *et al*, 1990:6–8), the focus of contextualists is on longitudinal qualitative data. This approach lends itself to a detailed understanding of the complex and dynamic processes of change (see Appendix). For example, Clark *et al* (1988), in their study of the changeover from electro-mechanical to semi-electronic telephone exchanges, use a compendium of different methods, including semi-structured interviews, non-participant observation, work diaries and group discussions. These methods are employed in order to examine technological change as a process, and to overcome the problems associated with the aprocessual and apolitical contingency approaches of writers such as Woodward (1980): 'Writers such as Woodward tend to see technology in a static fashion as having "impact" or "imposing itself" on organizational behaviour. Such an approach neglects the processes through which new technologies are implemented and operated and outcomes of change established and modified' (Clark *et al*, 1988:30).

They develop a framework for analysing the process of technological change based on three main elements: the stages of technological change; issues arising during change; and critical junctures in the process of change (Clark *et al*, 1988:31). They note that technology, as an engineering system which embodies certain social choices, may (amongst other things) define the 'design space' of outcomes which are shaped by organizational actors at critical junctures during the process of technological change (1988:29–32). In the detailed accounts of change, their research clearly demonstrates the importance of managers, trade unionists and workgroups in shaping the process of technological change in the workplace. The study not only identifies the independent influence of engineering systems on work, but also the important influence of individuals and groups during the unfolding of 'radical' (major) change programmes. In tackling the temporal dimension of transformative change, detailing the substance of the change (in this case, technology in the form of telephone exchange modernization), and incorporating an analysis of the politics of change, the research can be identified as being part of a broader international 'contextualist movement' which seeks systematic and detailed analyses of processes of change.

Similarly, the work of Child and Smith (1987) and Pettigrew (1987a) can be defined as contextualist research – the former, in their fine-grained case study of organizational change at Cadbury Limited, where they were particularly interested in the sectoral influence (context) on the process of transition; and the latter, in examining leadership and transformational change. Although there are noticeable differences between these studies (for example, whether the focus is on technology or 'firm-in-sector' perspective), there is a common methodology and research strategy which links them together. Each study has placed a high premium on longitudinal case studies and the collection of in-depth qualitative data (Child and Smith, 1987:584; Clark *et al*, 1988:224–8; Pettigrew, 1990:267–92). There is also a conceptual and theoretical overlap in their concern for:

1. the context in which changes are occurring;
2. the substance or content of the change programme; and
3. the process (rather than snap-shot analyses) of change.

What constitutes a contextualist approach is further clarified by Pettigrew (1987a; and 1987b), who advocates the need for vertical and horizontal levels of analysis. The vertical levels of analysis are taken to refer to outer (for example, environment) and inner (for example, interest-group behaviour) contextual factors. The horizontal level refers to the temporal interconnectedness between future expectations, present events and historical accounts. Research which is able to combine a processual analysis of change with an inner and outer organizational analysis of context is defined as contextualist: 'An approach that offers both multi-level or vertical analysis and processual or horizontal analysis is said to be contextualist in character' (Pettigrew, 1987a:656). To this extent, recent studies undertaken at the Work Organization Research Centre at Aston University, the New Technology Research Group at Southampton University and the Centre for Corporate Strategy and Change at Warwick University indicate the emergence of a processual/ contextualist approach to the study of organizational change.

With the growth in academic interest and the publication of case studies, the value of longitudinal, contextual approaches to understanding the dynamics of managing change is gaining increasing recognition. They highlight the importance of context in examining unfolding processes of change, yet, unlike contingency theorists, they are not drawn towards unidirectional episodic models of change. The focus is on the temporal and interconnected nature of change, and the influence of subjective attitudes and perceptions on the history and outcomes of change. Contextualists move beyond a rational model of change in attempting to explain the political arenas in which decisions are made, histories deconstructed, and results rationalized. In short, the grouping of research under what has been termed the contextualist approach includes those which seek to combine a fully historical perspective with emerging organizational dramas (Pettigrew, 1985b), and those which are concerned with more specific processual research (Clark *et al*, 1988). Whilst the perspective adopted here is more closely aligned with the latter, the historical antecedents in which change takes place are taken as critical to any detailed analysis of processes of change. Thus, from this discussion of the current body of pedagogical knowledge on managing change, there is clear evidence of a need to revise our use of conventional textbook models and to develop alternative 'contextualized' or 'processual' frameworks for understanding large-scale organizational change (Laughlin, 1991:209–32).

However, one of the major weaknesses of the contextualist approach stems from the richness and complexity of a multi-level analysis. For example, whilst the research findings adequately convey the complexity of organizational change, they have also tended to mask, mystify and create barriers of interpretation to the non-academic practitioner who seeks practical tools for action. The problem of translating propositions about understanding into guidelines for managers remains underdeveloped (Argyris, 1988:350), and is a major objective of the cases reported in the chapters which follow. As Buchanan and Boddy conclude:

> We are asked in this perspective to accept an intuitive definition of change as strategic, to put to one side as unimportant the control agenda of the project manager, and to work with a complex multi-

> variate and multi-layer model of process and context which, while of considerable interest to the researcher, does not constitute a 'user friendly' guide to practical management action. The logics of problem solving and ownership are subordinated by a preoccupation with the logic of legitimacy. The social and interpersonal dynamics of the processes Pettigrew addresses are not explored in a manner that facilitates the easy identification of practical advice.
>
> (1992:61–2)

Although they point out that it was not Pettigrew's intention to offer practical advice, they remain critical of this approach, both as a method for analysing data on change and as a perspective which serves to disable attempts to develop practical managerial advice (Buchanan and Boddy, 1992).

In an attempt to address these criticisms, the next chapter examines the main debates surrounding the transition towards new organizational arrangements and then builds on the contextualized approach in developing a non-linear temporal framework for analysing and explaining the process of organizational change. This alternative *processual* approach is then applied in the remainder of the book, which seeks to develop not only a greater understanding of the process of transition but also to develop a set of practical guidelines on the management of change.

3

THE TRANSITION TOWARDS NEW ORGANIZATIONAL ARRANGEMENTS

Introduction

There is an ongoing debate about the nature, process and consequence of introducing new production and service arrangements for the organization and control of work. Increasingly, this debate is being supported by new empirical evidence which seeks to identify the uneven and dynamic relationship between integrated automation and work organization (Webster, 1992); the consequence of change for work intensification (Turnbull, 1988); and the limits to flexible work and employment practices (Dawson and Webb, 1989). These studies have covered a range of different industries and manufacturing environments, with considerable emphasis being placed on the automotive industry (Dawson, 1991f; Sayer, 1986; Turnbull, 1988; Wood, 1990). The constituent elements of much of the work restructuring currently under way in industry represent a movement towards the development of multi-skilled self-regulatory workgroups who liaise with teamwork supervisors/facilitators on the shopfloor (Buchanan and Preston, 1991; Safizadeh, 1991). The main thrust of this change is to replace neo-Taylorite or Fordist type work structures with a more flexible model of management practice (see, for example, Clark, forthcoming; Storey, 1994). This new method of work organization (with a bias for action) stresses the importance of worker involvement, multi-skilling, and a team approach to production and process work tasks (Oliver and Wilkinson, 1988). The latter involves shopfloor employees in elements of industrial engineering which, in turn, influences worker involvement through placing greater emphasis on the quality rather than simply the quantity of output (Dawson, 1991c). In conjunction with other major changes, such as the push for TQM, cellular work arrangements and JIT manufacturing, these changes raise serious questions about teamwork, supervision and management control (Garraham and Stewart, 1991). In America (Womack, Jones and Roos, 1990) and Britain (Oliver and Wilkinson, 1988), the organizational adoption of these new production and service concepts has been referred to as the 'Japanization' of work. Although the term has also been used to refer to the direct investment by Japanese multi-nationals in the Asia-Pacific region, North America and Europe, it has more generally been used as an abbreviation for the introduction of Japanese industrial practices by non-Japanese companies (Bratton, 1991:378). Whilst Taylor and associates (1991) have argued that survey evidence indicating the widespread process of Japanization should be treated with caution (as there is often a discrepancy between corporate perceptions of plant operations and actual operations), there remains a critical debate on whether the adoption of Japanese production methods and labour-management practices is causing a general upskilling or deskilling of work. It is towards a clarification of these arguments and the development of an alternative approach to examining these transitions in operational work arrangements that this chapter is based. It is argued that a processual framework provides the most appropriate analytical approach to understanding the substantive, contextual and political processes of establishing new organizational arrangements.

The shopfloor challenge of new manufacturing and service strategies

The term new production arrangements has become the centre of a debate over the emergence of new forms of work organization in modern industrial economies (Elger, 1990; Lovering, 1990). It is often taken to refer to a qualitative shift in the way production is organized and signals a movement away from the detailed division of labour associated with neo-Taylorite and Fordist type production systems (Dawson and Webb, 1989). One of the most influential books in North America and Australia is Piore and Sabel's *The Second Industrial Divide*, which advocates that modern industry is replacing Fordist and neo-Fordist organizational structures with more flexible multi-skilled forms of specialist craft production. This movement towards 'flexible specialization' is seen to provide a new industrial strategy which is enabling firms to accommodate continual change and innovation on the shopfloor (Piore and Sabel, 1984: 17), and to mark the end of the detailed division of labour with the emergence of a more worker-oriented approach to factory organization (Mathews, 1989). The general characteristics of this emerging form of work organization are seen to comprise a broadening of job categories; the formation of work teams; decentralized decision-making; skill-based reward systems; increased training schemes; and better selection procedures (Littler and Quinlan, 1989:191). The extent to which these new practices are being adopted by industry is being influenced by the availability of technology, market imperatives, and the political processes of negotiating change within existing or developing frameworks of industrial relations (Badham and Mathews, 1989). Some commentators have argued for the promotion of a post-Fordist industrial relations strategy which places a premium on 'multi-skilling linked to career paths; wages linked to career developments; and career paths open to all workers covered by industrial relations agreements' (Badham and Mathews 1989:230). They suggest that such a transition would enable the direct democratization of the workplace through the trade union movement (Badham and Mathews, 1989:237). However, the outcomes of these changes for the organization and control of work remain in question, and continue to generate a heated and wide-ranging debate within the English-language literature (for example, Badham and Mathews, 1989; Lane, 1988; Lovering, 1990; Pollert, 1988; Smith 1989). But before it is possible to examine some of the implications of these changes for work, it is first necessary to clarify some of the terms and concepts used in these discussions and, in particular, the use of the term 'flexibility'.

The term 'flexibility' is used in four main ways in studies which have examined the emergence of new patterns of work (for example, Clutterbuck, 1985; Streeck, 1987). First, with regard to resource functionality, where functional flexibility is taken to refer to a 'firm's ability to adjust and deploy the skills of its employees to match the tasks required by its changing workload, production methods and/or technology' (NEDO, 1986:4). Secondly, manufacturing flexibility, which is generally taken to refer to the ability to rearrange and adjust existing plants and equipment to meet the changing requirements of a transformation in operations control, the process of production and/or product design. Thirdly, numerical flexibility, which refers to the ability to rapidly increase or decrease the numbers employed within a firm. Fourthly, financial flexibility, which refers to the ability to adjust labour costs, such as pay, to short-term changes in the level of business-economic activity (Atkinson, 1985:17). These concepts have been used to explain the emergence of a more general managerial strategy towards a model of the flexible firm with a core multi-skilled and functionally flexible workforce, combined with disposable unskilled peripheral groups of temporary employees (Clutterbuck, 1985:19). In so doing, it accords with elements of the upgrading thesis of flexible specialization (Piore and Sabel, 1984), the end of Fordism debate (Tolliday and Zeitlin, 1986), Japanization (Bratton, 1991), and the deskilling thesis of labour process theory (Braverman, 1974); and thereby raises the question of whether the current transformation in work is occurring within an existing Fordist or Taylorist framework, or whether these changes represent a movement towards new forms of production arrangements. Essentially, there has been a polarization of views between those who argue that the current changes represent more sophisticated techniques for reasserting managerial control (Armstrong, 1988; Thompson, 1990), and those who see the changes as signalling a general upgrading of skills and the end of Taylorist forms of work organization (Piore and Sabel, 1984).

The argument forwarded here is that, whilst real innovations in the organization of work are occurring (Dawson and Webb, 1989), they reflect neither a simple movement towards some ideal-type flexible firm or utopian vision of a new world order (Atkinson and Meager, 1986), nor the simple repackaging of old wine in new bottles (Pollert, 1988). These innovations represent a shift towards a collaborative system of industrial relations and teamwork practice, with a reduction in the level of direct supervision and a devolution of control responsibilities for elements of industrial engineering to shopfloor employees. The primary mechanism for control stems from the creation of a new set of values and beliefs (cultural control) which serve to reinforce co-operative teamwork and group regulation. These collaborative forms of industrial relations are generated and sustained by an overlapping of trade union and management interest towards restructuring work which improves the quality of working life on the shopfloor, and simultaneously increases management's ability to adapt production to changing market conditions. Although this suggests that the interest of management and workers need not be antagonistic (Dankbaar, 1988:26), this does not indicate that there is a more generalized commonality of concern and a mutuality of purpose (that is, it is only where the outcomes from collaborative change service the strategic intentions of conventionally conflicting groups that co-operative schemes exist). Moreover, the fragility of this common framework of interest may become evident when short-term objectives are achieved and longer-term issues reassert themselves on the political agenda of shopfloor bargaining. As Bratton (1991:393) concludes in his study of cellular work structures on manual engineering skills: 'The direction of change is not a simple one of upskilling or deskilling. Skills have a political dimension; they are shaped and determined by social choice and complex configuration of opportunities and constraints'.

Detailed empirical investigation is therefore required to understand the process by which functionally flexible, self-regulatory workgroups are created, and to explain the organizational ramifications of any associated change in the nature of shopfloor control. Wickens (1987) and Wood (1990), for example, both note that a change in management practice under new team-oriented systems of production required a reorientation of supervisory management. Their findings suggest that this renewed focus on teamworking is qualitatively different from the Swedish experience, and reflects (but is not a direct replication of) the Japanese approach. In Sweden, for example, the central aim of teamwork organization was to reduce the role of the supervisor through the formation of semi-autonomous workgroups, whereas in Japan the tendency has been to enhance supervision and to increase the density of supervisory personnel. In the case studies reported here, a number of manufacturers, such as Pirelli and General Motors, are attempting to develop teamworking on the shopfloor (see Chapters 5 and 7). In general, the tendency has been to enhance the function of supervision and reduce the density of supervisory personnel (Dawson, 1991d and 1991e). Under this new method of working, supervisors are a central element in being directly involved in industrial engineering and in co-ordinating and appraising workgroup performance. Nevertheless, whilst this development in teamworking is more closely aligned with the Japanese model, there are a number of significant differences. For example, in Japan supervisors may not only control and appraise workers but also act as a union shop steward in representing workers' grievances. There is therefore a tendency for union and supervisory roles to overlap, creating a situation where the development of supervision is integral to a system of collaborative industrial relations and the creation of flexible teamwork arrangements (Wood, 1990). In non-Japanese companies, even though many of the changes reflect a movement towards more flexible patterns of work (Curzon, 1986), with an emphasis on quality and teamwork practices (Wickens, 1987; Wood, 1990), the tendency has been to ignore supervisory issues which arise during workplace reform. For example, Elger and Fairbrother (1990:3–6) describe the changes at Lucas Industries as constituting a reorganization of working arrangements in the form of modular systems of operation which redraw the frontiers of control rather than simply establish a new system of co-operative work relations. Simple cellular structures form the basic organizational unit and involve 'new flexible job structures with multi-skilled staff and with indirect control activities being carried out by direct staff on-line' (Parnaby, 1987:2 quoted in Elger and Fairbrother, 1990:16). Nevertheless, this transition towards 'modularized' production arrangements has not been met by a redefinition of supervision, which in many cases remains the neglected function of shopfloor operations. As Buchanan and Preston conclude in their study of employee autonomy and the role of the first-line supervisor under a cellular manufacturing environment: 'The transition of the role of foreman from policeman to coach had therefore not taken place. Relationships with the shop floor were characterized by low trust and high intervention. The foreman had made only minimal concessions to participative management' (Buchanan and Preston, 1991:15).

These changes raise some interesting questions about the relationship between factory layout and strategies for increasing employee involvement in the work process. For example, Friedman (1977), from his study of the automotive industry in Coventry, concluded that there are two ends of a continuum of strategies open to companies in the pursuit of profit, namely, direct control as found under Taylorist forms of work organization, and responsible autonomy, where an individual or group of workers is given discretion over the direction of work with a minimum of supervision for the purpose of maintaining managerial authority. His claim that there has been a gradual shift towards strategies of responsible autonomy in modern industrial economies has been criticized for failing to take into account the high level of supervisory and technical control found under conventional automotive manufacturing layouts (Thompson, 1983:136). However, it is argued here that, by combining Friedman's characterization of managerial strategies for control with an understanding of the mechanisms for achieving shopfloor control, a useful categorization of the choices open to practitioners in the management of change can be constructed (see Figure 3.1.).

The main managerial methods of controlling employee behaviour have been summarized by Edwards (1979) who identifies three elements essential to the control of labour, namely: directing the activities of labour; monitoring the activities of labour; and disciplining the non-compliance of labour (Edwards, 1979:18). According to his historical analysis, the systems of control used by management to co-ordinate these three elements have undergone fundamental change. He suggests that it is possible to discern a typology of systems of control which have evolved as a result of conflict and contradiction in the management of organizations: that is, from simple forms of personal control systems (entrepreneurial control and hierarchical control) to structural systems of control (technical control and bureaucratic control). Entrepreneurial and hierarchical control involves direct personal control, either by the employer in the former case or by supervisory management in the latter (Edwards, 1979:25–36). Bureaucratic control is achieved through bureaucratic means in building formalized rules and procedures into the social structure of work (for example, personnel policies, disciplinary procedures and formal job descriptions), whereas technical control refers to the achievement of control through technical means which are built into the physical structure of the work process (for example, the automotive assembly line).

Whilst this historical framework provides useful insight into the development and variety of the means of management control, no account is given of strategies of responsible autonomy or those associated with a shift towards new patterns of work. As already noted, the high levels of supervision and technical control associated with the automotive industry are in some cases being called into question, with the movement towards modularized or cellular forms of work organization (see Dawson, 1991f; Elger and Fairbrother, 1990). This transition does not represent an incremental adjustment to existing structures but a radical transformation in work structures and control systems (Dunphy and Stace, 1990:69–70). It also highlights the general unevenness and variation in the process of organizational transition and the importance of local management, supervision and workplace union organization in processes of restructuring (Elger and Fairbrother, 1990:31–2). A key element shaping the process of transition towards teamwork and responsible autonomy is the creation of a new value and belief system which supports collaborative workplace arrangements and obscures or compartmentalizes traditional areas of shopfloor concern, conflict and resistance. This further dimension in the changing frontier of control is the Pandora's box of cultural control.

The 1980s obsession with culture as a vehicle for understanding organizations in part arose due to an upsurge in academic interest in the substantive content of new production arrangements, and the success of Peters and Waterman's (1982) book *In Search of Excellence*. The latter linked certain types of corporate cultures with competitive success, and forwarded the idea that culture provided the entry point for solving organizational ills (Turner, 1990:5). In contrast, the academic debates emphasized culture through identifying the greater dependency of management upon a committed and co-operative workforce (Oliver and Wilkinson, 1988). Although the passion for culture is levelling off, it remains an important ingredient of change and a difficult concept to define and analyse. For example, Adams and Ingersoll (1990:17) argue that there is often a basic misunderstanding of culture:

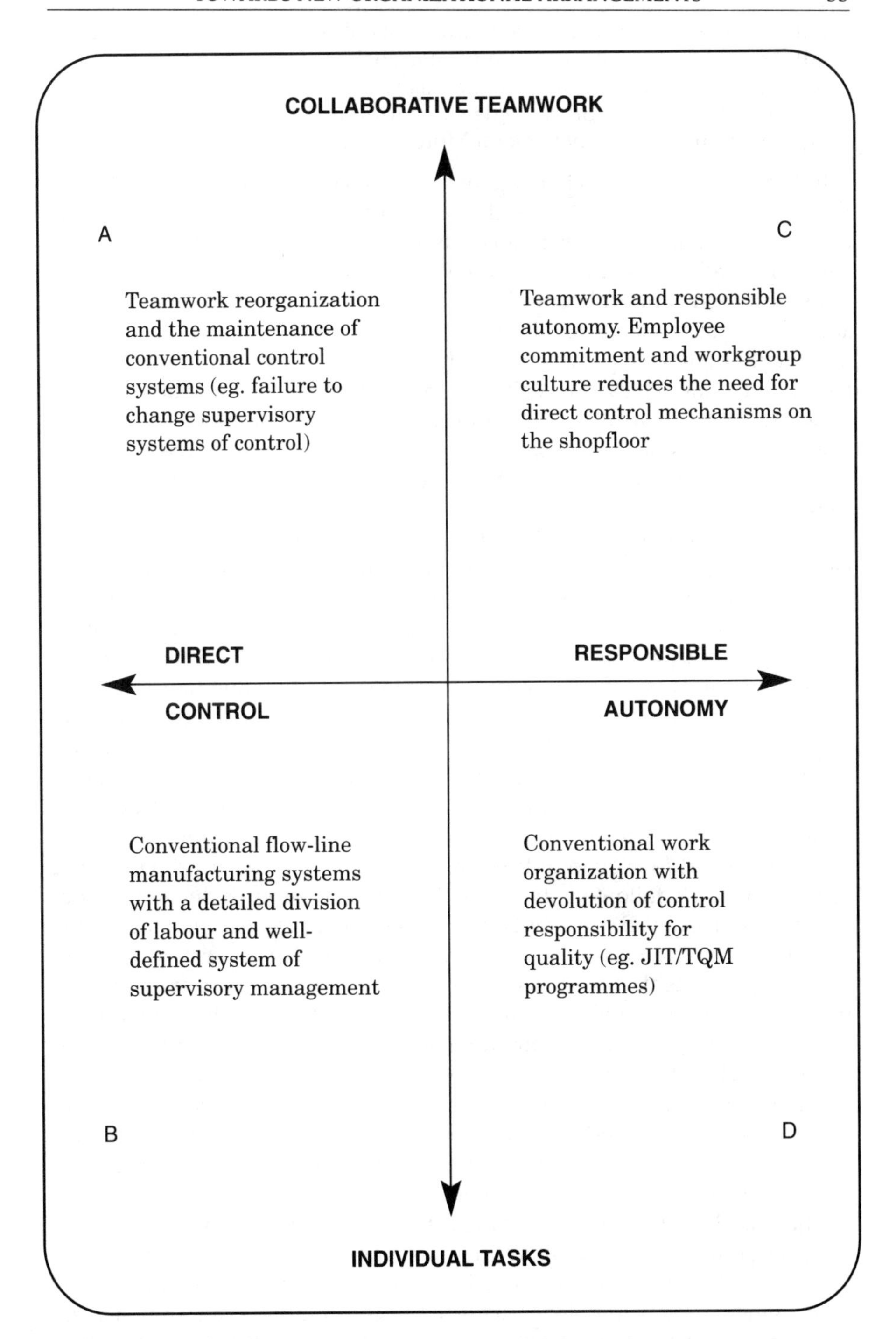

Figure 3.1 The organization and control of work

> Both academics and managers confuse subcultures as culture, and even talk as if such subcultures were mysteriously independent of the macroculture . . . After all, one could as easily discuss the subculture of the automobile industry, or even the subculture of General Motors, as the organizational culture of General Motors.

In recognizing that effective organizational change depends on changes in the shared interpretive schemes that inform action (Morgan, 1986:138), the main problem lies with engaging abstract belief systems with the more 'concrete' reality of shopfloor production. For the purpose of addressing this dimension here, cultural control is taken to refer to the predominant value and belief system as created, imposed and sustained by senior managers in the pursuit of more sophisticated methods of control over employee activity (Scase and Goffee, 1989:76). Whilst the interrelationships and relative weight between various subcultures is important (particularly in the case of professional culture as a mechanism for controlling behaviour across organizations), it is not feasible to enter into a lengthy debate (see Bloor and Dawson, 1994; Gagliardi, 1986).

Through combining these broad categories of control with a division of labour dimension, which ranges along a continuum from individual-based tasks to group work, it is possible to construct a provisional framework for analysing shifts in work organization under new production arrangements. The framework presented in Figure 3.1 allows for the co-existence of personal, structural and cultural control mechanisms with individual and work-group arrangements. The horizontal dimension refers to shopfloor control responsibility in the form of Friedman's (1977) responsible autonomy/direct control continuum, and the vertical dimension refers to the division of labour, in terms of a narrow range of single operator tasks at one extreme and totally collaborative teamwork at the other. By using these dimensions, it is possible to chart four quadrants of possible changes in the organization and control of work following the adoption of new production and service concepts. Quadrant B represents the conventional flow-line manufacturing systems with a detailed division of labour and well-defined system of supervisory management. Under this system, control over the pace and pattern of work is built into capital equipment (technical control) and little attention is given to employee commitment and collaboration. Consequently, management firefights and responds to problems of high levels of absenteeism and labour turnover, and shopfloor conflict and resistance is characterized by an adversarial system of industrial relations. In contrast, quadrant C represents a harmonious and collaborative system of industrial relations under new production arrangements. The emergence of a new system of industrial relations and work organization is seen to signal an end to Taylorist forms of work organization. These alternative arrangements are seen to include a commitment to participative decision-making and the formation of joint management–union (employee) consultative committees; an emphasis on teamwork; a philosophy or culture rooted in the ideas of flexibility, change and collaboration; the replacement of supervisors with facilitators; and an internal organizational system of co-operative customer–supplier relations. A new set of beliefs and values supported by a language of co-operation (cultural control) and system of rewards (structural control) acts as the primary mechanism for controlling employee behaviour on the shopfloor. Variations on these two ideal types are represented in quadrants A and D. The former refers to a change in work organization towards teamwork without restructuring supervisory management or conventional production control systems; the latter refers to the introduction of new ways of working, such as JIT management and TQM, which involves a devolution of control responsibility to the shopfloor without any major adjustments to the structural layout of the plant.

This framework for analysing shifts in the organization and control of work under new production arrangements emphasizes the importance of organizational values and beliefs systems for creating, developing and sustaining collaborative teamwork practice on the shopfloor. It also raises the critical questions of how these transitions are being managed, and what they mean for conventional workers who are expected to change their beliefs and values towards the nature and purpose of work. In addressing these issues, the chapters which follow adopt a processual approach in examining the process and outcomes of introducing new technologies and management techniques in British Rail, General Motors, Pirelli Cables, Hewlett Packard and Central Linen Service. The framework employed in these grounded case study analyses is briefly described below and particular attention is given to the development of an approach which is neither stodgy nor unreadable (a common criticism of previous processual presentations) but, rather, is easily understandable and of both academic value and practical worth.

A temporal framework for analysing transitions

In this section an alternative framework for analysing the process of operational change is formulated. Many of the initial ideas were formulated by the author as a member of the New Technology Research Group at the University of Southampton (see, Dawson, 1986 and 1988), and have been further developed in response to the work of Lewin (1951) and Pettigrew (1985a). Whilst there is a growing recognition of the need to examine the dynamic process of change (Hinings and Greenwood, 1988), the intention is not to model the pathways that environmental change or disturbance may take through an organization (see Laughlin, 1991:213–22) but, rather, to develop a framework for understanding the process and context of change as it unfolds within an organization. As Pettigrew (1990:269) has pointed out, much of the research on organization change is 'ahistorical, aprocessual and acontextual in character'. He argues for the encouragement of more detailed contextual and temporal analyses which are not misdirected by the biases in social science research towards the development of illusory grand theories of change (Pettigrew, 1990:270), and notes that: 'There are remarkably few studies of change that actually allow the change process to reveal itself in any kind of substantially temporal or contextual manner' (Pettigrew, 1990:269).

In developing an alternative framework for analysing change, attention has been given to the potential conflict of designing an approach which is both flexible and yet clearly defined, and also able to deal with the complexity of change whilst remaining uncluttered and of practical use. With these objectives in mind, it is suggested that the temporal aspects of change can be used as a means of breaking down the complex process of organizational transition into manageable portions. The three general timeframes advocated here are as follows:

- Conception of a need to change
- Process of organizational transition
- Operation of new work practices and procedures

During each of these timeframes a series of tasks, activities and decisions will be made by individuals and groups. In some areas decision-making activities may be influenced by outside agencies and groups, such as local and national governments and/or professional bodies and trade unions. In other areas, activities and tasks may result from the plans and preparations of management and/or the views, expectations and demands of certain employee groups or their representatives. In addition, certain individuals may act as major facilitators or inhibitors of change and prove instrumental to the 'success' or 'failure' of programmes which seek to establish new organizational arrangements. In practice, it is impossible to provide a definitive list of tasks, activities and decisions associated with the management of change. In the process of managing change an organization may move back and forth between various tasks and activities (and straddle the general timeframes associated with conception, transition and operation). Although there may be cases in which relatively stable systems of operation are never achieved, in the change programmes reported in this book they have all progressed beyond the stage of major upheaval to a period in which new patterns of working relationships can be identified and examined. With these caveats in mind, the remainder of this section explores in more detail the practical and analytical value of a temporal activity-based framework.

The conception of a need to change

The initial awareness of a need to change may either be in response to external or internal pressures for change (reactive), or through a belief in the need for change to meet future competitive demands (proactive). The latter has stimulated a wealth of research into the organizational adoption of management fads (Rumelt, 1974; Rogers, 1983; Lawler and Mohrman, 1985) promising a painless solution to raising international competitiveness (Mitroff and Mohrman, 1987:69). The increased complexity and uncertainty of international business markets has led some organizations to base change on imitation (which organizations are successful and what changes they have introduced), rather than on any conception of a need to adopt untried technologies or techniques (see, for example, DiMaggio and Powell, 1983; Thompson, 1967). Whether fads and fashions generate vital processes towards the evolvement and adoption of efficient innovations (Anderson and Tushman, 1991), or simply promote organizational inefficiency, is not of major concern here. What is important is how the conception of a need to change can be influenced by factors residing within the organization such as operational inefficiencies, industrial relations disputes or those which emanate from outside an organization – for example, through business press and media reports on the success of other organizations and the direct or indirect promotion of various management fads and fashions (see also, Abrahamson, 1991).

The process of organizational transition

Once a need for change has been identified, then the complex non-linear and 'black box' process of managing the transition commences. As already indicated, this period will comprise a number of different tasks, activities and decisions for individuals and groups both within and outside of the organization. In order to clarify this statement let us take the example of a firm where senior management have clarified a need to change because the organization is losing its competitive advantage or because there are major problems of labour turnover. Management then have to decide on the type of change they wish to introduce. This may be through a change in human resources, products or services (task), technology, or administration (Daft, 1986:269–86). In the case of new technology, a number of strategic objectives have been identified as influencing management's decision to embark on a programme of change. These include business market objectives; operating cost objectives; product quality objectives; and operating control objectives (see, for example, Boddy and Buchanan, 1986).

With regard to the first of these objectives, a change in technology may offer several possibilities for increasing an organization's ability to adapt to changing market conditions. For example, the flexibility of advanced capital equipment may permit the modification and redesign of production without necessitating any major structural alterations to the operating system. Alternatively, the new technology may enable a more effective utilization of existing resources and increase operating efficiency whilst reducing overall operating costs, and thereby improve an organization's business market position. Such an objective is achievable in cases where modern technology is introduced for the purpose of providing rapid access to accurate, up-to-date information on the disposition of material resources (see, for example, McLoughlin, Dawson and Smith, 1983).

Apart from improving a firm's market position and reducing operating costs through the more efficient utilization of resources, savings could also be made by reducing the total number of jobs required in the production of a given good or service (for example, Hines and Searle, 1979; Gill, 1985; Francis, 1986). Alternatively, the introduction of new technology could be used to eliminate management's dependence on in-house labour by transferring the use of labour from an employment to a contracting-out basis (for example, Edwards, 1979; Storey, 1983). The third objective of improving the quality of products or services produced may be particularly important in service industries where there is little to differentiate between competing services (Child, 1984:251). Buchanan and Boddy (1983) provide four case study examples which illustrate how new technology is introduced for the purpose of improving product consistency and quality. Finally, advanced technology may be adopted for the purpose of improving operational control through providing the rapid access of information and integrating previously diverse areas of operation (Dawson and McLoughlin, 1988).

The 'strategic decision' to adopt new technology, to introduce new products, or to change administrative structures would normally be taken at senior management level. However, the formulation of strategic objectives is not always as clearly defined as the example of a change in technology may suggest. For example, the research of James Quinn (1980) demonstrates how strategic decisions are often not highly formalized but, rather, take the form of what he terms 'logical incrementalism'. This involves the blending of behavioural techniques, power politics and formal analysis, in a logical incremental movement towards ends which are broadly conceived and revised in the light of new information during the process of strategic change. Quinn's findings illustrate how strategies can often be implemented prior to their final formulation (that is, during the conceptualization phase). This lends support to the need for a processual model which is able to accommodate the non-linear nature of complex processes of change within modern organizations (Quinn, 1989:20–36).

When a decision has been made on the general theme or content of change, then the task of search and assessment may follow, where members of an organization set out to find the best option for achieving a particular change objective. In our example, the search task would involve identifying the type of technology required (robotics, management information system, computer aided design), and the assessment task would involve an analysis of potential available products. In practice, many of these decisions may have been made at the outset, and may undergo revision as more information is collected on what is available in the market place, what costs are involved, and what the pay-back on investment is likely to be. The time-frame involved with this task may be relatively short involving a quick analysis of options, or it may instigate a major evaluation exercise requiring a team to visit other organizations and/or suppliers operating in different states and countries (see Chapter 8). In assessing possible options, a decision will generally be made on the choice and design of the system to be implemented. In the case of technology, whilst the choice of a piece of equipment may be made by senior management, the actual design of the system will often reflect the values and assumptions of design engineers (Davies and Taylor, 1976). For example, with computer technology, choices have to be made about hardware configurations and software architecture (although it should be noted that, whilst an existing organization may choose a ready-made system which comprises a hardware and software package, considerable modifications to the software can occur during the implementation and initial operation of the computer system).

System selection is also likely to influence the process of planning for the task of implementing change; for example, the logistics of managing the change (what pieces of equipment, where, in what order) and of ensuring that staff can use the new equipment (for example, how much training is going to be required), will be partly determined by the type of system selected. Moreover, in planning for change, decisions have to be made about the design of the organizational operating system: that is, on the organization of work in the daily operation of the new equipment. In the case of technology, Wilkinson (1983:89) argues that these decisions reflect social choices between either enhancing the existing skills and experience of operatives, or using technology as a means of degrading jobs and increasing management's control over the work process. The view proposed here is that management's strategic decision on the design of the organizational operating system will reflect certain social choices, as well as technical choices on the applicability of various technical systems to management's strategic objectives. In some instances, these choices may also be a response to certain external considerations, such as, for example, governmental pressure to buy British computer systems (see Chapter 4).

The task of implementing change has been well documented within the literature (see, for example, Boddy and Buchanan, 1986; Clark *et al*, 1988; Kanter, 1983; Pettigrew 1985a), and has been identified as an important 'negotiating' stage (Guth and MacMillan, 1989; Jacobs, 1983; Knights and Willmott, 1986). For example, Buchanan has noted that, while the pursuit of 'strategic' and 'operating' objectives tends to influence investment decisions, the pursuit of 'control' objectives 'influences the effect of technical change on the organization of work, operation, skills, and performance' (Buchanan, 1983:3). It is during the implementation of change programmes that occupational and employee concerns normally begin to influence the transition process (Dawson, 1988:58). For example, Edwards (1979) has argued that employee resistance to the imposition of management's implementation strategies can transform the workplace into a battleground of political dissension and control. However, these internal conflicts may not simply be a manifestation of workers' resistance to management but, rather, they may represent a complex political struggle between various occupational groups (managerial, supervisory and operative) with differing vested interests. In our example of new technology, the findings from contemporary research clearly illustrate how the effects of technology on work organization are dependent not only on the objectives, assumptions and values of those who make decisions about its use in organizations but also on processes of social choice and political negotiation between organizational factions during the implementation of new operating systems (Boddy and Buchanan, 1986; Clark *et al*, 1988). Consequently, a critical task in the introduction of new technology is the design by organizational practitioners of implementation strategies (McLoughlin *et al*, 1985), and the mobilization of certain key occupational groups may be an essential prerequisite to the successful management of change (see, for example, Weir and Mills, 1973).

The operation of new work practices and procedures
This final general timeframe is taken to refer to the period when, following the implementation of change, new organizational arrangements and systems of operation begin to emerge. During this period, a number of novel developments or contingencies may arise which may compromise the 'success' of management's implementation strategy. For example, unanticipated technical problems may undermine the usefulness of the system in its replacement of traditional methods. As a result, this may cause conflict and confusion among staff and management and threaten the establishment of new working relationships. Alternatively, if employees actively adapt and modify working practices around systems which have not been adequately 'debugged', then management may find it difficult to implement further changes. This point has been well illustrated by Wilkinson in his study of a plating company where management's attempt to modify new 'institutionalized' working practices was resisted by shopfloor employees (1983:39). Thus, the early stages of operating under new systems may be characterized by uncertainty, conflict and misunderstanding among employees, who may variously adapt, modify, reassert and/or redefine their positions under new operating procedures and working relationships set up by management during the process of organizational transition.

This is also the period in which a relatively stabilized system of operation may emerge comprising new patterns of relationships and new forms of working practices. It is during this timeframe, therefore, that the 'outcomes' of change can be examined and contrasted with the operating system prior to change. Although in reality it is often unrealistic to talk of an 'endpoint' of change (as the process continues *ad infinitum*) it does make sense to talk of the 'effects' of a particular type of change. In the case of large-scale operational change, it is possible to identify a period at some stage after implementation when the daily work routines of employees become part of the the operating system (which is no longer regarded as 'new'). Whilst the ongoing process of change will continue, this is the period which can be used to identify the outcomes of change on organizational structures and traditional operating practices.

These three general timeframes in the process of change provide a useful framework from which to begin a detailed examination of the issues surrounding the management of organizational transition. However, although every major change programme will have an organizationally defined beginning, middle and end, in practice it is not only difficult to identify the start and completion of change programmes (for example, there is often more than one organizational history of change and these may be reconstructed over time), but also to explain the complex pathways and routes to establishing new operational processes. Therefore, in examining the complex and 'black box' process of change there are considerable returns to be gained from developing a framework for data analysis. It is argued here that a useful way of tackling the problem of analysing complex change data is to construct data categories around the various activities and tasks associated with organizational transitions. For example, data categories for the activities associated with the establishment of new organizational arrangements may comprise: system selection, identification of type of change, implementation, preparation and planning, and search and assessment (for an illustration see also Chapter 4). These tasks are unlikely to occur in a tidy linear fashion throughout the process of change but, rather, will normally overlap, occur simultaneously, stop and start, and be part of the initial and later phases of major change programmes. Nevertheless, they are useful for locating and sorting data on change which might otherwise be too complex to deal with systematically. Although at a more general level there can be no definitive list of appropriate data categories, as these should be modified or revised to fit particular case examples and/or the planning requirements of different change programmes (for example, in many cases evaluation and appraisal may be a useful category to include), these categories do provide a useful starting point for locating and analysing change data.

For some readers the claim that a rational analytical structure should be used to ensure that reconstructed explanations are able to incorporate the non-rational and non-linear processes of change may appear paradoxical. However, it is argued here that a failure to deconstruct complex processes into manageable analytical sections is likely to result in highly abstract and largely impenetrable explanations which are of no practical value. In short, the construction of data categories is useful for sorting data on change and for aiding our understanding of what is a complex and dynamic process.

A processual approach for explaining change

In order to explain the ways in which the management of change is shaped at critical junctures during the process of transition, it is necessary to further develop our framework for analysing change. One way of doing this is to classify the major determinants of change and to locate these within the temporal framework developed above. The three major groups of determinants used here comprise:

- The substance of change
- The politics of change
- The context of change

The substance of change refers to the type and scale of organizational change. In this book, the concern is with the organizational processes associated with the introduction and use of new techniques and technologies (such as, just-in-time, total quality management, and management information systems). In each case, understanding the constituents of the change is an important prerequisite to understanding the process and outcomes of that change. In other words, what are the characteristics of the changes being introduced and how do they enable or constrain the options open to management during the introduction of a major change programme? In Chapters 4–8 the substance of each change programme is first discussed before processual analysis is undertaken.

The politics of change is taken to refer to the political activity of consultation, negotiation, conflict and resistance, which occurs at various levels within and outside an organization during the process of managing change. Examples of political activity outside of an organization would be governmental pressure, competitor alliances or the influence of overseas divisions of Multi-National Corporations (MNCs). Internal political activity can be in the form of shopfloor negotiations between trade union representatives and management, between consultants (working within the organization) and various organizational groups, and between and within managerial, supervisory and operative personnel. These individuals or groups can influence decision-making and the setting of agendas at critical junctures during the process of transformational change (see also, McLoughlin and Clark, 1988:42–4).

Finally, the context of change is taken to refer to the past and present external and internal operating environments as well as the influence of future projections and expectations on current operating practice. In this way, the context of change can be divided into the internal organizational context, and the context pertaining to the environment in which the organization operates. External contextual factors would therefore include changes in competitors' strategies and the level of international competition, government legislation, changing social expectations, technological innovations, and changes in the level of business activity, whereas the five key internal contextual factors comprise: human resources; administrative structures; technology; product or service; and history and culture.

Human resources refer to the individual members and groups of people who constitute an organization. This is the area on which OD programmes have tended to focus, namely, on improving the nature and quality of interpersonal work relations. More recently, greater emphasis has been placed on teamwork and intergroup development (see Chapters 5 and 7). Essentially, the personality, skills, established work relations and patterns of employee behaviour comprise the human contextual setting in which change is introduced.

Administrative structures refer to the allocation of tasks and the design of jobs and work structures. The structure of an organization, the formalized lines of communication, established working procedures, managerial hierarchies and reward systems are often all transformed in major administrative change programmes. In the work of Lawrence and Lorsch (1967) and Burns and Stalker (1961), it is shown how an organization structure may be defined in terms of the degree of complexity, formalization, differentiation, centralization and integration. Major changes in administrative structures may involve a movement from an organic towards a more formalized mechanistic pattern of arrangements, a shift from a function to a product structure or the creation of a matrix design.

The context of technology is used broadly to refer to the plant, machinery and tools (the apparatus) and the associated philosophy and system of work organization which blend together in the production of goods or services. Whilst, in practice, the focus of a major change in technology is on the equipment or apparatus (Batstone *et al*, 1987:2), this will ultimately necessitate a change in work tasks, skills, job content and supervision (see Chapters 4 and 8).

The primary product or service of an organization refers to the core business, whether this is providing an insurance service, baking bread, or manufacturing automobiles. This contextual factor constrains the options open to senior management in the strategic redirection of a company's good or service. For example, it is highly unlikely that a manufacturing firm would find it economically feasible to redesign plant and equipment for the purpose of organic farming.

Whilst it is analytically useful to separate the factors of human resources, administrative structures, technology and product/service, a change in one will often necessitate a change in another. Moreover, in examining these contextual factors as determinants of change, it is important to view them not only as they currently exist but as they are perceived to have developed over time, and how they have become legitimized within the organization. This contextual factor has been termed the history and culture of an organization.

History and culture refers to the contextual evolution of shared beliefs and assumptions within organizations. The concept is intended to incorporate both a historical perspective which can take account of multiple histories of the context in which change is taking place and an understanding of organizational culture. In the framework developed in this chapter, organizational culture is viewed as a multi-layered phenomenon comprising surface and deeper level elements and, following Schein, can be defined as:

> A pattern of basic assumptions – invented, discovered, or developed by a given group as it learns to cope with its problems of external adaptation and internal integration – that has worked well enough to be considered valid and, therefore, to be taught to new members as the correct way to perceive, think, and feel in relation to those problems.
> (Schein, 1985:9)

Surface level elements are taken to refer to those things in an organization which are readily accessible and which we can observe direct, such as espoused values articulated in company documents, office layout and dress codes. In contrast, the deeper aspects of culture relate to those underlying assumptions and beliefs which evolve as groups attempt to make sense of their collective experience within the work environment. This is what Schein (1985) refers to as the *essence* of culture, which can be uncovered from in-depth studies of organizational life.

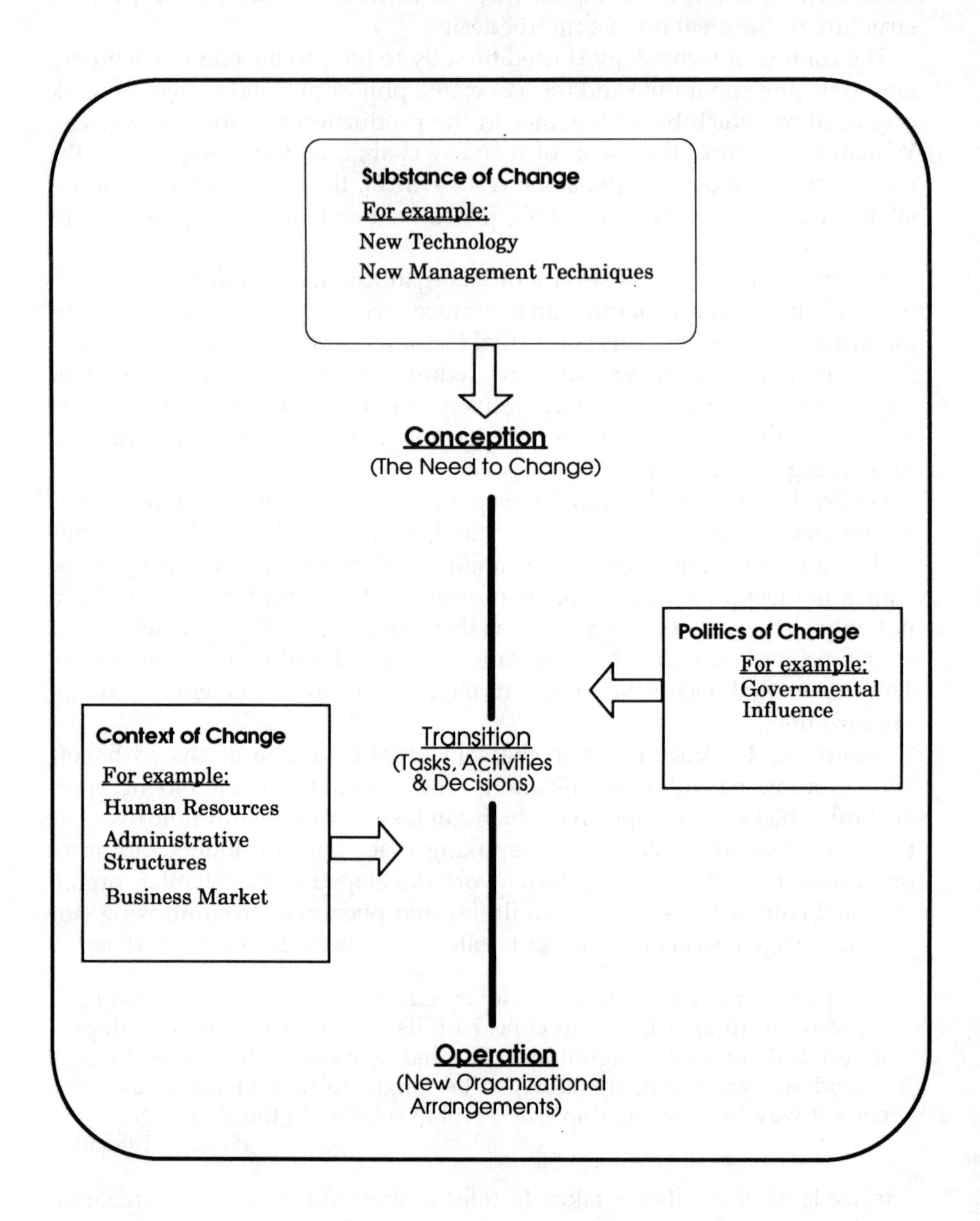

Figure 3.2 Organizational change: a processual framework

The more widespread concern and discussion of culture in programmes of change in part derives from the influence that culture can have on the way people perceive, think about, and ultimately behave in organizations. For example, cultural beliefs and assumptions, as well as organizational myths, legends and histories, can all exert a powerful influence on the behaviour of organizational members and may act as a form of internalized control. Although in the study of organizations it may prove possible to identify a dominant organizational value and belief system, most companies are characterized by the existence of separate subcultures, which in the case of countercultures may serve to challenge and change the core beliefs and values of the dominant organizational culture (Martin and Siehl, 1983). Furthermore, management may seek to establish new belief systems through the use of cultural change training programmes and/or by using their positions of power and influence to replace disruptive staff and reward those who conform to the newly prescribed set of values (Bamber and Patrickson, 1994). For these reasons, it is important to take account of the history and culture of organizations in contextual examinations of the process of change.

Through combining the three general timeframes of change with this threefold classification of factors shaping the process of organizational change (that is, the substance, context and politics of change), it is possible to construct a processual framework of organizational change. This alternative model (for analysing and explaining the process of managing organizational transition), is presented diagrammatically in Figure 3.2, which is intended to convey the interconnectedness and complexity of dynamic processes of change through combining a threefold classification of factors shaping the process of organizational transformation with a clear representation of the temporal nature of change. As a diagrammatic representation of the processual framework employed throughout the remainder of the book, Figure 3.2 should be referred to by the reader whenever necessary.

The final element of this alternative framework that requires some further elaboration centres on the changing significance of factors as shapers and determinants of change during different time periods in the process of organizational change. As Clark *et al* (1988:222) have noted: 'Apart from its analytical and explanatory value in particular cases, the processual approach also sensitizes us to the fact that there are no fixed outcomes of change under a given . . . system, simply outcomes at particular moments in time'.

Typically, the initial conceptualization of a need to change and the strategic decisions on the substance of change and system selection will be made at senior management level (Child, 1972). These decisions are likely to be influenced by management's strategic objectives, the state of the business market, and the availability and applicability of new technologies, techniques, products and services to particular operating systems. During the planning and implementation of a major change programme, project management, authority relationships, training, timescale, budgets and so forth will be the main focus of attention. Once implementation is under way and initial operation of the new system commences, then factors such as business market considerations are likely to decline in significance, whereas occupational and employee concerns are likely to increase in importance and influence the outcome of management's strategic objectives behind the introduction of the change programme. Finally, under ongoing processes of change of a comparatively stable system, occupational and employee responses will further serve to shape the operational use made of the new forms of work organization and employment relations. At this later period, employees and occupational groups will adapt to change and, in the process, they are likely to redefine the consequence of change for their positions within the new organization structures and operating practices imposed by management during the initial operation of the new system. In short, external influences tend to decrease in importance at each successive time period in our framework of the process of change, whereas occupational and employee concerns will tend to become more organizationally significant towards the latter periods associated with major change programmes. It is also worth stressing that, in practice, the pertinence of these factors in shaping organizational adaptation is likely to vary both between and within existing organizations (see Chapters 4–10).

Conclusion: making sense of the transition process

This chapter has set out to provide an explanation of the academic debate on the challenge of new organizational arrangements and in particular, on the implications of new technologies and management techniques for labour flexibility and the organization and control of work. A processual approach to managing transitions has been formulated and the key determinants of change have been classified into three broad categories, namely, the context, politics and substance of change. It has been argued that within organizations there will always be a number of periods (sometimes overlapping and rarely distinct) associated with any major change programme. Although the appropriate number of categories identified for analytical purposes and the order in which they take place are likely to vary between organizations, there remains a historical timeframe within which change progammes take place. In other words, in order for an organizational transition to occur, there will have been some initial conceptual stage of the need to change, a period of transition in which the old methods of working are replaced by a new system of operation, and a time when the emergence of new working practices and procedures can be clearly identified as forming part of the production or service arrangements of a changed organization. Furthermore, whilst the scale of change may decrease during the latter period of major change programmes, change within organizations should be viewed as an ongoing process.

Within these three general timeframes, it is analytically useful to construct a number of data categories around the various tasks and activities associated with the establishment of new organizational arrangements. Such a framework makes it easier for the researcher, consultant and practitioner to identify, analyse and explain factors which shape outcomes at different moments or periods during the process of organizational transition. In the chapter that follows the example of computer technology and corporate change within British Rail is used to demonstrate the utility of this approach for explaining the transition towards new organizational arrangements.

4

APPLYING A PROCESSUAL APPROACH: THE COMPUTERIZATION OF FREIGHT OPERATIONS AT BRITISH RAIL

Introduction

In this chapter the processual framework developed in Chapter 3 is applied to a historical reconstruction of the factors which facilitated the successful introduction of a fully operational computerized management information system in British Rail's Freight Division. It demonstrates the importance of internal and external variables in shaping the process of change and illustrates the weakness of studies which attempt to explain the dynamic and processual nature of change from single events or incidences.

The case in question concerns British Rail's decision to invest £13 million in a new computer information system to improve management control of freight operations. The system, known as Total Operations Processing System (TOPS), has been in operation since 1975 following a four-year implementation programme. This investment was one of the first large-scale ventures by British industry in the application of on-line real-time computer information technology. The decision to computerize was taken at senior management level, and the strategic intentions behind the introduction of TOPS comprised various 'business market', 'operating', 'product', and 'cost' objectives. These objectives were shaped by the opportunities offered by computer-based technologies and the nature of railway freight operations, each of which are discussed below. This is followed by an analysis of the conception of a need to change and the identification of the TOPS computer system. Other tasks associated with the change, such as the search and assessment of options, the preparation and planning for change and workplace implementation, are all examined, and the key 'problems' which surrounded the initial operation of the system are discussed. The case concludes by summarizing the main findings and outlining the lessons to be learnt from the management of corporate change in a large 'conservative' organization. But, first, it is necessary to examine some of the debates surrounding the substance of change (which in this case is computer technology) prior to embarking on a case analysis of British Rail.

The organizational implications of computer technology

The debate on the effects of computer technology on organizations was initiated in the late 1950s. Leavitt and Whisler, in their now well known article, 'Management in the 80s', stated that:

> Over the last decade a new technology has begun to take hold in American business, one so new that its significance is still difficult to evaluate . . . The new technology does not yet have a single established name. We shall call it information technology. It is composed of several parts. One includes techniques for processing large amounts of information rapidly, and it is epitomized by the high speed computer.
>
> (Leavitt and Whisler, 1958:41)

At this time, much of the debate centred around the issue of whether computer technology would be used to centralize or decentralize production operations control (see, for example, Hoos, 1960; Burlingame 1961; Myers, 1967) and the question of whether the intermediate layer between top management and the workforce would be eroded or enhanced as a consequence of computerization (see, for example, Whisler, 1970; Stewart, 1971). Some commentators argued that middle management would be replaced by computer controlled information systems, and that line management would become reduced to a basic routine monitoring function (Mumford and Ward, 1965; Whisler, 1967). Others argued that, although the effects of computerization on middle management would be small, junior management and supervisory jobs would tend to become either fully or partially 'automated' (Stewart, 1971). Alternatively, it was also argued that certain aspects of supervisory line management (for example, co-ordination and overall understanding of the problems of ground-level operations) would be heightened and their role as technical problem-solvers strengthened (Ashen, 1960).

The early studies of Mumford and Banks (1967) and Whisler (1967), claimed that computer technology would lead to a reduction in the number of clerical staff; the displacement of departments through increased integration; the centralization of control (which would increase the 'visibility' of decisions made by middle and lower level managerial staff); and an erosion of the control responsibility of first-line supervisors. For the purpose of examining the relationship between computer technology and organizational adaptation, these early debates raised three points worth emphasizing here. First, that computer technology may enable an organization to either centralize or decentralize decision-making authority. In other words, technology does not determine organizational structure: rather, this is determined by the way in which the technology is introduced and used. Secondly, that strategies which promote centralization are likely to erode the control responsibilities of lower line management, supervisory and operative staffs. Thirdly, that strategies which promote decentralization may either reduce or increase the control responsibility of supervisory management and/or operatives. Thus, even these early studies clearly indicated the importance of examining the process by which technology is introduced into the industrial enterprise in order to explain the emergence of new forms of work organization.

With the growth in size of industrial enterprises and changes in technology, more extensive, formalized information control systems have been developed. These control systems, concerned with processing information (in order to co-ordinate diverse and spatially distant activities), have been further enhanced following developments in telecommunication networks and the converging developments in microelectronic and computing technology (see, for example, Barron and Curnow 1979; Benson and Lloyd 1983). Recent developments have served to reduce the cost and size of computer information systems whilst improving their performance and reliability. This has led to the widespread application of computer-based systems which provide 'real-time' (as-it-happens) information on which 'intelligent' decisions can be based. The significance of these more recent developments in microelectronics and computer technologies have been well documented elsewhere and need not be discussed in detail here (for example, Forester 1980 and 1985).

There are, however, two essential points worth stressing. First, that information is a key resource in the control of diverse and spatially distant production operations. Secondly, that comprehensive computer information handling systems are currently available to organizations. According to Crowe and Jones, these developments enable organizational practitioners to make a choice between either centralizing or decentralizing operations control: 'The computer . . . can make efficient centralization possible . . . or it can equally make for efficient decentralization to take place making available to all locations the appropriate information required for decisions' (Crowe and Jones, 1978:7).

The organizational significance of modern computer systems derives from their ability to capture, store, manipulate and rapidly distribute information on which decisions can be made. For the most part, these systems have been used to improve the efficiency of hierarchical organizations, through replacing traditional manual reporting systems of communication and control. Thus, it is not the information being processed which is new but, rather, it is the sudden availability, accuracy and immediacy of this information to management which has changed the nature of operations control within these organizations. Moreover, through maintaining an historical record of, for example, fluctuations in the supply and demand of resources, managements are also able to evaluate potential strategies for changing the future level or method of resource provision. Nevertheless, whilst this information processing technology is bringing about a new diversity of operator tasks (Cavestro, 1989:217) and has the potential for improving management decision-making through the provision of accurate up-to-date information on current or past performance, the consequence of change for the organization and control of work remains an important area of managerial choice, as Appelbaum and Albin (1989:247) argue: 'Computerized-control technology alters the balance of work tasks and decision-making between people and machines, increasing the scope managers have to redesign jobs so that the skill content of work is increased or decreased'.

This claim indicates the importance of examining the process by which new technologies are introduced into organizations, and this is the objective of the case study which follows. Furthermore, in using this case to illustrate the utility of the processual approach developed in Chapter 3, it is important to first say something about the context of railway freight operations.

The context of railway freight operations

Railway freight transits consist of a complex and interdependent set of 'time sensitive' cycles of operations. The problem of management control centres on the task of providing an adequate supply of resources (wagons, locomotives, train crews) to meet changing customer demands, and then to integrate freight transits over a national rail network. Information on the location and disposition of resources over the entire network has to be captured, transmitted, processed and disseminated. This information then has to be utilized in the control and integration of a number of interdependent cycles of operations: for example, about the route to be taken, the provision of train crews (and relief), the type of locomotive required, the compatibility of wagons, and their integration into existing and planned passenger and freight train services.

The basic elements of this cycle of operations are as follows (see Figure 4.1):

- A customer is provided with empty wagons for loading.
- The loaded wagons make a local trip to a marshalling yard.
- The wagons are marshalled into a train and a locomotive (including train crew) is attached.
- The train makes a trunk trip to another marshalling yard.
- The locomotive is detached and the wagons are shunted according to their individual destinations.
- The wagons make a local trip to the customer unloading point.

The control and co-ordination of these operations rest to a large degree on the availability and accuracy of information about the location and disposition of resources (in particular, empty wagons) and the movement and composition of freight trains. This is made even more imperative by the regular occurrence of contingencies in railway operations, including fluctuations in demand for freight resources, resource shortages, train delays and locomotive failures, which require the daily rescheduling of planned operations and services.

The conception of a need to change

During the 1960s, British Rail's freight operations faced an acute economic problem (Hirst, 1974:40–56). Whilst the Beeching Report had made an

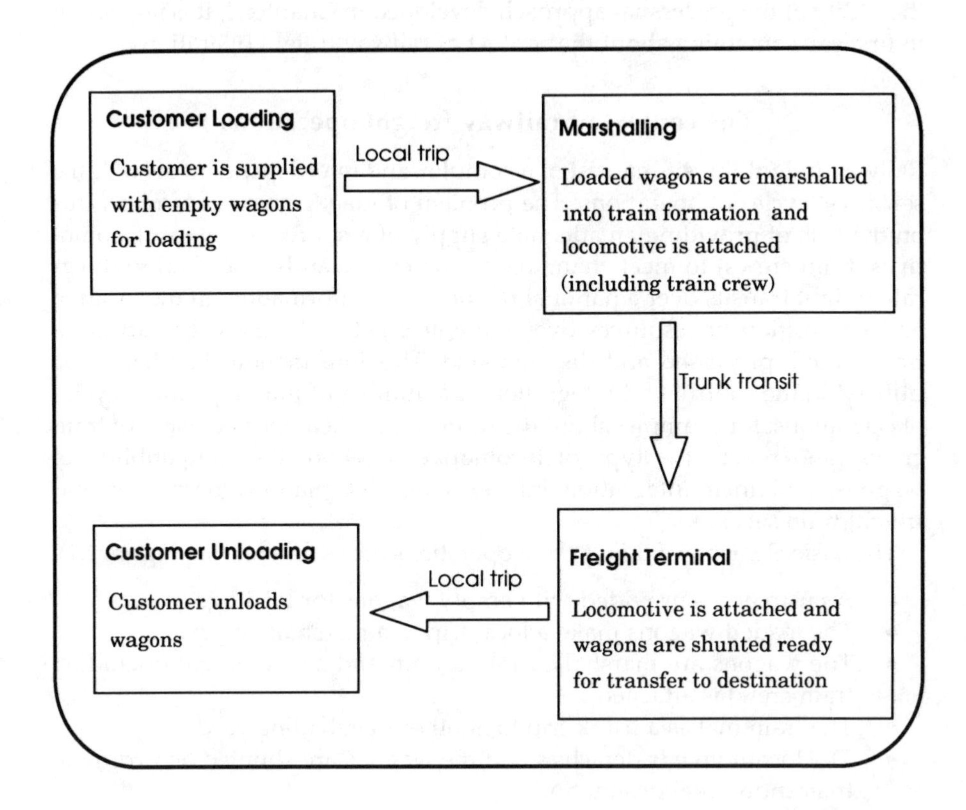

Figure 4.1 Cycle of operations in freight transits

attempt to arrest the decline in the passenger business (see for discussion, Pryke, 1971: 249–55), little had been done to reshape the ailing freight business which suffered from increased competition from other types of transport – in particular, road haulage of small consignments – and a decline in the industries which most used rail transport (Ferner, 1985). In 1956, 21% of freight tonnage was moved by rail, compared with 75% by road (McLoughlin *et al*, 1983:6). By 1967, British Rail's share of the market had fallen to 11% and road haulage had increased to 84.6%. In 1967, just over 6% of British Rail's receipts came from the haulage of freight, 48% of which came from the carriage of bulk commodities such as coal, coke, iron and steel, which accounted for 75% of railway freight tonnes carried (McLoughlin *et al*, 1983).

By the late 1960s the bulk of British Rail's freight business was concentrated in the carriage of bulk commodities, in the face of a rapid decline in small consignments more suitable for road haulage (see, for example, Pryke, 1971 and 1981). There was growing concern that the freight business could not remain viable, since the industries which provided the bulk of its freight traffic were either declining or growing only slowly: for example, coal and coke tonnage carried by rail fell by 27% between 1956 and 1967 as a result of the decline in the coal industry (Reid and Allen, 1970:107–10). By 1967, British Rail had accumulated a working deficit plus interest charges of £153 million, largely as a result of the decline in freight business (Hirst, 1974:64).

In the preliminaries to the 1968 Transport Act, the then Labour Government expressed concern over the position of the freight business. British Rail responded by undertaking a series of planning exercises aimed at finding a way to improve productivity. In these, the unavailability of accurate, up-to-date information was identified as the key factor contributing to the gross underutilization of resources, and consequently was singled out as an area where improvements needed to be made. Thus, the opportunities afforded by new computer technologies to improve this situation influenced the British Railways Board in their strategic decision to computerize the freight information system. It was felt that computer technology could be used to arrest the decline in freight traffic by enabling the better utilization and control of resources, and hence improve the speed and efficiency of freight transits.

The principal problems associated with controlling the pre-TOPS freight system were seen to derive from the manual hierarchical system of freight information control, in particular, three inter-related characteristics of the pre-TOPS system. First, management relied on daily physical checks for its information about the disposition of resources. At headquarters, day-to-day decisions about resource allocation (especially the supply of empty wagons to meet customers' loading requirements) were contingent upon the provision of information through hierarchical manual reporting procedures which listed the location and status of wagon and locomotive fleets. Secondly, the effectiveness of manual reporting procedures and information flows was undermined by a combination of the parochial attitudes of railway freight supervisors and the impossibility of validating the information provided by staff responsible for checking wagons. The need to satisfy local requirements and respond to fluctuations in customer demands meant that 'figure adjusting' in daily returns was widespread, and that stores of unreported wagons and 'spare' locomotives were accumulated in individual local areas as a matter of course. Thirdly, customers had no knowledge of the whereabouts of their consignments. Once despatched, their wagons were 'lost' until such time as they arrived at their destination. Despite the attention of a small army of wagon inspectors, it was estimated that only 80% of the wagon fleet was accounted for in each daily distribution report (McLoughlin *et al*, 1983:8).

All these factors combined to produce a grossly inefficient utilization of material and human resources. These operating inefficiencies resulted in a wagon fleet which, despite substantial reductions post-Beeching, was still too large for the size of the network and volume of freight traffic. In addition, there was an over-provision of locomotives and train crews due to the variability of demands for freight services. Thus, the decision to computerize was a response to internal operating problems associated with accurate information flows for the control of railway freight operations.

Identification of type of change

The availability of computer technology and external business market pressures both played a part in influencing the strategic decision to computerize the freight information system. This was supported by British Rail's 1971/75 Freight Plan, which unequivocally recommended computerization, claiming that it would stem the loss-making trend and make possible an expansion in British Rail's share of the freight market. It identified the need for a 'real-time' computerized freight information system which would enable the more effective utilization of resources in the day-to-day control of railway freight operations. Moreover, it was also suggested that, if a suitable computer system could be obtained from another railway, this would minimize delays, reduce the risks involved and enable considerable savings in development costs (British Railways Board, 1970).

The 1971/75 Freight Plan set out the specifications from which a 'world tour' of railway computer systems could be judged. These specifications were as follows:

1. More effective distribution and utilization of freight rolling stock.
2. More effective pre-planning of yard and terminal operations.
3. The availability of accurate information to provide guaranteed transits from source to destination.
4. Prompt response to customers' requests for information on the location of loaded and empty wagons.
5. Provision of a database for a comprehensive management information system.
6. More efficient control of locomotives and train crews.

7. Prompt assessment of the practicality of meeting customers' needs for the running of special trains at short notice.
8. More effective re-planning of the total workload, particularly short-term planning of the highly variable element of the freight business.
9. Provision of an efficient system of traffic regulation and the means to decide on the priority of freight train movements

(Arnott, 1979:1)

After reaching a decision to computerize British Rail's system of freight information control, senior management then had to decide on which system to purchase to achieve their strategic objectives.

Search and assessment of options

A team of British Rail executives, appointed by British Railways Board, travelled overseas to examine existing computer freight information systems. The team investigated systems in France, Germany, Japan and Canada. The TOPS computer system, developed by the Southern Pacific Railroad in Canada, was identified as the system that most closely met the requirements listed above. Unlike the experimental nature of computer systems used elsewhere, TOPS had been developed over 10 years and represented a tried and tested system which had also proven to be a commercial success (McLoughlin *et al*, 1982:4).

The development of the original TOPS computer system began in the early 1960s when, in the face of increasing competition, Southern Pacific Railroad (which deals almost entirely in freight traffic) was facing a financial loss for the first time this century. A cutback in the space programme at around the same time had left International Business Machines (IBM) with a surplus of high level computer programmers and, at the initiation of Ted Strong (an entrepreneurial vice-president of IBM who had links with Southern Pacific Railroad), a collaboration was agreed on the development of a computer information control system for Southern Pacific Railroad's freight operations. In 1968, Southern Pacific Railroad had devoted 660 person-years of effort to the development of TOPS software programs. By the end of the 1960s, TOPS was a 'comprehensive' and 'proven' computer system (Dawson, 1986:90).

Systems selection

In June 1970, representatives from Southern Pacific Railroad carried out a feasibility study on the applicability of TOPS to the very different operating practices on British Rail. The Southern Pacific Railroad team made a number of visits to different British Rail regions, talked to management at all levels and concluded that TOPS could be used successfully in British Rail. A team from British Rail then re-visited Southern Pacific Railroad and began to probe the possibilities more deeply and to determine realistic timescales for inclusion in the submission for investment approval to put to British Railways Board and, later, to the government.

The major benefits to be derived from the TOPS investment were judged to be savings on wagon costs through better utilization of rolling stock and a reduction in the size of the wagon fleet; reduced operating costs through improved utilization of locomotives and train crews (with computerization it was expected that 250 locomotives and 1,200 train crews could be saved by 1980); and increased traffic retention through improving the quality of services by ensuring that 90% of train movements occurred as planned in the timetable. In the event, the savings from improved wagon utilization alone were seen as sufficient justification for investment in the TOPS computer system.

The draft submission for investment approval for the TOPS computer system was presented to the Investment Committee in March 1971, and from March until June financial debates ensued over the investment, especially because of its speculative nature. In addition, the decision to purchase TOPS software and IBM hardware was met with considerable vacillation within British Railways Board and the Department of Transport, where considerable pressure was exerted to 'buy British'. However, the TOPS software was designed for use with IBM hardware, and an equivalent British product was yet to be developed. As it turned out, the Investment Committee agreed to implement TOPS on the casting vote of the chairman.

In October 1971, the scheme was submitted to John Peyton, the Minister of Transport Industries who, in giving his approval for the TOPS investment, stated that the personal views of the chairman and the chief executive that the project should go ahead weighed heavily with him in his decision. The major advantages of the TOPS computer system over a 'home-grown' system were seen to be in the shorter lead times involved; savings in development costs; and the availability of specialist expertise from North America on a consultancy basis.

The TOPS computer system

The TOPS computer system is an operations processing system and comprises: a hardware configuration; software architecture; and operating procedures. The basic hardware consists of mainframe computer equipment and numerous peripheral devices. The mainframe computer equipment comprises two identical 370/168 IBM computers. One is always 'on-line', in the sense that it is connected to outlying terminals and is continually executing the TOPS Control and Application Programs. The other computer is described as 'off-line', which means that it does not deal with everyday programs but is essentially a backup to the 'on-line' computer in case of breakdown (see Figure 4.2). However, it should be noted that some TOPS programs always run off-line.

The software architecture consists of a number of computer programs which control the computer in the execution of its tasks. The five major program types in operation on the TOPS system are:

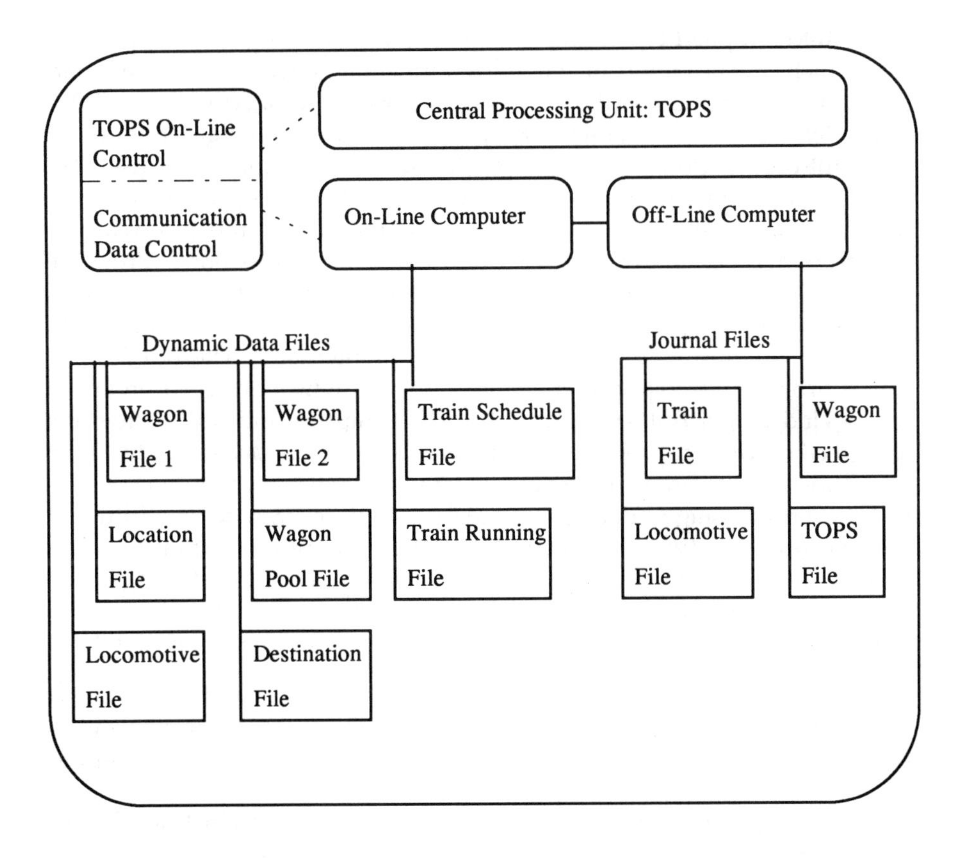

Figure 4.2 Total operations processing system

1. IBM Support and Utility Programs.
2. IBM Operating System.
3. TOPS Control Programs.
4. TOPS Application Programs.
5. TOPS Support and Utility Programs.

The IBM-supplied Operating System is a suite of programs supplied by IBM which covers a range of generalized functions such as transferring data to and from peripherals (the peripheral devices associated with the TOPS computer system are essentially for the purpose of receiving data, producing print-outs of processed data, and for storing data for future use). The IBM Support and Utility Programs are specific function programs for use off-line to undertake common computer activities; for example, copying the data from disks to tapes for security purposes. The TOPS Control Programs are general function programs used on the on-line computer for controlling the handling and processing of TOPS messages (originally supplied by TOPS Inc., but now maintained and developed internally). The TOPS Application Programs are specific function programs which are used on-line to process individual TOPS messages. The TOPS Support and Utility Programs are specific function programs for off-line activities associated with TOPS, which include the preparation of disk data to be referenced on-line, and the historical processing of data generated by the on-line system. In addition to the five program types outlined above, there are also a variety of other specific function application programs which have been developed by British Rail since the initial introduction of the TOPS computer system.

The basic operating procedure of the TOPS computer system is as follows:

1. Clerical staff send and request information about train and wagon movements by entering 'messages' through computer terminals in local offices which are connected by land lines to the TOPS computer system at headquarters.
2. The 'message' is then passed through Communication Data Control (CDC), where facilities exist for re-routing 'messages' to and from individual terminals via different land lines as and when transmission problems occur.
3. Finally, the 'message' is passed through the TOPS Computer Centre, where it is automatically fed into the computer system for other processing.

An example of how TOPS is used to control the train movement cycles is provided in Figure 4.3; in this example, the following procedures would be undertaken by the TOPS clerks to report changes to the computer in the wagon's status and location as it makes this journey. The *release* procedure notifies that wagon B498585 status has changed from *inposition* (that is, loading/unloading) to *normal* (that is, available to move). The *transfer origin/destination* procedures report the wagon's movement on a local trip from the siding in Drinnick Mill to the main marshalling yard at St Blazey. On *release*,

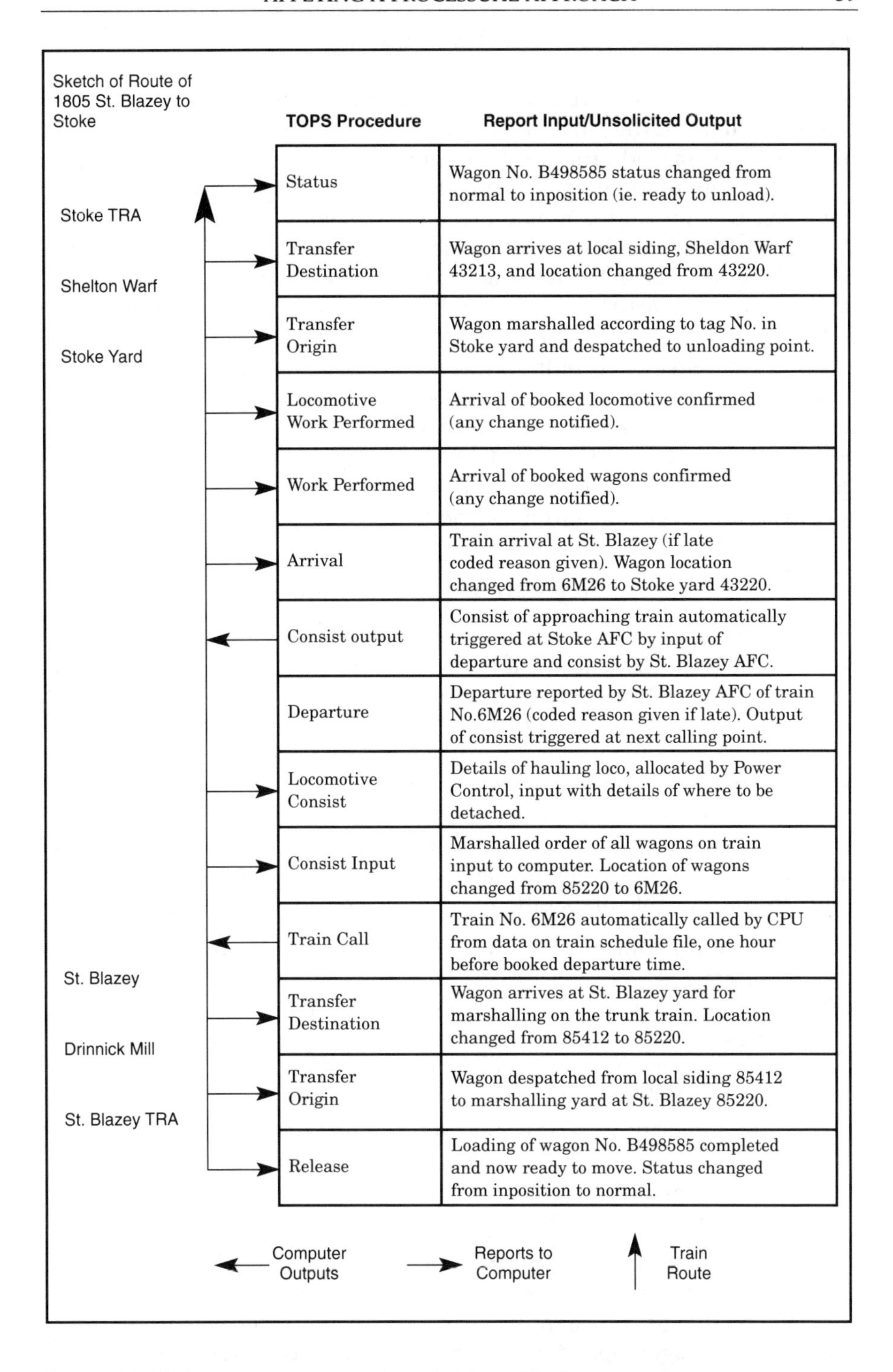

TOPS Procedure	Report Input/Unsolicited Output
Status	Wagon No. B498585 status changed from normal to inposition (ie. ready to unload).
Transfer Destination	Wagon arrives at local siding, Sheldon Warf 43213, and location changed from 43220.
Transfer Origin	Wagon marshalled according to tag No. in Stoke yard and despatched to unloading point.
Locomotive Work Performed	Arrival of booked locomotive confirmed (any change notified).
Work Performed	Arrival of booked wagons confirmed (any change notified).
Arrival	Train arrival at St. Blazey (if late coded reason given). Wagon location changed from 6M26 to Stoke yard 43220.
Consist output	Consist of approaching train automatically triggered at Stoke AFC by input of departure and consist by St. Blazey AFC.
Departure	Departure reported by St. Blazey AFC of train No.6M26 (coded reason given if late). Output of consist triggered at next calling point.
Locomotive Consist	Details of hauling loco, allocated by Power Control, input with details of where to be detached.
Consist Input	Marshalled order of all wagons on train input to computer. Location of wagons changed from 85220 to 6M26.
Train Call	Train No. 6M26 automatically called by CPU from data on train schedule file, one hour before booked departure time.
Transfer Destination	Wagon arrives at St. Blazey yard for marshalling on the trunk train. Location changed from 85412 to 85220.
Transfer Origin	Wagon despatched from local siding 85412 to marshalling yard at St. Blazey 85220.
Release	Loading of wagon No. B498585 completed and now ready to move. Status changed from inposition to normal.

Figure 4.3 Train movement cycle (adapted from BR documents)

the wagon is allocated a *tag* number which indicates its next marshalling yard beyond St Blazey (in this case the tag is 43T). The *train call* procedure is an 'unsolicited output' from the computer informing St Blazey, one hour before departure is due, that the 1805 to Stoke is scheduled to run. Yard staff report the marshalled order of the wagons for the train to the TOPS clerks who input the information to the computer as a wagon *consist* listing the numbers, weights and commodities of the wagons making up the train. Wagon B498585's location is changed from Stoke Yard, 43213, to train 6M26. In addition, details of the hauling locomotive are supplied by the control organization. The *departure* procedure reports the actual time the train leaves St Blazey giving a coded reason if late. On receiving this information, the computer automatically outputs the full *consist* of the train at the next booked calling point, which in this case is Stoke freight yard, location number 43220. The *transfer origin/destination* procedures report the movement of wagon B498585 from Stoke yard to its unloading point at the customer siding at Shelton Wharf, location number 43213. On arrival at the siding, the wagon's status is changed from *normal* to *inposition*.

Preparation and planning

A central feature of the TOPS investment strategy was the speed of implementation which was required if the various strategic objectives concerning cost savings were to be achieved. In order to ensure that implementation went smoothly, two years were given over to the preparation and planning of how the changes were to be introduced. If the investment was to bring the necessary improvement in freight service operations required to rescue the business, it had to be implemented within budget by 1975. Despite the advantages of 'buying-in' a proven system, a considerable implementation task had still to be faced and the trade unions convinced of its necessity. This required considerable preparation and involved:

1. extensive modification of the TOPS software to suit British Rail's requirements;
2. the construction of a new computer centre and outlying local freight centres;
3. the enhancement of the British Rail telecommunications network to cope with TOPS data transmission requirements;
4. a programme of staff education and training (especially for the supervisors and staff responsible for exploiting the system); and
5. occupational and employee consultation and negotiation and the actual cut-over and operation of the TOPS computer system.

Unlike previous and subsequent innovations within British Rail, it was decided that the TOPS project organization should be deliberately constructed on cross-functional lines, incorporating under the overall control of one project manager, operating, computing and telecommunication specialists (see Figure 4.4). This particular organizational design was the product of

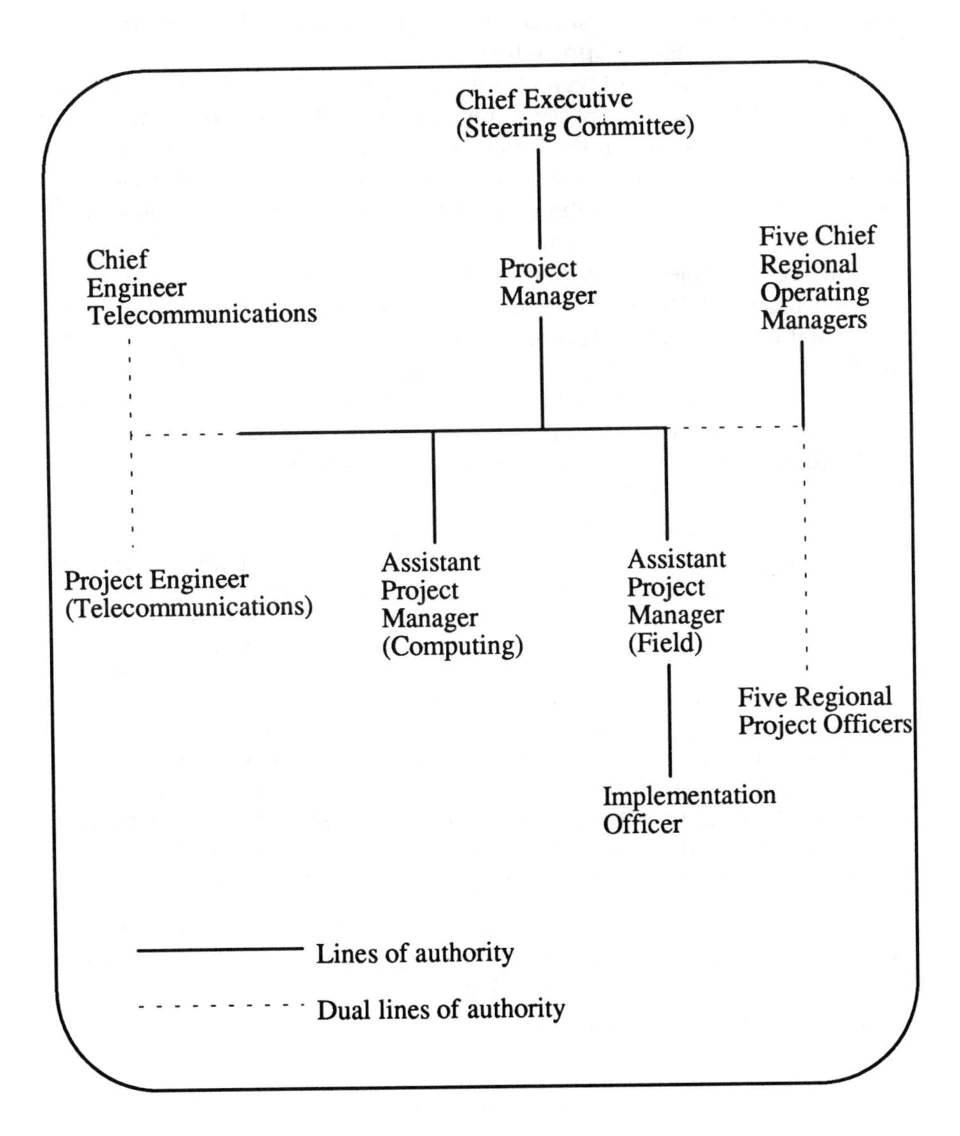

Figure 4.4 TOPS project organization

the senior British Rail management who developed the TOPS implementation strategy. Two points worth emphasizing are: first, that the project manager was invested with considerable authority and had a direct channel left open to the British Railways Board Chief Executive; and secondly, that the cross-functional project organization was instrumental in avoiding interdepartmental rivalries and procedural delays.

The high level backing given to the TOPS project allowed for the necessary 'rule-bending' and 'by-passing' required of such a tight implementation schedule. The decision that the Project Manager should be a senior member of the operating department who knew nothing about computers had ensured that TOPS implementation would take into account operating requirements of British Rail's railway freight network. Moreover, through ensuring that the TOPS project would be represented on the top operating body within British Rail (the daily 'operating conference'), it was possible to avoid the formal bureaucratic jungle and overcome individual managerial resistance. In the words of the TOPS Project Manager: 'I had the trust and backing from my colleagues to provide for them a workable system for operating staff. This obviated a lot of time which would otherwise have been involved in meetings, explanations and arguments on how the system should be developed for use on British Rail'.

In the Project Manager's view, the authority vested in him was a critical factor in achieving some of the major changes in management operating practice which the TOPS computer system made possible:

> I had heard that the intention was to draft Management Services resources to me on loan as necessary, and it did not appeal to me in the slightest. If I was going to run the project I wanted to run it my way, with a team completely identified with it and determined to share in its success. Knowing all too well the strength of the establishment I didn't dissipate time and effort making an issue of it, but went ahead building up the kind of joint organization I considered essential . . . I can understand the annoyance when the *fait accompli* was realized, but without it TOPS would at best have been delayed, and at worst failed.

Within this framework, a specialist implementation team was formed to carry out the task of implementing the system in each local area. The plan adopted was to introduce TOPS to the freight network in stages over a period of approximately two years.

Implementation

In setting up the implementation team, the strategic decision was made to combine the task of implementation with that of training. The decision was based on an immediate advantage of 'buying-in' an already developed and operational system, in that lessons could be learned from railways which had already implemented TOPS. One such lesson was the need to coordinate implementation with staff training, as they can quickly become out

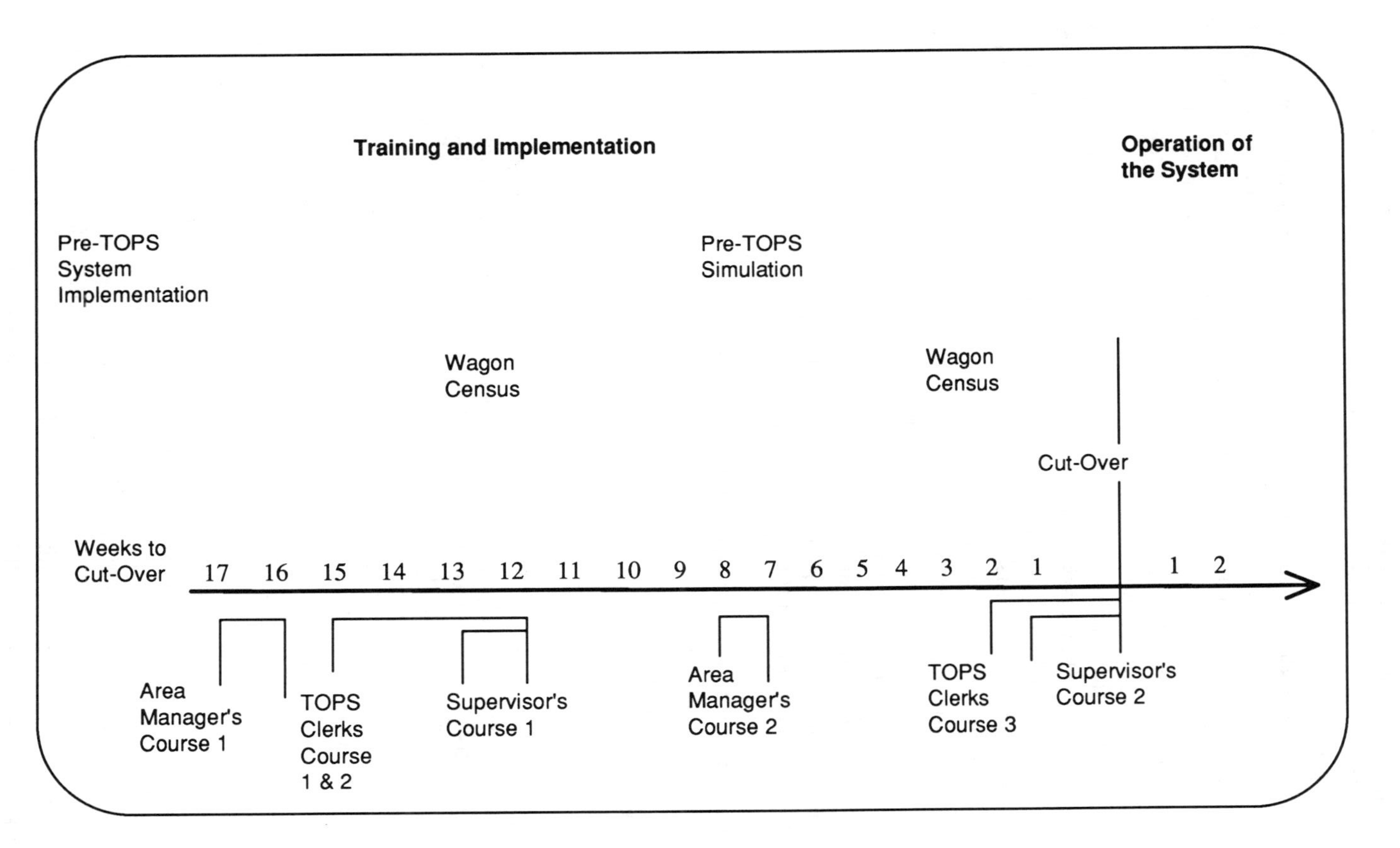

Figure 4.5 Implementation and staff training of TOPS in local areas

of phase. Through bringing the two under the authority of the implementation team, the organization's established training facilities and procedures were by-passed.

As each local area was 'cut over' to TOPS, the implementation team would move on to the next area, and so on. At the peak of the implementation programmes, several areas were being 'cut-over' simultaneously. During this period the team, which consisted of a combination of salaried staff seconded from operating jobs, management trainees and other management staff, numbered over a hundred.

The mobility of the team was achieved by converting 'condemned' railway coaches into travelling classrooms. This enabled the team to act as 'trainers' and 'implementors', and to see the staff at each location through the entire conversion process. The basic programme of training and implementation is summarized in Figure 4.5. However, these timescales were often compressed, reflecting, as the implementation officer stressed, that it was often 'ad hocery' rather than planning which was the key to the team's success.

The TOPS implementation team adopted a militaristic-type task-force approach to computerization. During interviews, members of the team stressed the *esprit de corps* generated within the team fostered by an almost regimental discipline. In the words of one of the team: 'if you weren't fired with enthusiasm for the project you were fired from the project'. This authoritarian task-force approach, combined with a high level of management commitment, generated what can best be described as a 'culture of change' within the organization. The 'unity' of the project team was reinforced through the design of a TOPS logo, the publication of a TOPS newsletter and the manufacture of a TOPS tie. In addition, the commitment of the TOPS team was strengthened by senior management support:

> After every one of the TOPS offices was cut over I personally made a visit to the terminal. Not a red carpet or white-washed coal stacks affair, but to satisfy myself as to the quality of the equipment, working conditions and staff morale. To sit down and personally key enquiries into the terminal concerning current operations . . . Another feature was that I let it be known that promotion to Area Manager was dependent on the chap satisfying us that he had TOPS 'under his skin'.
>
> (TOPS Project Manager)

These factors had a galvanizing effect on the project team, which was passed on to the staff they were training. This bolstered the 'culture of change' and generated the view that change could happen quickly. The project team promoted confidence in the use of the TOPS computer system and bridged the transitional gap between implementation and initial operation. As implementors, they also became progressively more proficient and self-confident at each cut-over. This had a steam-roller effect which made it all the harder for the remaining areas 'off-TOPS' to resist computerization. This point has particular significance in understanding occupational and employee responses to change.

Initial operation

The implementation of TOPS was remarkably free from occupational and employee conflict and resistance. There appear to be a number of reasons for this. First, the initial effect of the TOPS computer system was to create jobs rather than reduce them. Moreover, all three rail unions agreed that the decline in the freight business had to be arrested, and computerization afforded this possibility whilst also initiating the creation of new positions rather than displacing jobs. A large number of TOPS clerks were required to operate the computer system. This factor brought support from the Transport Salaried Staffs' Association (TSSA), which represents the majority of white-collar employees in the industry.

Secondly, operating with the TOPS computer system was seen to involve additional duties, rather than fundamental changes in the skills or work roles of manual staff in marshalling yards. The concern of the union representing these staffs (the National Union of Railwaymen (NUR)) was to negotiate extra payments in recognition of the added responsibility involved in reporting information to the local freight centres. The union argued that the job of the shunter involved the additional task of checking and providing accurate information on freight movements and train formations (a task demanded by the characteristics of the technology). On this basis, an extra grade-related payment of 145 pence to 175 pence per week was agreed with management (Bagwell, 1982:68).

Thirdly, national trade union support was also turned to good advantage by management in 'smoothing-over' local areas of resistance as TOPS 'cutover' progressed. The leaderships of both the TSSA and NUR were instrumental in resolving local disputes which threatened to delay implementation. They provided what management regarded as 'constructive assistance' in the formalizing of procedures for appointing new staff required to operate the TOPS computer system.

Fourthly, while the TOPS computer system could have been used for the recording and monitoring of the work of train crews and TOPS clerks, the exploitation of this 'labour control' capability was not considered a major priority by management. As already noted, the main motivation for introducing TOPS lay in the improvement in the control of material resources made possible by improving management information and performance through computerization, rather than the application of the new technology to directly monitor the work and performance of manual and white collar staffs. Furthermore, management was able to allay the drivers' union's (Associated Society of Locomotive Engineers and Firemen (ASLEF)) concern over the 'Big Brother' connotations that such a use of the computer would have for its members. Thus, management's strategic intentions behind the introduction of TOPS was supported by the railway unions, which consequently influenced the process of change and employee response to the emergence of new working practices and procedures (see also Dawson, 1987 and 1988).

The response of the railway unions was one of co-operation rather than resistance to the introduction of TOPS, convinced, no doubt, of the dire consequences of a failure to adopt the new technology as a means of improving operational efficiency. An editorial in the TSSA journal in 1975 emphasized the union's view of TOPS' significance:

> The project is now well and truly in operation and everything possible should be done to ensure that its potential is known amongst freight consigners, so that traffic which could best be conveyed by rail is switched to that mode of transport . . . British Rail has acquired what is regarded as the most advanced freight control system in the world. If it is going to help to bring better service to the customer and more freight to the railways, then there should be a 100% effort to ensure its success . . . The industry and its customers stand to gain by its success; that is the spur making it work.

Although the implementation and initial operation of TOPS was free from major industrial relations difficulties (through being given general trade union support), 'pockets' of resistance and conflict did occur in various local areas. For example, on the Western Region, management's implementation strategy had to be modified (a number of sub-strategies were adopted) in order to deal with ground-level resistance to change. These 'political' conflicts brought considerable delay to the implementation schedule, with the result that although the Western Region was the first to start implementing TOPS in 1972, it was the last to finish. The size of the problem was indicated by one headquarters manager who recounted that 'the industrial problems in South Wales put the whole of the Cardiff division back about a year.'

The TOPS implementation teams were modified to deal with local resistance. This was achieved through developing locally based implementation teams which, in this case, consisted of a TOPS person from Western Regional Headquarters, local management, local supervisors, and the involvement of freight yard staff.

The major source of resistance in South Wales derived largely from management's implementation strategy, which had not taken adequate account of the key role which the supervisor holds in absorbing local frustrations and industrial relations conflicts. The large marshalling yard in question acted as a 'semi-autonomous community', being located within a railway village where the 'top-down' authoritarian approach from a headquarters implementation team was not taken to kindly. As one supervisor put it: 'we weren't entirely satisfied with the chaps that came with the implementation team'. Another supervisor who formed part of the local implementation team recounted the difficulties, and supported the claim by Weir and Mills (1973) that the supervisor can often act as an important 'catalyst' in ensuring the relatively smooth transition of an organization from one state to another:

> We had problems, you know, getting people to accept it, getting people to operate it accurately, because if it's not accurate it's worthless, because the rubbish into the computer is going to be the rubbish out. So

> you've got to have it accurate. And this is the thing with the human element, you've got to watch that the staff don't skimp it, it's got to be done properly or it's worthless. In the initial stages we kept our eye on everything. The TOPS people had been instructed if there was anything wrong, for them to ring back here and for us to put it right and to get it back in there. We had problems in the beginning . . . a month or five weeks and things began to follow a pattern. But even now, the problem is that you've got this human element that you've got to involve in the system, and it all depends on the individuals concerned.
>
> (local implementation team supervisor, 1982)

These findings illustrate how occupational and employee response can influence the process of computerization and, in particular, management implementation strategies. In the South Wales Region, management strategy was composed of a series of sub-strategies which comprised both positive actions and reactions, as well as omissions and elements which could not be foreseen in planning for the implementation of computer technology.

Conclusion: the process of managing change

The case example of the computerization of British Rail's Freight Division illustrates the processual nature of large-scale change programmes. It has been shown how management strategy, technology, occupational and employee response and the nature of the operating system, in addition to other various determinants of change, do not have equal explanatory significance at different time periods during the process of transitional change. For example, the decision to computerize was taken at the corporate level of the business organization of British Rail. Strategic management's decision to introduce a computerized freight information system was largely a response to external business market competition and internal operating inefficiencies. Moreover, British Rail's 1971/75 Freight Plan unequivocally recommended computerization, claiming that it would stem the loss-making trend and make possible an expansion in British Rail's share of the freight market. It identified the need for a 'real-time' computerized freight information system which would enable the more effective utilization of resources in the day-to-day control of railway freight operations. It was also suggested that, if a suitable computer system could be obtained from another railway, this would minimize delays, reduce the risks involved, and enable considerable savings in development costs. As a result, the strategic intentions behind the introduction of a computerized freight information system consisted of various business market, operating, product and cost objectives, which were, in turn, influenced by the nature of railway freight operations and the availability and capacity of computer-based freight information handling systems. In short, the decision to introduce the TOPS computer system was based upon:

1. the specific recommendations of the 1971/75 Freight Plan;
2. the capacity of the TOPS computer system to provide 'real-time' information on the disposition and status of freight resources;

3. the availability of the TOPS computer system as a developed operational and commercially successful system; and
4. the absence elsewhere of any similar system at the same stage of development or with the same capabilities.

whereas the design of the system involved:

1. the extensive modification of the original TOPS software to suit British Rail's requirements;
2. the enhancement of British Rail's telecommunications network to cope with the TOPS data transmission requirements;
3. the construction of a new computer centre at British Rail headquarters and the employment of specialist staff; and
4. the deployment of TOPS clerks at outlying Area Freight Centres, and the creation of a new senior supervisory position to exploit the information generated by TOPS.

(see Dawson, 1990a)

Consequently, both the decision to introduce a computerized freight information system and the choice and design of that system depended primarily on management's strategic objectives, and the availability of computer information technology and its applicability to railway freight operations.

The implementation and initial operation of the TOPS computer system was, from senior management's viewpoint, a success. This was due to three main reasons: first, the effectiveness of management's implementation strategy and 'task-force' approach in circumventing organizational procedures and practices likely to delay final cut-over, and in challenging traditional operating culture; secondly, due to the absence of any intractable industrial relations problems during implementation and the support of trade union leaders for the project; and, thirdly, the financial basis for introducing TOPS was based upon a short implementation programme with little margin for delay or overspending. Consequently, as the official opening of the TOPS computer system was held within schedule on Monday 27 October 1975 (just two weeks after final cut-over), this signified the achievement of an important managerial objective.

There are a number of factors which explain why the implementation and initial operation of the TOPS computer system was largely free from occupational and employee conflict and resistance. First, the initial effect of the TOPS computer system was to create jobs rather than reduce them. Secondly, operating with the TOPS computer system was seen to involve additional duties rather than fundamental changes in the skills or work roles of manual staff in marshalling yards. Thirdly, while the TOPS computer system could have been used for the recording and monitoring of the work of train crews and TOPS clerks, the exploitation of this labour control capability was not a major managerial objective. Fourthly, national trade union support was turned to good advantage by management in smoothing over local areas of resistance as TOPS cut-over progressed. Nevertheless, some local 'pockets' of resistance did occur, particularly in the South Wales Region. This served to influence management's implementation strategies rather than the outcome of computerization. This involved the setting up of local implementation teams which incorporated ground-level supervisory and shunting staff participation. Thus, the modification of management's national implementation strategy illustrates how managerial sub-strategies can emerge as reactions to pressures and problems rather than as clear-sighted proactive decisions and choices.

The empirical analysis of the TOPS computerization project has demonstrated the utility of the processual framework of managing change outlined in Figure 3.2. The substance (computer technology), politics (for example, management strategy and trade union response) and context (British Rail freight operations in the 1970s) were important groups of determinants which shaped the process of this large-scale organizational transition. The case also illustrates the temporal aspect of change by highlighting how external factors influenced the decision to change and choice of technology, whereas occupational and employee influences tended to become more significant towards the later task of technology implementation. In the Pirelli example which follows, the process of establishing a TQM programme is examined, and particular attention is given to the implications of change for a shift along the organization and control of work dimensions presented in Figure 3.1. Together, these two chapters demonstrate the value of a processual approach to understanding the process and outcomes of organizational change.

5

TOTAL QUALITY MANAGEMENT AT PIRELLI CABLES

Introduction

The case study presented in this chapter examines the implementation of Total Quality Management (TQM) at Pirelli Cables. A major objective is to critically assess the implications of the Pirelli transition for the emergence of a new manufacturing philosophy based on teamwork, employee involvement and collaborative customer–supplier relations. Drawing on the framework developed in Chapter 3 (see Figure 3.1), attention is given to the extent to which the adoption of TQM can be explained as a movement from a conventional flow-line manufacturing system (with a detailed division of labour and well defined system of supervisory management), towards one based on teamwork and responsible autonomy (where employee commitment and workgroup cultures reduce the need for direct control mechanisms on the shopfloor). Although, in practice, the emergence of new organizational arrangements is unlikely to match any of these two extreme pre-characterized forms, it should be possible to locate workplace change somewhere along the two continua which comprise direct control and responsible autonomy on the one hand, and individual and team-based work organization on the other.

In applying these two dimensions, two further alternatives or outcomes are possible (represented by quadrants A and D in Figure 3.1). Both of these can be described as a hybrid method of work organization where there has been no concomitant change to either the existing supervisory system of control or the conventional system of work organization. For example, if TQM is used to promote collaborative teamwork through reconfiguring tasks from an individual to group basis without providing any real discretion or autonomy in the organization and control of work, or if there is a devolution in control responsibility for elements of industrial engineering and quality control without restructuring towards teamwork on the shopfloor, then these new forms of work organization would comprise a mixture of 'old' and 'new' methods of workplace arrangements.

In examining the process and outcomes of change, data is largely drawn from senior executive interviews and in-house documentation of Pirelli's Australian operations, with shopfloor responses to change being discussed elsewhere (see Dawson, 1993). The case analysis provides an overview of the change programme and identifies a number of obstacles to the successful management of the transition process. The problems experienced by Pirelli are used to illustrate the unpredictable nature of large-scale change and form the basis from which some of the guidelines on the management of change are formulated in Chapter 10. The chapter concludes with a summary of the main defining characteristics of the company's TQM programme and a discussion of the consequence of change for the emergence of new organizational arrangements. In the next section, some of the confusion which surrounds TQM is briefly examined prior to embarking on a processual account of the management of organizational change.

Total quality management

The growing interest in TQM as a philosophy for achieving continuous improvements in quality and gaining employee commitment has sparked a plethora of popular articles and texts on how to make more effective use of employees in the pursuit of quality, flexibility and productivity (see, for example, Oakland, 1989). The works of Deming, Juran, Ishikawa and Taguchi have become modified and adapted by a growing number of consultants, who both aid and hinder the organizational introduction of TQM. As Roberts (1990) has noted, too many organizations assume that quality is a 'quick fix' package to be purchased, rather than a transformational change in the nature of organizational operations. The tendency for organizations to be misled by 'flashy presentations and snappy illustrations' has been highlighted by Barnett's (1991) account of the prevalence of the Taguchi approach in Australia. He claims that it is an astounding, if unhelpful, achievement that Taguchi exponents have popularized experimental design even though it is widely known to be 'inefficient and flawed' (Barnett, 1991:11). He concludes that: 'Total quality management must be founded first and foremost on solving people problems and, second, on "picking the eyes out" of appropriate proven techniques, and using them intelligently. Fadism must be avoided and "quality hype" replaced by social application and teamwork' (Barnett, 1991:13).

The hype, fadism and consultant-driven claims which surround TQM are significant factors which have influenced the widespread organizational uptake of this new management technique (Dawson and Palmer, forthcoming). In practice however, TQM remains a comparatively new managerial philosophy aimed at the continuous improvement of service delivery and/or product manufacture to meet changing customer expectations. Through incorporating an externally based definition of quality (rooted in customer expectations), rather than relying on internally defined systems (based on established specifications and standards), the philosophy of TQM centres on a competitive dynamic process towards the attainment of 'the best service' or 'best quality product' within changing markets. Quality is no longer viewed as a stable state but, rather, as a future possible state based on current expectations. As tomorrow's potential, it stands as an achievable goal which, once attained, is redefined in order to maintain employee commitment to continuous improvement. The ongoing dynamic of continuous improvement is therefore built into the TQM perspective at the outset, and stands in marked contrast to traditional conceptions of quality which are based on the setting of internal standards and measurement (although it should be noted that both existing and improved formal quality standards generally form an integral part of TQM programmes). For example, the Chief Executive Officer (CEO) of Wallace Company, which received the American Malcolm Baldridge National Quality Award in 1990, indicated that, after receiving the award, the company set about documenting their processes to gain certification by the International Standards Organization (ISO), in order to compete in European markets (Hill and Freedman, 1992:81). This illustrates how the broader philosophy of TQM may be influenced, and at times constrained, by the competitive demand for standardized processes for firms operating in international markets. In this sense, the drive for quality has its roots in both traditional quality assurance practices for setting standards and the more philosophical approach which emphasizes the need to meet changing customer expectations. As a result, some programmes focus more on the quantitative statistical elements of process control and some of the attitudinal and employee involvement elements, and as Robson (1989:71) writes: 'The TQM process calls for a gradual reduction in policing whether this be via traditional quality control mechanisms or via management control devices'.

For many commentators, this quest for a 'the quality revolution' is seen to stem from the writings of an American engineer, W. Edwards Deming (Brocka and Brocka, 1992; Dobyns and Crawford-Mason, 1991; Tenner and DeToro, 1992). Deming was invited to Japan in 1947 to assist in the Japanese population census (Gabor, 1990). In a series of seminars to Japanese executives, Deming applied and developed his systematic approach to productivity and quality management. Gabor (1990), has summarized this philosophy as consisting of the following six principles:

- Quality is defined by the customer.
- Understanding and reducing variation in every process is a must.
- All significant, long-lasting quality improvements must emanate from top management's commitment to improvement, as well as its understanding of the means by which systematic change is to be achieved.
- Change and improvement must be continuous and all-encompassing. It must involve every member in an organization, including outside suppliers.
- The ongoing education and training of all the employees in a company are a prerequisite for achieving the sort of analysis that is needed for constant improvement.

- Performance ratings that seek to measure the contributions of individual employees are usually destructive.

In recognition of Deming's contribution to Japanese industry, the Deming Prize was created in 1951. This award is given to the company that is appraised as having attained the highest level of quality that year. According to Deming, poor quality is generally 85% a management (or systems) problem and only 15% a worker problem. Within Japan, these problems with the system of management were identified and tackled through the use of 'quality circles'. Essentially, a quality circle is a group of employees who meet regularly to undertake work-related projects designed to advance the company, enhance working conditions and improve quality, through the systematic use of quality control concepts (see also, Vries and Water, 1992:33). The 'circle' participants are taught a range of quality control concepts or problem-solving techniques, which can be used to identify problems, determine how to rectify these problems and communicate to management and employees the need to resolve these problems.

Although Quality Circles (QCs) originated in America, they have not proven to be particularly successful in Western companies (see, for example, Littler, 1985:25–7). This lack of success has been discussed by Hill (1991b), who claims that Japanese companies have used their organizational reward systems to ensure that employees and particularly managers, (voluntarily) co-operate with circles, and that Japanese QCs were only one part of an organization-wide system of quality improvement (550–1). In comparing the British QC programme he concludes that there was: an absence of top management involvement; a failure to match authority with an increase in employee responsibility for quality; only partial consideration of the cultural change aspects of quality management; and a failure to incorporate middle managers into QC programmes. (Hill, 1991b:556). The essential difference with the Western adaptation of quality circles and the current move to introduce quality management, is that the former was introduced as a stand-alone participative scheme, whereas the latter is being used as a total organizational approach to quality improvement through employee participation. This change in the substance of quality initiatives can be traced back to developments in Total Quality Control (TQC), which was a term first used by Armand Feigenbaum in 1956 to convey the view that quality is the responsibility of all groups within an organization who should work together in a systematic effort to achieve TQC (Campbell and Davies, 1992:4). He claimed that everybody should be involved in the process of satisfying customer requirements and that quality should not be the preserve of a small group of specialists in Quality Assurance (QA) departments: 'Total quality control's organization-wide impact involves the managerial and technical implementation of customer-oriented quality activities as a prime responsibility of general management and of the main-line operations of marketing, engineering, production, industrial relations, finance, and service as well as the quality-control function itself' (Feigenbaum, 1991:13).

Thus, the lack of success with QCs is now being 'potentially' offset by a TQM approach to managing employee attitudes and behaviours (Hill, 1991b:565–6) which, whilst drawing on the work of Deming, encourages organizations to tailor basic quality principles to their own particular circumstances (Hill, 1991a:401). The tendency for organizations and consultants to adopt different conceptions of TQM has resulted in a number of different models or approaches to implementation (see, for example, James, 1991; Whittle, 1992:8–13). For example, Forker (1991) has categorized variations in definitional variables into five different approaches, namely innate excellence (transcendent approach), quantity of desired attributes (product-based), satisfaction of consumer preferences (user-based), conformance to requirements (manufacturing-based), and affordable excellence (value-based). For the most part, however, the two major thrusts of the prescriptive literature centre on the view that, first, companies should restructure to encourage multi-skilling and innovation on the shopfloor; and, secondly, that companies should develop high-trust co-operative cultures to support process improvement through employee involvement programmes. Typically, these views are not based on any systematic analysis of empirical data but, rather, on cursory summaries of quality management strategies, anecdotal evidence and the development of neat prescriptive market-driven consultant packages (Dawson and Palmer, 1993:116). In an attempt to redress this tendency, the following sections examine the process and consequences of introducing TQM in Pirelli Cables.

Pirelli Cables Australia Limited

The Pirelli Group was founded in Milan in 1872. It employs approximately 69,000 people worldwide and has a total turnover in excess of $10 billion. This European multi-national corporation manufactures a diverse range of products including tyres, (which accounts for 40% of sales), electrical cables (43%) and industrial and motor vehicle components. The Pirelli Cable sector operates 63 production facilities in 12 different countries, and employs a workforce in excess of 20,000. The three key product categories comprise power transmission, telecommunications, and industry, building and miscellaneous applications. The company is committed to innovation and product development and is a market leader in submarine cabling and optical telecommunication systems.

Pirelli Cables Australia Limited (PCAL) was established in 1976, with the creation of a new plant at Minto, near Sydney, for the manufacture of power and telephone cables and building wire. In 1992, PCAL consisted of three manufacturing sites and eleven sales branches (including one in New Zealand). The Minto site specializes in power and building wire cables; Dee Why operations in New South Wales are responsible for telephone cable manufacture; and the two plants in Adelaide service the automotive and white goods market. In the case study reported here, attention is given to the senior management of change within the Australian operations of Pirelli Cables.

Initiating a change strategy: the choice of TQM

TQM is currently being adopted by Pirelli operations worldwide. There is a corporate TQM manager who has global responsibility for co-ordinating TQM activities (although in a number of Pirelli companies the initiation of change has occurred locally), and quality is defined within the Pirelli Group as: 'Without exception, providing a uniform and reliable product which meets our customers' requirements at a realistic cost' (Pirelli Document, 1991).

In the case of PCAL, the senior executive identified a number of operational problems that required management action. Their conception of a need to modify existing operations focused attention on problem-solving strategies. In considering a number of alternative strategies, attention was directed towards TQM following the considerable publicity given to the topic via the media and the Australian Government (see Sprouster, 1984) and the establishment of a National Industry Extension Scheme (NIES) (which offered seminars and part-funding for the introduction of TQM under government accredited consultants). The Managing Director was also attracted by the straightforward and practical approach to problem-solving which TQM espoused. Following a period of discussion, in which members of the executive attended seminars and familiarized themselves with the notion of TQM, a decision was made to appoint a consultant to facilitate the introduction of this new management philosophy. As the managing director recalled, whilst the decision to introduce TQM in European and South American operations was largely based on the finding that successful businesses (and in some cases competitors) were using TQM, in Australia: 'It was more of a case of: "Gosh, we've got some problems here, what can we do?" People were talking about TQM in terms of being a common-sense approach to problems. So we decided to adopt it, and we're still in the process of getting it to work' (Senior Executive Interviews, 1991).

On the basis of potential savings from reducing operating inefficiencies (there was no formal cost-benefit analysis, although a limit of $200,000 was placed on accumulated expenses and external costs), PCAL embarked on a programme of change. As one of the senior executives explained: 'We didn't have to carry out an accurate assessment to see that the thing could be justified financially.' With labour accounting for only 10–15% of total operating costs, the main concern was with reducing material waste and process inefficiencies. A proposed TQM programme was included as part of an annual budget that was submitted and ratified by corporate management (although it should be noted that any corporate intervention at this point in the strategic decision-making process would have been highly irregular). Typically, policies set at the national level would be supported by corporate management in Milan. Close liaison between national operations and the international cable group is maintained through regular visits by Pirelli's senior managers worldwide. By maintaining regular contact and clear lines of communication, expectations are affirmed and the boundaries between acceptable and unacceptable policies are clarified. Whilst the nature of this relationship may appear informal, it is, in practice, tightly controlled. As the managing director indicated:

> In practical terms, we submit an annual budget to Milan, saying what we expect to sell next year, what costs we expect to incur, our capital expenditure plan, et cetera. I will go and present that at the end of the year. It's interesting that they never ever reject anything, but you get the message of the things that they're not keen on, or what they don't want us to do.
>
> (Senior Executive Interviews, 1991)

Once the decision to introduce TQM had been made and the annual budget agreed, the senior executive team set about evaluating various different consultant groups. Although the practical details of implementing TQM were beyond their expertise, the executive team had a fairly clear understanding of the type of approach they were looking for. Essentially, TQM was identified as a potential vehicle for solving problems and facilitating good management practice:

> I think that the ideas are common sense. That you measure things before you take action, you take action, you measure them again afterwards and you record the change. They're all common sense ideas. The idea that you get everybody in the organization contributing, so that you're not wasting any of your resources. You get an input from people very close to the problems, because they're in a better position to see things. It's not a complicated philosophy. It's all common-sense ideas and you say: 'Yeah, if everybody did that then we're going to be better, aren't we?'
>
> (Senior Executive Interviews, 1991)

After a series of consultant presentations, senior management decided to employ Blakemore Consulting to carry out the task of implementing TQM in their three operating sites. Blakemore Consulting's approach was well structured and clearly outlined in three supporting manuals. The twelve steps to achieving the objectives of 'long-term management commitment to quality management and continuous improvement' were set out as follows:

1. Set up management workshops and a firm commitment.
2. Select and train facilitators.
3. Identify pilot areas.
4. Select the steering committee.
5. Select working committee.
6. Select and train project team group.
7. Identify problems and set standards.
8. Apply TQM tools to the task of solving problems and improving the process.
9. Encourage presentation to management.
10. Cement mechanism in place.
11. Participate in the ongoing process.
12. Celebrate achievements.

(Blakemore Consulting, 1987)

This approach was positively appraised by senior Pirelli management, who argued that the successful introduction of TQM should result in a disciplined approach to shopfloor activity, combined with a shift in culture towards greater employee involvement and participation. Prior to TQM, problem-solving was haphazard and largely ignored shopfloor employees as a key resource for identifying, measuring and solving production problems. The TQM approach offered a programme of culture change directed at increasing employee involvement and worker harmony, through the formation of TQM groups versed in the use of statistics (although it should be noted that whilst statistical information formed part of the Blakemore presentations, team members are not familiar with statistics). The approach also supported the managing director's view that changes initiated from the shopfloor were more likely to be accepted by employees than those imposed by management:

> I wasn't overly primed to introduce a lot of new practices, we don't think that they would accept that. It was more a case of looking for them to generate ideas, and I still think that that's probably the right direction. Because I think the teams involved will often solve the problem in terms that you wouldn't be allowed to introduce as management. You can't say that any man on this machine will do the job this way. Whereas if it comes from them there is no problem.
>
> (Senior Executive Interviews, 1991)

The implementation and initial operation of TQM

In March 1989 the managing director made a senior management appointment to the position of TQM manager, for the purpose of co-ordinating and controlling the introduction and operation of a TQM manufacturing philosophy. In the words of the TQM manager: 'My job is to co-ordinate all the TQM teams, to try and change the philosophy of our services, to introduce TQM philosophy into our operation, and to report to the steering committee on progress. I answer directly to the MD.' (Senior Executive Interviews, 1991).

The TQM manager, in close collaboration with Blakemore Consulting, set about implementing TQM across the whole of Pirelli's business operations in Australia. This was a major task which would ultimately involve the training of approximately 600 personnel. During the first twelve months, 22% of Pirelli personnel were trained in various aspects of TQM. At the outset, only three teams were formed in the Minto plant in New South Wales. These original teams served as a pilot project for TQM implementation. Over the following twelve months, a number of new teams were added as new problems were identified, and some of the newly formed teams were disbanded once objectives had been achieved. Although many of the original teams (which focused on major manufacturing problems) have continued, whenever practicable, there has been an interchange of personnel. Some of these groups have proven particularly successful: for example, by

March 1991 two of the original TQM teams that focused on scrap rates and machine breakdowns had reduced scrap rates from 9% to below 6% and machine breakdowns from over 500 hours a week to 117 hours.

As more teams were developed, the TQM manager set about defining 'standards of excellence' in order to provide a goal or target for TQM teams to achieve. The six phases normally associated with the formation of TQM teams and the setting of standards of excellence were as follows:

1. The steering committee would decide on a problem that needed investigating.
2. A facilitator would be chosen for a particular TQM team (for example, works engineer for machine breakdowns).
3. Shopfloor volunteers would be selected for the various TQM teams (they would normally be approached by the facilitator in the first instance).
4. The facilitator would be asked to establish an achievable target, and the TQM manager would then attempt to push the facilitators beyond their initial recommendation.
5. The proposed objectives set for the TQM team would be checked against worldwide standards of excellence provided by Pirelli's corporate headquarters in Italy.
6. The standards of excellence are documented and the TQM teams are expected to work towards achieving clearly defined targets.

From the outset, 6–8 people was deemed the most appropriate size for group work, with larger groups being too bulky and cumbersome – although there were some initial problems with the groups, such as trying to do too much too quickly and not ensuring a mix of personnel in the groups (in particular, operators, technical and supervisory staff). These early experiences have been built upon and, with a clearly defined problem and a good mix of people, the TQM manager argued that the remaining key ingredient to successful teamwork was the facilitator:

> The secret of success, as I've found it, is to have a good facilitator. If the facilitator is good, he makes sure these people know what day he's going to meet. He makes sure that the people are there on time. He makes sure that minutes are kept of the meeting. He also displays the minutes of our meetings in the shop so those in the teams can look up on these boards and anything that the teams decide is displayed on the board. And that gives the guys that are down there a chance to see what's happening. It also gets them interested in what we're doing, so they eventually get them involved.
>
> (Senior Executive Interviews, 1991)

The facilitators report directly to the TQM manager and are responsible for the running of their TQM teams. They direct, monitor and evaluate performance, and are directly involved in the selection of new team members. All new team members receive two days' training in TQM, and receive supporting documentation on the TQM philosophy and TQM statistics. Although Blakemore Consulting's approach was seen to over-emphasize the statistical side of TQM, particularly with operating staff, the training programme was evaluated as being a major ingredient in the successful introduction of a total quality programme. The training sessions provided the initial forum in which traditional values could be questioned through the presentation of an alternative, and yet scientific, approach to problem-solving. It also introduced employees to the concept of group work, and to the benefits of working in a team.

The topics for team project investigation were determined by the TQM steering committee in collaboration with other 'appropriate' personnel. As one middle manager commented:

> The steering committee determined what the projects are. So we haven't gone about picking projects where we can simply get good results. The important part is to tick off the tall poppies. What are the ones that are going to have the biggest impact on our business? Let's fix them then let's go to the next one. Let's not tackle the easy ones, let's tackle something that is going to have an impact and so the steering committee determines what those projects are.
>
> (Management Interviews, 1991)

During the first year of TQM, there were a lot of teams working on a range of shopfloor problems. These teams were later reduced in number and their objectives more clearly defined. By June 1992, there had been an increase in the number of 'focused' TQM team projects. On the shopfloor, graphs showing efficiency rates are located next to machines undergoing investigation. These were known locally as 'magic lanterns', and were seen to provide a source of motivation for TQM teams. This move towards teamwork was seen as important in attaining greater resource flexibility. The TQM groups, in fostering a team spirit and breaking down traditional boundaries, represented the first step towards teamwork on the shopfloor. Although the way the plant was organized, in terms of machinery and equipment, allowed little opportunity for people to work together within groups, the setting up of machines could be organized on a group basis. For example, teams could be used to co-ordinate quick machine changeovers, and then operators could be allocated the task of monitoring particular machines. In this way, the shopfloor could combine flexible machine operators with co-ordinated group work for machine set-up. Although some of the biggest monetary benefits have been in reducing scrap levels and eliminating over-use of materials, the increased flexibility of labour and the improved system of communication signals a more significant change in the nature of production operations. Not only has there been a 'knock down of barriers between departments' but also far closer liaison between production personnel in different operating sites. For example, inter-company visits have been organized for supervisors, and collaborative meetings are arranged to prevent the multi-site problem of 'reinventing the wheel'. Consequently, whilst the tangible benefits of TQM are important (for example, one team which investigated power savings was able to save the company $16,000 a month in electricity bills alone), these should not be over-emphasized at the expense of overlooking other more 'subjective' benefits, such as the development of team spirit, commitment and the shopfloor acceptance of change. Furthermore, there were also a number of unanticipated benefits consequent to particular changes; for example, in tackling the problem of customer delays and reducing deliveries from 12–14 weeks to 8 weeks, there was also a marked reduction in work-in-progress with considerable savings on material costs. Whilst it is often difficult to identify direct causal relationships, the senior executives were convinced that TQM had made a major contribution towards productivity increases. For example, over a two-year period, productivity increased from 30 to 61 kilograms of finished product per operator hour. Moreover, this figure includes the 240 weekly operator hours taken up in the 'non-productive' time associated with the 30 TQM teams operating within Pirelli. This raises the TQM paradox that so-called 'non-productive' time can, in the longer term, be more productive than the continual engagement of labour in direct operations. As will be seen in the Hewlett Packard case which follows, conventional notions of 'time is money' are being called into question under new manufacturing philosophies. The emphasis is no longer on maintaining systems operations at any cost but, rather, on solving process problems, reducing non-labour costs and increasing the quality and reliability of products. In successfully implementing TQM into their Australian operations Pirelli Cables have started to embark on a strategy towards the adoption of new production arrangements. However, before discussing some further implications of this change, the next section briefly outlines some of the major obstacles that arose during the process of introducing TQM.

Unforeseen obstacles in the management of change

During the period of initial operation a number of unforeseen problems arose. At this time, considerable emphasis was being placed on getting results in order to highlight shopfloor achievements at steering committee meetings. As one of the training officers commented:

> I think it had its problems along the way. We may have taken off a bigger chunk that we could chew at the time. That is to do with pressures of getting results. The bottom line is that management want to see their bottom line figure of dollars improve just like that. The reality is that you can't do that. People were being pushed and pushed and pushed.
>
> (Training Officer Interviews, 1991)

This emphasis on getting results sometimes distracted attention from the importance of gaining employee commitment towards and acceptance of TQM as a new shopfloor operating philosophy. During the first 6–9 months of the programme, middle management did not play a very active role in the project. Although a monthly review committee was set up, this started to lose focus on the broader objective of total organizational change. The emphasis on shopfloor change resulted in TQM becoming increasingly divorced from management and, as a consequence, the review meetings were cancelled and the executive were given responsibility for progress reports, in an attempt to draw them into the programme. This reorganization of the TQM reporting and command structure was aimed at facilitating a greater functional integration between different departments, such as production, accounting and marketing, and incorporating management into the system of continuous process improvement.

The separation between different management functions had been a long-standing issue that the managing director sought to resolve:

> We would identify that we've had a problem in the company of too rigid barriers between functions. And I would say that we've probably done a number of things to try and reduce them in one way or another – management training, executive training, through to TQM. They're all beginning to remove those barriers.
>
> (Senior Executive Interviews, 1991)

The executive claimed that, in their experience, TQM was a tool that fitted well with production because production lends itself to measurement. They claimed that it is often easier to isolate a production process, collect statistical data, analyse the problem, propose a solution and implement the change, compared to service processes. For example, when TQM was applied to areas in financial accounting, in an attempt to reduce accounts and minimize delays in issuing documentation, it never survived the 'chaos' associated with the preparation of the monthly accounts. In part, this was explained by a lack of commitment, but it was also constrained by the custom and practice of operating a 'calm-and-crisis' system of financial accounting. In the view of the executive, once TQM has become a permanent part of production greater attention would be placed on the application of TQM to accounting (although it should be noted that in May 1992 the financial team had achieved their target of reducing the number of days required to produce the monthly accounts) and marketing.

One of the major problems which Pirelli faced in implementing TQM was in gaining employee commitment at the middle management and supervisory level. Resistance to TQM was largely in the form of questioning its relevance to their area of operation. TQM, as a tool for solving process problems, assumes that problems exist, and that production workers are best placed for identifying solutions. However, the problem of dealing with unexpected operating contingencies, both technical and human, were central to the jobs of line supervisors who would tackle these problems as part of their daily work routines. Consequently, the introduction of a system that offers to take away the 'problem' of firefighting also poses itself as a threat to the jobs of front-line supervisors. In other words, if supervisors define their job (and their reason for being) in terms of dealing with disturbances in production, and if TQM is heralded as a new methodology for solving production problems through group employee participation schemes, then supervisory resistance is a reasonable response to a change that questions their position within the organization. The resistance of supervisory personnel to the TQM project may also be explained by a failure to integrate supervisors into the implementation programme. For example, the TQM manager argued that, if he was to introduce TQM from scratch, he would first win over his supervisory staff by running a two- or three-day supervisory training session. Thus in retrospect, one of the major lessons learned from the programme was the importance of supervisory personnel to the successful management of change:

> What we've found through TQM is that most of our foremen badly needed training. They were very very poorly trained in the art of management. And also our operators were very limited in their skills. And so we started to interchange people. We found if we had a man away we would stop a machine all day (whereas now we have several men that can drive the one machine), and we have a skills chart where each man has got what he can do against his name. If someone's away the foreman just looks up his skills chart and designates someone else. And that has given us an enormous saving in time and labour from absenteeism.
>
> (Senior Executive Interviews, 1991)

For the employees at Pirelli's Minto plant, there was some concern that TQM groups were solving company problems, and yet there were no financial rewards for any savings their solutions achieved for production. The view that an operator would rather make a good product than a bad one forms part of the TQM philosophy, and it is assumed that this is its own reward. But shopfloor personnel also sought active recognition of their contributions and, in response to comments from employees, senior management presented everybody on the Minto site with a $100 voucher at the end of 1990. However, the longer-term issue of appropriate rewards remains unresolved, with management taking the view that, if the change makes the job easier and less stressful, this is sufficient reward:

> When we started TQM, once results were achieved, we had people who were members of the group presenting back to management what they did and how they achieved it. That happened once and then it stopped. I think the teams need to start getting back into the feel that they have an audience. It gives them more of a sense of ownership of the project.
>
> (Training Officer Interviews, 1991)

Another issue that arose on the shopfloor was the question of the maximum number of teams that an employee should be able to join. Initially, the idea was to have lots of different teams and to continually move employees around. However, in practical terms this created problems, as employees could be in four different teams all of which met once a week. As the meetings are held in company time, employees were spending less and less time on the shopfloor and the allocation of labour in planning work became a significant supervisory headache. In response, the decision has been made that employees can only be members of two teams and that, in some cases, it may be more appropriate to meet fortnightly rather than weekly.

In overcoming these obstacles during the introduction of TQM, a number of lessons have been learned on the management of change. These include the need to involve supervisors at an early stage during the process of change; the importance of developing appropriate reward and recognition systems; and the inappropriateness of evaluating the 'success' of change in terms of monetary benefits, without regard to the strategically significant attitudinal changes which may accompany TQM. In summarizing the other major lessons learned from introducing TQM, the managing director stated that:

> You can't stand back too far from it and expect it to carry on happening. Almost every scheme has to have the full support of the chief executive, and TQM should have the full support of the executive. The other one is that you have to get it to work through the management – not alongside of it. Don't do TQM as a separate thing to managing the company because it's supposed to be about managing the company, the two work well together. You also have to be very specific. If you try to cover a big area then you jump all over the place and effectively get nowhere – we did that for four or five months in Adelaide and got nowhere. Whereas if you concentrate on one area, that's when things start to happen. When you see a team that has not made much progress, it's invariably because they have strayed from the principles of TQM (they haven't stuck to measuring it). I guess the lesson is, stick to the rules of the game and you should make progress. TQM means participation from all the people in the company towards gaining continuous improvement in the company performance.
>
> (Senior Executive Interviews, 1991)

Conclusion: the third dimension to organizational arrangements

The case of PCAL highlights how TQM is often part of a whole series of changes that are being introduced by modern manufacturing organizations. TQM, in encouraging greater employee involvement and the development of team spirit, has facilitated the smooth transition of other changes (such as the move towards award restructuring and enterprise agreements), and can be broadly defined as a management philosophy for continuous improvement in company operations. The eight main elements of the Pirelli TQM programme comprised:

1. A management philosophy of change.
2. An emphasis on continuous product, process and service improvement.
3. A focus on 'internal' and 'external' customer–supplier relations.
4. The application of systematic measurement techniques.

5. Quality standards were defined as the responsibility of management and decisions on product and service quality were viewed as the responsibility of all employees (they were driven by data and then implemented by teams).
6. There was a commitment to total employee involvement.
7. A climate of trust, co-operation, and a non-adversarial system of industrial relations was a primary objective.
8. Quality improvement was viewed as a dynamic and ongoing process.

Furthermore, the general absence of any major industrial relations problems surrounding the introduction of TQM has been instrumental in the successful management of change. Whilst the trade unions were informed of the changes under way, their position has been one of non-participant observer rather than active negotiator:

> He told them what we were going to do, but there certainly wasn't any objection. They didn't really want to take a position on it. I think that they took the view that if the work force accepted it, then they wouldn't complain – although they wouldn't actively promote it or work against it. And I think that they've had zero involvement since then . . . I honestly believe that in the UK it would be very difficult to introduce it without having a negotiation. So to some extent, I'm surprised that it hasn't been more difficult here.
>
> (Senior Executive Interviews, 1991)

From the experience of this company TQM can be described as a philosophy of change which centres on the management of continual improvement through involving employees in group problem-solving of processes, rather than end-product quality issues. In the process of trying to establish this new operating philosophy there have been three main areas of change. First, through a reconstitution of control structures and, in particular, in the unforeseen and yet fundamental redefinition of middle and supervisory management. Secondly, in the development of TQM teams and the implementation of a system of positive reinforcement for employee involvement. Thirdly, in attempts to apply these changes outside the organization for the purpose of improving customer–supplier relations. For example, there is now a collaborative Pirelli and Telecom TQM team that has facilitated closer relationships between the two companies. On the supplier side, attempts are being made to reduce the 'quarantine area' of supplies (the need for incoming quality inspections) although, with the large number of small suppliers, this objective has yet to be achieved.

The first two elements of this transition would indicate a movement towards quadrant C in Figure 3.1, where the development of a workgroup culture of employee commitment would reduce the need for direct control mechanisms on the shopfloor, and enable the formation of self-supervising workgroups. However, in the case of Pirelli this transition is still in its early phases, and the failure to change supervisory systems of control and integrate middle management into the programme of change has combined with the nature of the workflow itself, to prevent the immediate realization of teamwork and responsible autonomy on the shopfloor. Nevertheless, the movement towards internal and external systems of co-operation and participation (in terms of customer–supplier relations), suggests that the relational dimension might more usefully be treated as a third dimension (rather than being subsumed under control) and added to our initial description of companies operating under new production arrangements (refer to Figure 3.1.). This third relational dimension can be represented by a continuum that characterizes the contract between suppliers and users and distinguishes between a traditional adversarial approach and a more collaborative negotiation.

The more conventional adversarial method of contract formulation is perhaps the most common, and is based on a zero-sum notion of profits and costs. It could be described as 'market-mediated': typical of arrangements for the buying-in of products or processes that are well defined and understood. This form of contract is based on short-term commitment and a simple price bargain where contractual arrangements are clearly stipulated and formalized, with predefined delivery timetables and penalty clauses. It requires the user organization to have resolved qualitative uncertainties internally (user needs and problems would be pre-defined and suppliers would have matched these with solutions). The only remaining uncertainty is the price of the good, and the adversarial mode is well-adapted to such quantitative flexibility.

In contrast, the firm may choose to manage the uncertainties externally by collaboration with suppliers. The degree to which problems may be resolved by externalizing them is varied. The whole task could be devolved to consultants, but at the cost of loss of control and greater financial expenditure for the user organization, and a failure to develop in-house capabilities. More typically, a collaborative approach will be adopted, requiring a problem-solving model of contracting, the creation of trust between partners, joint participation and the objective of mutual benefits and rewards. It involves the establishment of structures to facilitate exchange of information between the customer and the supplier about user needs and problems in implementation and use. The development of the partnership is based on reciprocity and a shared belief that low cost and high quality are mutually compatible. Contractual arrangements are initially more flexibly defined, but collaboration necessitates a longer-term mutual commitment that is likely to militate against financial flexibility, such as changing orders in the light of market reversals.

In the case of Pirelli, the forging of closer relations with customers and suppliers, combined with active participation on the shopfloor and greater functional integration, signals a transition towards an alternative model of organizational arrangements. The initial elements of a new manufacturing philosophy are beginning to emerge, based on teamwork, a greater devolution of control to the shopfloor, and the development of collaborative customer–supplier relations. In this sense, many of the new practices being introduced on the shopfloor have implications beyond a single organization, and signal the emergence of *collaborative organizational networks* where closer co-operative relationships are formed and maintained with major customer–supplier firms (for a fuller discussion see Chapter 10). These changes in the nature of relationships, both within and between modern organizations, are still in their early stages and indicate a shift in emphasis away from traditional contractual arrangements and towards relationships based on trust, reciprocity and collaboration.

6

JUST-IN-TIME AT HEWLETT PACKARD

Introduction

Just-In-Time (JIT) systems of operation are increasingly forming a central part of the strategic management of change in European, American and Australian corporations. The term has been broadly used to describe an operational philosophy which seeks to improve the quality of output, eliminate waste, and reduce costs and material handling. More specifically, the central aim of JIT is to make products to order rather than for stock, and to ensure that work is done only when it is needed. Machine set-up times and operating methods are re-examined to allow changes of machine tools to be made quickly, thereby reducing overall cycle times. Customer orders are given to workers responsible for the final stages of production, who pull the necessary materials and sub-assemblies from workers upstream. Materials are delivered in small lots, on demand, near their point of use. The supplier base is reduced, and the purchasing firm works closely with suppliers to ensure that parts and sub-assemblies meet technical specifications and quality requirements (Dawson and Webb, 1991:120).

This movement towards a system which reduces inventory, improves quality and encourages collaborative customer–supplier relations, marks a shift in employee relations and a reconfiguration of technical systems of production. Within the literature, the quantitative benefits and strategic advantage of adopting JIT have tended to dominate recent debates (see, for example, Womack *et al*, 1990), with far less attention being paid to the qualitative change in operative relations (see, for example, Delbridge, Turnbull and Wilkinson, 1991:2). However, as a production/operations philosophy, JIT often includes other key elements, such as teamwork and the devolvement of responsibility for the identification and problem-solving of production problems. Consequently, many of the elements associated with collaborative workgroup arrangements discussed by the General Motors case (see Chapter 7) and the quality issues raised in the Pirelli example (see Chapter 5), are relevant to the programme of change described here. They also highlight how there are a number of common threads which run through these differently labelled schemes for workplace transition, such as: the movement towards teamwork practices; the emphasis on employee commitment; and the tendency to devolve responsibility for quality control to shopfloor employees.

In discussing these recurrent themes, this chapter examines the introduction of JIT manufacturing at the Telecommunications Division of Hewlett Packard (HP) in Scotland. From this examination, two further issues are raised which centre on the emergence of new work disciplines and the contextual redefinition of JIT. In contrast to the many commentators on JIT, who see it as only being appropriate to large volume manufacture (see, for example, Sayer, 1986), the example of HP reports on the process by which JIT (the substance of change) is modified to accommodate the manufacture of low volume, high quality products (the context of change). By so doing, the case illustrates how JIT manufacturing systems are often misconceived and inappropriately described as a well-defined and consistent system of operations. In evaluating these changes particular attention is given to the relationship between the job of the production manager and JIT within a small-volume production environment, and the organizational implications of 'non-work' activities resultant of producing just-in-time.

The chapter begins by examining the nature of change and the competitive advantages which are seen to surround the introduction of JIT. This is followed by an overview of HP and a description of their operations in South Queensferry, Scotland. The introduction of JIT is then discussed, and the importance of technology and the existing system of employee relations in facilitating the smooth and successful management of change is highlighted. This is followed by a brief analysis of the job of production manager and a questioning of the utility of umbrella definitions of JIT. The final section examines the development of team activities and the transition towards new work disciplines, focusing on the emerging problem of managing 'non-work' situations. The chapter concludes by suggesting that JIT, as a new manufacturing philosophy, challenges many conventional assumptions both about the nature of production management and about the value of traditional work disciplines rooted in the notion of 'time is money'.

Just-in-time manufacturing

The new production arrangements associated with JIT are believed to have originated in Japan in the 1960s where, because of an over-supply of steel, shipbuilders were able to reduce their inventories from one month's supply to only a few days' worth (Dawson, 1989:2). The basic idea of JIT was further elaborated by the Toyota Motor Company in Japan, which developed a formal management system (known as the Toyota Manufacturing System) to meet customer demands for different models and colours with minimum delay. By the late 1970s, many successful Japanese companies had adopted this approach to meet their own particular needs. The success of these early endeavours highlighted the potential competitive advantages of JIT, and by the 1980s this new production method had started to be introduced into Western companies. In Britain and America, particular attention was given to the Kanban subsystem of JIT manufacture. In essence, Kanban (which means 'visual record') is the name given to two cards: the '*requisition Kanban*' which is used to authorize the movement of standard containers between work stations; and the '*production Kanban*' which authorizes the production of a standard container of parts at a work centre. The unique feature which separates a true Kanban system from other card systems is the incorporation of a 'pull' production system, which refers to a system where products are produced only on demand. In this way, JIT manufacturing has been described as 'a production system to produce the kind of units needed, at the time needed and in the quantities needed' (Monden, 1981:29–46).

To achieve this perfect symmetry between supply and demand, production should be operating at or near zero-defects. This requirement has led many organizations to introduce quality programmes in tandem with JIT, and to change their materials management and inventory control systems (Dawson and Webb, 1991:120–2). Consequently, the introduction of JIT manufacture rarely involves a simple set of techniques for minimizing costs through restricting expenditure commitment; it more often develops into a type of operational philosophy aimed at eradicating waste and improving the quality of output (Delbridge *et al*, 1991:6).

In developing a JIT system, Lubben (1988) identified five basic principles which should be used to guide a company introducing JIT. These are as follows:

1. Each worker or work unit is both a customer and supplier.
2. Customers and suppliers are an extension of the manufacturing process.
3. Continually seek the path of simplicity.
4. It is more important to prevent problems than to fix them.
5. Obtain or produce something only when it is needed (just-in-time).

He claims that, through following these basic principles, considerable savings on costs can be made (for example, through reducing the number of suppliers and eliminating the stocking of inventory), and concludes that the adoption of JIT is necessary for regaining competitive advantage in international markets: 'The Japanese were not content with being merely as good as the other suppliers; they wanted to be the best. In order to accomplish this feat, the Japanese manufacturer learned how to obtain the optimum productivity from the minimum amount of material, equipment and labour.' (Lubben, 1988:21)

The main benefits of adopting a JIT manufacturing system have been classified into five main groups (see for example, Schonberger, 1982):

1. *Costs*: where JIT is able to reduce inventory costs and lower scrap levels.

2. *Quality*: through the fast detection and correction of poor quality parts, in conjunction with the higher quality of parts purchased.
3. *Design*: in being able to make a fast response to engineering change.
4. *Administrative efficiency*: through a reduction in the number of suppliers and a simplification of customer–supplier communication systems.
5. *Productivity*: through a reduction in rework and inspection and reduced parts delay.

In a radical critique of JIT, Delbridge and associates (1991) argue that these business-economic gains are achieved through increased employee exploitation. They disagree with the 'consultant rhetoric' that JIT involves 'working smarter, not harder' and, following Gordon (1976), make a distinction between the quantitative and qualitative efficiencies which stem from JIT. Quantitative efficiency is seen to derive from a reduction of inputs to achieve the same or higher level of output; and qualitative efficiency is seen to stem from the development of more sophisticated mechanisms for the complete subjugation of labour. They suggest that, whilst a great deal of attention has been given to the quantitative or technical aspects of change, the effects of JIT on employee relations have not been well documented (Delbridge *et al*, 1991:6). Whilst both of these dimensions are examined in the case study which follows, it is worth first outlining the four key areas of JIT manufacture. For our purposes, these can be categorized as comprising:

1. Optimized manufacturability.
2. Employee involvement with production problems.
3. Flexible resource functionality.
4. Development of collaborative customer–supplier relations.

Optimized manufacturability centres on increasing manufacturing flexibility through reducing the need for unnecessary functions (such as inspection and rework loops), and designing products for manufacturability. New product designs aim to minimize parts whilst ensuring that components are both easy to obtain (whether by purchase or in-house fabrication) and easy to assemble. A second essential cornerstone of JIT's philosophy of continuous system improvement is getting employees involved in identifying production problems, collecting and analysing data, and then suggesting possible solutions. Staff are expected to be aware of and to indicate any opportunities that may exist for reducing inefficiencies or waste present in the manufacturing system. Flexible resource functionality is taken to refer to the development of a functionally flexible workforce, which can be redeployed to match a shift in labour requirements for production. For example, this may be achieved through multi-skilling and the breaking down of traditional job demarcations, or through the ability to retrain and relocate staff without recourse to formal negotiations and industrial relations procedures. The final element, of developing collaborative customer–supplier relations, rests on the establishment of long-term relationships based on a system of mutual trust. A tighter and more integrated system of production control is achieved when the customer can be confident that the supplier will be able to deliver an agreed quantity of quality components or purchased materials, just-in-time to be transformed into fabricated parts.

Hewlett Packard in Scotland

Hewlett Packard (HP) is an American multi-national corporation which was founded by Hewlett and Packard in the 1930s. The company designs, manufactures and services electronic products and systems for measurement and computation. HP is committed to growth through the development and marketing of new state-of-the-art high quality products (in fact, over half of HP's revenue comes from products under three years old). In 1990, HP's orders were $13.5 billion and net earnings reached $739 million (Hewlett Packard, 1990:21). As a successful high-technology corporation, HP operations are run with the help of approximately 2,500 minicomputers and 85,000 personal computers, workstations and terminals linked into a worldwide communications network (Hewlett Packard, 1989:6). This emphasis on leading-edge technology is combined with an emphasis on good employee and customer relations in the research, development, manufacture and marketing of HP products. This combination of productive, personal and corporative aims is highlighted in the company's corporate objectives, namely:

1. To achieve sufficient profit to finance our company growth and to provide the resources we need to achieve our other corporate objectives.
2. To provide products and services of the highest quality and the greatest possible value to our customers, thereby gaining and holding their respect and loyalty.
3. To build on our strengths in the company's traditional fields of interest and to enter new fields only when ideas we have, together with our technical, manufacturing and marketing skills, ensure that we can make a needed and profitable contribution to the field.
4. To let our growth be limited only by our profits and by our ability to develop and produce technical products that satisfy real customer needs.
5. To help HP people to share in the company's success, which they make possible; to provide job security based on their performance; to ensure them a safe and pleasant work environment; to recognize their individual achievements; and to help them gain a sense of satisfaction and accomplishment from their work.
6. To foster initiative and creativity by allowing the individual great freedom of action in attaining well-defined objectives.
7. To honour our obligations to society by being an economic, intellectual and social asset to each nation and each community in which we operate.

(Cressey, 1984:9–10)

Operations in the UK began in 1961 with the establishment of a manufacturing and research and development plant at Bedford. In 1992, the three main UK operational sites comprised Bristol and Pinewood in England, and South Queensferry in Scotland. The company employs approximately 95,000 people worldwide and over 1,500 at South Queensferry. The South Queensferry site is located in an area north of Edinburgh known locally as 'Silicon Glen', in which over 300 other high-technology industries can be found. The Scottish operation consists of two divisions: the Queensferry Telecommunications Division (QTD) and the Queensferry Microwave Division (QMD). The latter was established in 1984 to manufacture products for the European mobile communication and cellular radio market. QTD was founded in 1966, to develop, manufacture and market, test and measure equipment and computer-based systems for the worldwide telecommunications industry. Each division acts as a self-contained business unit, and it is with the introduction of JIT in QTD that this chapter is most concerned. At this time, the division had an organization structure which consisted of a divisional manager and seven functional managers (Product Assurance, Business Accounting, Marketing, Manufacture, Printed Circuit, Engineering, and Personnel). Under this structure, the manufacturing organization comprised three production units, metal fabrication, production services, process engineering, product engineering, order processing and production planning, and materials management, and it was within this manufacturing group (which included supervisors and test engineers) that most of the material was collected on the process of introducing a JIT philosophy to manufacturing operations.

The introduction of JIT

> It was a shift in corporate manufacturing. It was probably driven by a need to reduce, as I say, inventory, increase quality – there was a tremendous increase in quality: a phenomenal increase in the quality of the product. Also, basically, to give more ownership to the people – if you like, to the shopfloor. That's not a term which we use in HP, by the way, but it's the one that's most commonly used when you talk to people outside.
>
> (Management Interviews, 1987)

The introduction of JIT was viewed as a new approach to manufacturing which would enable a reduction in make cycles (which stood at 15/16 weeks) and allow for the faster implementation of design changes. The system was also seen to offer the opportunity for reducing work-in-progress, scrap and rework which, in turn, was expected to diminish inventories, the central objectives being to lower costs, increase quality, and to be better placed to meet customer demands through more flexible patterns of work.

Under the old system, the delivery of a new instrument would often take over 20 weeks from the initial order, through manufacture to final delivery.

Essentially, the flow of instrument manufacture was 'pushed' from stores (materials) to automatic insert (where the components are automatically loaded into circuit boards), manual load (where manual operations are undertaken), assembly wire (where the PC boards are combined in instrument build) and, finally, test (where the product is tested for quality and reliability). Manufacturing was based on predicted and actual demand which forms part of the master schedule. This was the operating plan from which the supervisors were expected to work. They were under pressure to meet pre-set targets and to set priorities around the task of achieving operating efficiencies rather than deliverable products. Raw materials were gradually built up into parts which were combined into sub-assemblies and which were later assembled into products. This multi-levelled approach to the construction of products resulted in high inventories, both of parts and assemblies, and to the maintenance of costly and inflexible manufacturing arrangements (for example, in the inability to use material committed to one application for a different application). In short, the operation of a 'push-system', with the automatic initiation of parts and materials from the central master schedule, meant that most parts were built for stock, with the consequence that, whilst high levels of operating efficiencies were achieved (up to 95%), most of this was in the form of unfinished products and work-in-progress.

Over a period of two years, QTD moved from a system of operations based on a just-in-case-or-worse scenario philosophy to one based on just-in-time manufacture. Within the context of an HP worldwide move towards the adoption of JIT, responsibility was devolved upon each division for implementation. Schonberger's book on Japanese manufacturing techniques became the 'corporate bible' and through a series of seminars on JIT, and with the strong support and backing of corporate management, QTD managers were convinced that JIT was a vehicle for maintaining a competitive edge in the market place:

> HP is the largest single manufacturer of electronic instruments in the world. I've seen what happened to a lot of really strong British industries, where they've been killed by the Japanese – taken to the cleaners totally. They'd started to make inroads in the States into the electronics thing, and it really was a case of if we didn't respond I really think HP would have gone. At the end of the day, I think it was self-preservation.
> (Management Interviews, 1988)

In managing the transition to JIT, a lot of time and attention was given to the potential problem of overcoming employee resistance to change. Communication and employee involvement were central to the process of convincing staff of the necessity and importance of the change: 'An awful lot of it really was just selling the idea to somebody: convincing them it's a good idea. Tell them the reasons behind it; show them; explain; then do it again and again and again' (Management Interviews, 1988).

The change was initiated on an incremental basis, with a run quantity being halved from 10 to 5. This initial step reduced inventory and highlighted major material problems. Whilst these problems served to support the sceptics' claim that JIT should stay 'Just-In-Tokyo', it also illustrated how problems can be compounded by a system obscured by large quantities of inventory and work-in-progress. In tackling these material problems, local management also set about changing working practices. A number of teams were set up and given responsibility for particular instruments. A 'pull system' was instigated where only material which was going to be used was 'pulled' from stores, and nothing moved forward until it was needed by the next stage or group in the manufacturing process. In this sense, the concept of internal customer–suppliers was implemented, where nothing was delivered until it was required and nothing was requested until it was needed. Once this had become established, significant benefits were recorded. For example, changes in the organization of materials handling resulted in a reduction in the number of people in stores and a fall in the average kit time from four weeks to two days.

In implementing these changes, local management set about devolving ownership of the production process to employees. This was accomplished through combining JIT with a Total Quality Control (TQC) methodology, where the former was defined as: 'a commitment to excellence in which all functions focus on continuous process improvement, resulting in increased customer satisfaction'. The five fundamental elements of TQC comprised:

1. *Customer focus*: through replacing the notion of conformance to a standard with that of user's satisfaction; that is, the customer determined whether or not quality had been achieved.
2. *Management commitment*: the need for senior management support and backing.
3. *Total participation*: through the concept of 'next process is our customer', every employee is part of the system for achieving customer satisfaction.
4. *Systematic problem-solving*: data are collected at strategic points in the transformation process (between input and outputs), and statistical methods are used to measure and analyse performance.
5. *Statistical quality control*: the use of simple statistical techniques to compare factual changes with perceived trends.

For QTD, it was not possible to separate TQC from JIT: the two systems went hand-in-hand in implementing a new approach to manufacture. Over a period of two years, QTD has moved from a push system of operation to JIT manufacture. As one manager recalled:

> It probably took about a couple of years to get from system one to something that you could probably define as system two. But I would say it probably went backwards in the first six months of those two years. If I was being honest, we probably ended up worse after six months from when we started. But looking back, it's probably because we tried it in isolation, which was doomed to failure. Because if you

didn't get the systems to back you up then they were still grinding away, turning out material.

(Management Interviews, 1987)

In the case of production control, a pull system has been established between the lines, PCB assembly and stores. The supervisor is no longer simply involved in implementing planned schedules but, rather, responsibility for changing planned operations to meet local fluctuations in the supply and demand of resources has been devolved upon him or her. The basic operating philosophy is based on the concept that materials should never be collecting storage costs but should be continuously involved in the production process. In adopting this approach, make cycles were reduced from 8–10 weeks to 2–3 weeks, and average delivery was reduced from 24 to six weeks.

The transition to JIT also involved greater emphasis being placed on developing and maintaining good customer–supplier relations. This has resulted in a distinction between core suppliers who provide unique parts, and the more peripheral suppliers who supply common parts. With common components, HP adjust their suppliers according to the more conventional criteria of cost and ability to deliver. In contrast, longer-term and single-sourcing relationships are built up with core suppliers, emphasizing deliverability and quality. For example, delivery objectives and performance measures were agreed with key suppliers, who were invited to attend an 'in-house' seminar on JIT. The open-door seminars focused on the productivity solution for poor production practice through setting out the major components and competitive advantage of implementing a JIT manufacturing philosophy. In this sense, HP not only attempted to persuade suppliers to take on JIT but actively engaged in its adoption and development through teaching suppliers how to use JIT techniques.

This transition towards a manufacturing system which is able to provide the customers with what they want when they want it requires a high level of collaboration and flexibility in customer–supplier relations. The onus is now on the supplier to provide quality components and materials in order to eliminate the costs associated with the inspection of deliveries. This change in customer–supplier relations places a premium on communication, trust and the development of long-term relationships. By instituting these changes, purchasing was able to increase on-time delivery from major suppliers from 46% to 95%; to significantly reduce the amount of time spent on firefighting; and to lower the level of back orders from 800 to 25 orders.

On the question of employee relations, HP already had in place a comprehensive system of employment policies which encouraged employees to be flexible and to become part of the company. Their approach to personnel included such factors as:

1. *Premium salaries*: ensuring that HP employees are paid higher salaries than their major competitors (although individual salaries are largely determined by performance appraisals).

2. *Benefits package*: a range of benefits are available including profit sharing, stock purchase, medical care, subsidized lunches, holidays and life cover.
3. *No redundancy*: this policy had become entrenched and produced an atmosphere in which the employment effects of change were not feared.
4. *Single status*: all employees are known by their given names and all have access to the same facilities.
5. *Internal promotions and training*: individual advancement could be attained by working within the company rather than having to seek external appointments.
6. *Employment policies*: the company was non-unionized and dealt with 'people policies' and industrial relations issues on an informal basis.

The policy of no redundancies reduced the threat posed by labour-displacing change. HP's record of maintaining security of employment served to strengthen employee commitment to the company and to facilitate the successful management of change. On this issue, it is worth pointing out that HP does not offer job security but employment security. In other words, there is an expectation that employees will learn new skills and progress through a series of jobs during their employment at HP, which is combined with an expectation that their employment with HP is guaranteed. This commitment to sustaining good employee relations was further substantiated by the practice of management which was primarily concerned with instilling values associated with the maintenance of employee commitment:

> There has been much less resistance to change within HP than there probably would be in other comparable companies. I mean, everybody's afraid of the unknown, me as well. Change for change's sake is lousy; there's got to be a reason behind it. But no, I think there's probably been a lot less resistance to change within HP. It's probably made it easier because there has been this belief that, no matter what happens, at least I'll still be employed here; I can go and buy the groceries. It makes a big difference, it really does.
>
> (Management Interviews, 1988)

The absence of trade unions, a commitment to employment security and the dynamic and ongoing process of technological change, provided a context in which the transition to a new manufacturing philosophy could be accomplished with the minimum of disruption to divisional operations. Nevertheless, even within this context change took time, and was marked by an initial downturn in production prior to the introduction of a fully operational system. Moreover, there have been a number of interesting changes in the role and function of production management, and the attitudes required of employees working under JIT, that warrant further discussion, and these are examined in the section which follows.

Production management and the redefinition of JIT

Working in collaboration with six production line supervisors, the production manager will deal with a whole range of issues from production engineering to problems of materials control. The four basic tasks comprised planning work, monitoring its progress, dealing with contingencies, and reporting to supervisory staff and higher levels of management. For example, once a week there is a manufacturing meeting at which the production line managers can report on existing operations, discuss new ideas, debate potential problems, and be notified of any changes which require attention. Each line manager would also have a weekly meeting with the supervisor in order to pass on information and discuss any current problems. For both line managers and supervisors, dealing with unforeseen events or contingencies can take up a considerable portion of any given day. The main types of contingencies can be divided into technical and human contingencies. Human contingencies refer to situations which require active participation in the management of employee relations, whereas technical contingencies usually require the management of technical intervention, such as in arranging for a fault in the production process to be remedied. This emphasis on problem-solving was viewed as being essential to the smooth running, maintenance and development of production units operating under JIT. The production manager, in collaboration with supervisors, steers operations in an attempt to minimize disturbance and improve production performance. As one production manager commented:

> Really, a lot of my job is just oil work, you know, keep it going and don't let anything interfere with it. It's my belief that if you can get people to take a pride in their end product, then really half the battle's won. You're home and dry. If the people are working together and believe in their product, then as a line manager you really don't have an awful lot to do. My greatest fear really, is I suppose, that something will destroy that. Because if you destroy it, then it would take months to get it back again: you just can't replace that sort of thing overnight; it just won't work. You have to build up a mutual trust, a mutual respect, a mutual understanding; and if something destroys that you won't get it back tomorrow, period.
>
> (Management Interviews, 1987)

In steering the JIT system of operations to ensure the smooth running of production, open communication and the development and maintenance of relationships based on trust and honesty were identified as integral parts of management. This was viewed as being particularly important, given the ongoing changes experienced at HP, such as through the continual design and development of new products, the introduction of new technologies, and the local implementation of corporate strategies for growth. Moreover, the early communication of these changes and the need to relocate personnel and encourage the development of new skills, was seen to be a major function of production management, and all three production unit managers agreed that JIT had made this aspect of their job easier. The main benefit was in terms of increasing the visibility of production and enabling effective decision-making in both routine and non-routine situations. Management control of the process had been enhanced in terms of planning, directing, monitoring and adjusting process operations to meet fluctuations in the demand and supply of resources. The greater flexibility of labour brought about by the introduction of JIT was one example of this. As a production manager commented:

> One of the elements of JIT that is important is the flexibility of labour that allows you to move people around. If sometimes only one person goes off sick and you don't have labour flexibility it clogs up your flow of material. So what I have encouraged is cross-training between functions, between PC assembly and instrument assembly and vice versa.
>
> (Management Interviews, 1987)

The ability to redeploy labour and adjust workgroup arrangements is of particular value in the manufacture of high-technology/low volume products. For example, if a production manager requires one-and-a-half people to process a weekly batch of 10 instruments and s/he is unable to split an employee's time across two separate processes, then this acts as a major resource constraint. In breaking down these barriers and increasing functional flexibility, QTD have been able to adapt JIT to the manufacture of small volume, high quality products (many commentators on JIT see it as only being appropriate to large volume manufacture). Their experience demonstrates how JIT is often misunderstood and inappropriately described as a well-defined and consistent system of operations. Clearly, whilst there are certain key elements to JIT, such as manufacturing to order, developing collaborative customer–supplier relations, reducing inventory and minimizing set-up times, the way in which these various elements are combined often differs across organizations and even between distinct manufacturing operations operating on the same site of a single company. This confusion which surrounds JIT is summed up by one manager who stated that:

> I think we're trying to do things differently and we're using the term JIT as an umbrella term, without anyone else having a very clear idea of what JIT is. We'll cheerfully talk about the philosophy of JIT and what-have-you, but if you try and pin anybody down as to what they actually mean, they would be shifting their ground all the time. You know, it's one of those Alice in Wonderland type experiences where people use words to mean exactly what they mean without disclosing to other people what they're actually meaning. So it's quite difficult. Certainly, we're talking about JIT. We're certainly practising some of the things that are related to JIT, like getting the cycle times down and set-up times for machines. But I suspect we're not able to practice JIT as people can who are in the manufacture of large quantities of goods.
>
> (Management Interviews, 1988)

One of the major pitfalls or dangers of adopting JIT is accepting a 'banner' definition with no regard to the operating context in which you are trying to introduce the system. As another HP manager explained:

> I would suggest to anybody who's embarking on JIT: don't just go under a banner, because it doesn't work, because I've tried it. I've said, 'Let's do just-in-time', because people interpret it differently, so you try and break it down into elements. And you work away at these elements and you find, possibly, you may have some success.
>
> (Management Interviews, 1988)

In the case of QTD, they have adapted JIT to batch operations and now function with a hybrid production system which could be described as sub-batch processing. For example, if they require a batch of 15 instruments in a week, they will now work in product groups to build 3 a day. In order to move to a full-blown JIT system, the other elements in the chain (such as supplier organizations) must also adopt similar methods of manufacture. The interdependencies between previously distinct areas of organizational activity are highlighted by JIT. For example, with the movement towards teamwork and the integration of previously discrete operations into the line (such as PC assembly and fabrication), there has been a move to reduce the number of supervisors whilst increasing their span of control. With fewer supervisors to liaise with, the production managers found that there had been improvement in the flow of information and interpersonal communication:

> The actual information available to the line manager is just beyond belief to what it was 10 years ago. We had the usual production chasers and people who ran around with pieces of paper, running from here to there, saying, 'Fred needs this now. When am I going to get it?' 'Oh, I haven't got it.' You'd go and see the buyer and he'd say, 'Well, that was ordered three weeks ago. They promised it last week.' 'Have you done anything about it?' – that was the way it was, whereas now the flow of information is just vastly superior. It's just unrecognizable, and it's technology that's made that possible.
>
> (Management Interviews, 1988)

Breaking time: the transition to new work disciplines

The transition to a JIT system of operation had a number of unanticipated implications for traditional time-centred work disciplines. Continuous productive activity over a defined period of time was the commonly recognized (and internalized) work discipline expected by companies of their shopfloor employees. A JIT system questions this focus and breaks open the convention of time-based work disciplines through introducing the notion of productive 'non-work' activities. In practice, one of the biggest hurdles to operating under a full-blown JIT system was seen to stem from the need to change staff attitudes towards time and work disciplines. Under the old system, for example, operatives were required to engage in productive work tasks throughout their turn of duty. It was assumed that increased worker effort would lead to increased output and competitive advantage. However, operating with JIT, the emphasis has switched from continuous productive effort to continuous process improvement. The quantity of worker output is no longer the main concern: rather, attention has turned to the quality of finished products and the minimization of material costs. Under JIT, work is organized around teams, whereby a group of employees will be given responsibility for an instrument or product group, and if there are any problems during the process then work is stopped while supervisors and managers set about solving the fault. This emphasis on getting things right first time, and solving unexpected problems as they arise, marks a significant reversal in operating procedures. For example, prior to JIT, employees would continue working regardless of the problem, in an attempt to maintain high levels of operational efficiency. In contrast, today employees are expected to stop work until the problem has been accurately identified and solved. This questions traditional assumptions about work and the 'need' to look busy but, as one manager explained:

> It's actually cheaper to have people sit and read a book or knit than to make stuff that you don't want. Because you have to pay their salary both times, but in one case you have to provide them with the raw materials as well . . . We had whole areas that were simply storing thousands of printed circuit boards, thousands of them! Years ago you would have said: 'Great! We've got all these, I'm okay for the next month.' I mean, it just becomes crazy. You have enough inventory to hide any inefficiencies.
>
> (Management Interviews, 1987)

Consequently, there are periods when employees are not required to be engaged in productive work, and these periods of 'non-work' can prove stressful for employees and supervisors alike:

> There are times when your JIT philosophy requires that we have excess capacity – excess labour capacity so that you can handle the peaks; so it does mean that you may have people sitting doing nothing sometimes. And people can't get used to that; people feel that they must be inefficient. But, in fact, it's actually more efficient than the mass production approach of having so much stuff around that people are actually spending so much of their time either storing all this excess material, or fixing it, or chasing bits for it, and generally looking after it.
>
> (Management Interviews, 1988)

One way of coping with this extra time was to involve employees in TQC groups. The new teamwork arrangements have been fostered by the transition from a functionally orientated outfit into a product-oriented organization, in which TQC has been used to increase the participation and involvement of staff in process and product issues. However, not all employees were enthusiastic about getting involved in TQC groups and taking on extra responsibilities:

> What you find is that there are operators who are keen to be involved in TQC teams and there are others who are not interested. And if people

> don't want to do it there's no point in really forcing them to do it. There is a bit of a problem in that some of the operators are really not interested, they just want to come in here at seven, do their job and go home at night. But there are some bright girls out there who are quite keen to take part in teams and discuss the processes that they get involved with, and make suggestions as to how things could be done better.
> (Management Interviews, 1987)

Thus, involving employees in these team activities was not always a feasible option. Local managers were aware of the stress induced by 'non-work' periods and the need to relocate staff, and this employee relations aspect has become a central part of the production manager's job. Once again, good communication and an open and supportive approach were identified as the best methods for handling these situations. Nevertheless, whilst the shift in attitude required by JIT was at times difficult to embrace, the culture of HP was generally viewed as an enabling factor for successful change management. Moreover, as a non-unionized company, QTD did not have to consult and negotiate with employee representatives over major programmes of change. As one manager described it: 'it must be a big advantage that we don't have a union structure, and the culture of the company is such that people have always accepted the need for change'. Good working and employment conditions, the absence of trade unions, and the continual and ongoing nature of product change have all served to facilitate the relatively smooth transition from a traditional batch manufacturing environment to one based on a JIT philosophy.

Conclusion: the management and philosophy of JIT

This chapter has shown how managing the transition to JIT manufacture is often less clear than indicated in the literature. In the case of HP, JIT was not applied to mass production but, rather, to the manufacture of a small quantity of high-technology products. The greater labour flexibility experienced at HP was identified as being of particular value to low volume manufacture, where an employee's time could be allocated to more than one process. This change was also welcomed by the production manager who, as a result, was better placed to deal with daily operating contingencies. In this example, the common conceptions of JIT were not only found to be misleading and inappropriate, but also carried with them the ultimate danger of undermining any attempts to successfully introduce this new system of operations management.

In terms of our processual approach, the conception of a need to change was initiated by corporate management, who formulated a strategy for ensuring the adoption of JIT in all their manufacturing operations worldwide. Once formulated, these proposals were discussed with senior managers at other locations, and then devolved down the managerial command hierarchy for divisional site implementation. In other words, the process of change originated at the senior executive level, whilst implementation strategies and work reorganization schemes were developed at the local level. For example, it was the general manager at HP South Queensferry who allocated responsibilities for the planning and implementation of change, following which local management set about developing a programme for using JIT within their own departments. This approach to devolving responsibility for the implementation of strategic change has been further promoted through the application of TQC methodology. This technique has proven particularly fruitful in encouraging HP personnel to take ownership of their local production problems. As illustrated in the case, employee participation in change programmes is no longer viewed as a series of one-off events but, rather, as an ongoing process. As a result, the company has managed to inject and maintain a culture of change at the local level, which has facilitated the smooth uptake of innovations appropriate to operating within a rapidly changing international market. HP engineers are currently training suppliers in the use of JIT, reducing the number of suppliers and exploring the standardization of supplier computer systems for components specification. They have even been part of a BBC video production for management education on the introduction of JIT (BBC, 1989), and continue to place a high priority on the development and maintenance of collaborative customer–supplier relations.

On the issue of new organizational arrangements, traditional work disciplines rooted in the notion of 'time is money' have been replaced by a new philosophy of working just in time to meet customer demands. The pace and pattern of work is no longer set by the need to meet efficiency targets regardless of costs but, rather, centre on the principle of manufacturing quality products to order. This has resulted in the notion that the work of product assembly should stop, in order to carry out the legitimate 'non-work' of fixing the process. This change in manufacturing philosophy challenges the conventional discipline of 'clock time', and in many cases created feelings of guilt among workgroups who found it equally difficult to stop work when they had built the required amount of goods for that day. A number of managers interviewed recounted the story of production workers secretly maintaining a store of work in progress 'just in case' they were hit by unexpected problems in the following day's production. Consequently, this new manufacturing technique also represents a significant change in manufacturing philosophy away from the traditional conception that increasing production rates is the best method for meeting delivery dates, towards reducing make cycles, improving process operations and ensuring quality production. In this sense, JIT represent a new manufacturing philosophy which challenges many of our traditional notions about production and operations management.

In concluding this chapter it should be remembered that, like the other studies reported in this book, the successful management of change is influenced not only by the substance of the change but also by the context in which change takes place and by political decision-making processes. For example, in a review of the literature on JIT, Sohal, Keller and Fouad, (1989) emphasize the importance of contextualizing change and taking account of local factors, such as trade union agreements and existing management practice. In this case, two contextual factors worth highlighting are the existing system of employee relations and technology. On the first count, change took place within an environment which had created and sustained an harmonious system of employee relations. Labour costs only accounted for a small percentage of total operating costs and the company continually strived to ensure that the working conditions of its employees remained above the standards set by comparable competitor firms. On the second count, the transition was managed within the context of a high technology company associated with innovation and change. The ongoing developments and application of advanced technology contributed to the smooth transition to JIT manufacture in at least three important ways. First, through the availability of accurate production information; secondly, by enabling a reduction in the number of parts required to manufacture a product; and, thirdly, through a movement towards digital instrumentation which enabled the more rapid and global computer-based testing of finished products. Moreover, the availability of information via workstations linked to computerized manufacturing systems made it possible to identify material and to examine the potential implications of process change. Developments in technology have also brought about a significant decrease in the number of parts required to manufacture complex instruments. This change, combined with a compression in the timeframe for instrument tests, resulted in a dramatic reduction in product make cycles. In this sense, the context of ongoing processes of technological change have further facilitated JIT manufacture.

7

CELLULAR MANUFACTURE AT GENERAL MOTORS

> Having worked for hardware for 32 years I would say that, personally, this is probably the biggest turnaround in the hardware plant that I can remember. I don't think that I've ever seen anything like it. I consider myself to be pretty lucky to have been able to see it and even more so to be a part of it. The people are very, very proud to have someone come in and have a look at it (national and international manufacturing companies). They really take great delight in that, to think that they can show off something that is very successful.
>
> (Local Management Interviews, 1991)

Introduction

This chapter provides a case study analysis of the process of transition from a traditional machine-centred job-shop working environment to a cellular manufacturing facility at General Motors' hardware fabrication plant in South Australia. Particular attention is given to the conception of the need to change and the use of other workplace change initiatives to stimulate and promote employee acceptance and recognition of the personal benefits which can be accrued from change. The importance of employee and trade union support is emphasized and the successes of a number of earlier initiatives are described and assessed as being central to the creation of an harmonious climate of industrial relations prior to workplace restructuring. The shopfloor transition to cellular manufacture is then examined and it is shown how the identification of the change programme was not determined by senior management but, rather, derived from the ideas and enthusiasm of plant level management. The commitment and cohesion of the local management team is identified as a major factor influencing the success of this locally induced change programme. Finally, in examining the long-term consequences of change and their implications for the emergence of new production arrangements, the issue of teamwork and supervision raised in the Pirelli case is further elaborated and discussed. It is argued that whilst the transition to cellular manufacture has resulted in a movement from individual to team-based work practices, this change has not resulted in a system of work organization which is able to accommodate a broader range of employee behaviours. The traditional individualistic model has been replaced by a collective teamwork approach which employees are now expected to embrace not simply for the benefit of the company, but also for their own personal development.

In detailing these changes the chapter commences by examining cellular manufacturing as a hybrid form of automation and a refinement of conventional group technology techniques. The major theoretical concerns surrounding these 'innovations' in work reform are outlined, and their implications for teamwork, supervision and management control discussed. The empirical section commences by providing some background information on the Australian automotive components plant. This is followed by a case study analysis of plant restructuring. The key factors which enabled and constrained the process of change are identified, and particular attention is given to management strategy, union involvement and the consequence of change for supervisors and employees working under the new production arrangements. The objective is to analyse shifts from 'old' to 'new' production arrangements and to critically appraise these findings with other comparable empirical research (see, for example, Bratton, 1991; Buchanan and Preston, 1991; Elger and Fairbrother, 1990). The chapter concludes with a critical appraisal on the organizational implications of 'flexible workcells' and a brief comparison of these findings with those of Pirelli and Hewlett Packard for changes in the organization and control of work.

Group technology and cellular manufacture

In the late 1960s and throughout the 1970s, Group Technology (GT) became a popular panacea for solving the problems of employee relations on machine-paced automotive assembly lines. Many of the principles were adapted from Russia in the 1940s (Petrov, 1968), where it is reported to have been used by Mitrofanov and Sokolovskii (Gaither, 1990:147) and later applied to automotive and associated supplier companies in Western industrialized countries. For example, in the famous Volvo experiments in Sweden and the Volkswagon programme in Germany, workers were decoupled from the assembly line and organized into teams. In the latter case, they received training in all jobs, operated in groups of seven on a two-shift system, were free to rotate job assignments, and were expected to meet a set quota of seven engines per team per day (Gill, 1985:68). Although by the mid-1970s GT had spread to around 10% of batch engineering firms in Britain, computerized information systems were not generally available for setting up reliable GT production systems (Gill, 1985:69). However, with the more recent developments in technology, many of these initial constraints have been overcome and have enabled group participation programmes to be introduced into batch as well as process operations (Safizadeh, 1991:63).

This convergence of historically different manufacturing processes is highlighted by the seminal work of Joan Woodward (1980) who, in a study of a hundred manufacturing firms in South East Essex, categorized firms according to whether production was standardized or one-off. (One-off products were further subdivided according to whether production was non-continuous or continuous. She also differentiated between manufactured or 'integral products' and processed or 'dimensional products'.) On the basis of these distinctions, Woodward listed eleven categories which can be located under one of three general stages in the historical development of manufacturing operations. These comprise:

1. unit and small batch production;
2. large batch and mass production; and
3. process production.

(1980:35–44)

She argued that it is possible to identify certain stages in the development of production systems which are associated with certain characteristic forms of organizational structure. Her work suggests that, with each movement from unit production towards process production, there will be a growth in the command hierarchy and an increase in the proportion of supervisory personnel to non-supervisory personnel (1980:56–7). At the first-line supervisory level, a 'curvilinear' relationship was shown to exist between types of technology and span of supervisory control (Woodward, 1980:61–2). These similarities at the extremes indicated the way work was organized into small primary groups in process and unit production firms. In contrast, large batch and mass production industries were unable to successfully delegate or decentralize control, as Woodward notes:

> There was greater variation in the way in which production operations were planned and controlled between firms in the middle ranges of the scale than between firms at the extremes . . . Life in firms in the middle ranges of the technical scale was (generally) less pleasant and easy-going than in firms at the extremes.
>
> (Woodward, 1980:66–7)

The constraints on work organization associated with the technical configurations of process, mass and batch production, are increasingly being called into question with the search for a new theory of manufacturing (Drucker, 1990). Developments in technology, combined with the adoption of new production and service concepts, have resulted in a 'trend' towards exploring alternative methods of organizing work (Safizadeh, 1991:63). Particular attention has been given to the development of flexible, team-based manufacturing methods which are able to respond to the increasing volatility of trading conditions, product and process changes, and heightened competitive pressures, (Schonberger, 1982 and 1986). This movement towards teamwork complements many of the early principles of group technology which demonstrated that significant improvements could be achieved by the grouping of technology (dissimilar tools and machining equipment) and labour (differing skills and trades) into work units or cells for the purpose of manufacturing related parts that are similar in their processing requirement (Ham, Hitomi and Yoshida, 1985; Opitz and Wiendahl, 1971). In other words, through grouping parts which require a similar combination of different operations it was shown that plants could be restructured around a component's processing requirement rather than a machine's functional purpose (see Biddle, 1990).

These early principles of GT have been further developed and explored by an increasing number of academics (Ang and Willey, 1984; Ashton and Cook; 1989; Gallagher and Knight,1973; Knight and Wall, 1989; Shtub, 1989) and American and British manufacturers, who have looked for alternative methods of improving their competitive position without having to rely on large capital investments (for example, Ferranti, Rockwell, Kawasaki Motors and Scania-Vabis). In particular, there is a growing interest in the hybrid system of cellular manufacture, which can be described as a composite of both the flow-shop dedicated to mass production of one product and the job-shop which is concerned with the manufacture of a large variety of parts. According to Wemmerlov and Hyer (1989b:1511), the main aim is to 'reduce set-up times (by using part-family tooling and sequencing) and flow times (by reducing set-up and move times, wait times for moves, and using small transfer batches) and therefore to reduce inventories and market response times'.

These group-based approaches to manufacturing contrast sharply with the traditional job-shop layout where machines are usually grouped by function. For example, all grinding machinery might be located together and all drilling machinery might be installed at a separate location within the same plant (Blackburn, Coombs and Green, 1985). Consequently, the succession of operations necessary for the manufacture of components would often require semi-finished parts to be moved to different locations throughout the entire plant, incurring considerable costs in the routing and storage of parts in various stages of completion. This functional layout of machinery also encourages the manufacture of parts additional to requirements, in order to achieve an apparently high level of operating efficiency through maximizing machine utilization (see also Gallagher, 1980). In the automotive components case discussed later, lines of machines which performed particular operations were grouped together, such as press blanking, press forming, rotary deburring, spot welding and projection welding. Once an operation was completed, the batch of parts was placed into a storage area and later retrieved and marshalled on a flatbed tram for destination to its next manufacturing operation. Under such a system, considerable time, equipment and labour was required to schedule the processing of parts; monitor the operating system; physically move the semi-finished parts around the plant; and to ensure quality checks through the employment of a small army of inspectors.

Whilst, in theory, there is considerable management and academic interest in new manufacturing philosophies, there are few practical examples of the full-scale cellularization of an entire plant. There is also, perhaps as a consequence, a general absence of systematic research on the process and outcomes of adopting cellular manufacture. For these reasons, the example of GM's automotive manufacturing plant is significant, as it represents an unusual and rare case of the total rearrangement of existing plant and equipment, and the development of multi-functional operators under a fully operational workcell system of production. However, before detailing these changes, a brief overview is presented of GM's automotive component manufacturing plant in South Australia.

General Motors-Holden's Automotive Limited

General Motors-Holden's Automotive Limited (GMHAL) produced the first all-Australian automobile in 1948. The company's origins in the transportation industry can be traced back to 1854 when James Alexander Holden started a leather and saddlery business in Adelaide. In 1919 a new company, the Holden Motor Body Builders Ltd, was formed, which merged with General Motors (Australia) Ltd in 1931 to form General Motors-Holden's Ltd. In 1951 the Holden became Australia's top selling car, and in the year 1988–1989 GMHAL produced 53,360 VN Commodores, posting an operating profit of $24 million after tax and extraordinary items. Today, GMHAL operates as part of a new joint venture, United Australian Automotive Industries Ltd (UAAI), which was formed as part of the Federal Government's plan to increase the efficiency and international competitiveness of the Australian automotive industry. UAAI co-ordinates the activities of GMHAL and Toyota Motor Corporation Australia Ltd (TMCA). Although both companies maintain their own dealer networks through which their products are sold, there is close collaboration in the utilization of materials, plant and equipment.

The automotive component manufacturing plant undergoing change to cellular manufacture is situated on GMHAL's site at Elizabeth in South Australia. The GMHAL complex is the operating headquarters of GMHAL; it covers an area of 123 hectares; it is located 25 kilometres from Adelaide; and it currently produces 350 cars per day. The hardware plant was the first plant to be constructed at the Elizabeth complex in 1959. Its original charter was to produce small components, such as brackets, braces, filters, seat wires and door frames required in the production of motor vehicles. Over 1,500 people were employed over a three-shift system, and they were able to manufacture some 3,500 individual parts and small assemblies. Today, the Elizabeth site employs approximately 4,600 staff (of a total GMHAL staff of 6,411 as at June 1989). The hardware plant produces a wide variety of small- to medium-sized press-formed and welded components, such as door frames, petrol tanks, cross-members, control arms, and brackets in general. It covers an area of over 3,000 square feet, and has over one hundred presses from 25 to 350 ton capacity.

Creating a climate of change

The process of change at GM's component manufacturing plant has occurred over a period of years. Whilst the research was conducted between 1989 and 1991, the process of change was initiated in the early 1980s when the plant attracted the attention of senior management, who were sceptical about the feasibility of the plant as a competitive manufacturer of small components for vehicle assembly. In 1981, a new plant manager was appointed and given the task of turning the plant around within five years (failure to achieve this major change would result in the closure of the plant). The plant manager set about tackling the problem of inefficient operations through a continual series of meetings and discussions with his local management team. Working within a tight financial budget, they developed a five-year change programme centred around improving the methods and practice of human resource management. From an analysis of current operations, they identified a number of small components which could be manufactured more economically by outside suppliers. The consequent need to reduce production operations and direct and service personnel created a climate of uncertainty which acted as an 'invisible barrier' to change.

In an attempt to overcome potential resistance to change, the local management team developed three major strands to their five-year plan. The first centred on improving the work environment. The conditions on the shopfloor provided a good illustration of the consequences of over twenty years' neglect by employers of the need to maintain and improve environmental working conditions. There was poor lighting, the ventilation was inadequate for some welding operations, the whole plant was painted a depressing battleship grey, and the floor was hidden by a layer of oil and grease. Operating under these conditions, employees would emerge in grey oil-stained clothing by the end of a shift. As one machinist recollected: 'When I first started here you could walk down any one of those aisles and you'd have oil this thick up the side of you . . . there's very, very little of that now. The basic area is cleaner, it hasn't got that oil-stinky smell and I think a lot of people appreciate that' (Shopfloor Interviews, 1989).

The plant was also extremely noisy, with lines of presses operating simultaneously, resounding and amplifying the mechanical clatter and clang of regimented machines at work. For many employees, this was the nature of small component manufacture in the automotive industry. Although there was nothing pleasant about the working environment, the culture of the shopfloor and the attitudes of the staff were a reflection of this traditional operating environment and the historical legacy of the functional layout of 25–350 tonne presses. Within such an environment, it was difficult to imagine that it could be any other way. The idea of physically rearranging 250-ton presses was an idea, and not one which could be easily translated into practice. It was not simply the technical logistics of relocating large pieces of machinery; there were also the human implications of the breaking of routines and traditions, the financial cost associated with such an exercise and, in particular, the costs involved in a loss of production during the implementation of change.

It was within this context that the local management team identified the need for a well-planned programme of employee involvement. This began with a series of actions aimed at demonstrating the commitment of local management to introducing changes which would improve the quality of working life within the plant. Following a series of meetings with senior shop stewards and employees, the shopfloor was cleaned; machines were painted yellow and surplus staff were assigned tasks associated with improving the 'housekeeping' of the plant. These simple but effective measures initiated the mobilization of employees behind management's plans to update and improve plant operations as a whole. Once the seeds of employee commitment to change had been generated, the second major thrust of the local management's five-year plan was implemented. The basic aim was to achieve employee accountability through non-monetary incentives. Essentially, this involved devolving responsibility for quality control to operators; developing staff training programmes; and encouraging employee participation in identifying and discussing production problems. These objectives were achieved by sending a selection of staff on a series of training sessions, and then establishing a group of staff within the plant committed to the development, implementation and evaluation of Quality of Work Life (QWL) programmes.

The final strand in local management's plan was to improve industrial relations and develop better communication between plant managers and shop stewards. The main objective was to achieve full union involvement and co-operation, and to develop and maintain a relationship of trust between local management and union officials. The major union involved in the change (the Vehicle Builders Employees' Federation) was highly supportive of management's plans, and the Amalgamated Metal Workers' Union (AMWU), although less involved in the change, also claimed that there was plenty of open discussion. On the electrical side, the senior shop steward of the Electrical Trade Union (ETU) recalled that:

> All the unions sat down with Barry Matthews [Plant Manager] and management, and there was a new concept put to us in regard to work cells. And basically – I can only speak from the ETU's point of view – we didn't have a major problem with it, but we made one point very, very clear to the company: that if they were going to go down that road we want total involvement as far as the electrical side is concerned, and that we wouldn't tolerate outside contractors. So we reached an agreement on that. We gave a total commitment to the company that from the day we started we would be committed – committed as such that we would supply the labour and also any overtime or any outside of normal working hours: we would be totally committed to that.
>
> (Union Interviews, 1990)

There is now a far more harmonious climate of industrial relations, and the union representatives have been instrumental in allaying employee fears and anxieties over the implications of change for employment. This shift in the attitude of employees and their representatives towards management and the process of change was central to creating a climate in which a major transformation in work operations could be accomplished.

The shopfloor transition to cellular manufacture

The shopfloor transition to cellular manufacture can be traced back to the arrival of a new plant manager who suggested to the production superintendent that they should start trying to implement group technology on an incremental basis. This part-time approach accomplished little until the setting up of the QWL group and the selection of the senior shop steward of the Vehicle Builders Union (VBU) to act as a full-time QWL co-ordinator. At this stage, the production superintendent set about introducing a type of group technology system through identifying groups of parts and tagging them all the way through the plant. The intention was to work within existing plant arrangements in grouping the parts together rather than machines:

> It achieved some good things as far as having control of the parts, and it gave us a chance to have a look at the things that went wrong with quality. But what it didn't do was eliminate excessive material handling. The parts still had to travel some enormous distances throughout the plant backwards and forwards.
>
> (Local Management Interviews, 1991)

As a result of these initial experiments, the local management team decided that there were two major problems. First, although it was possible to tag particular groups of parts, no individual or group ever had complete control over the part from start to finish. Secondly, because there was no change in material handling, there was unlikely to be any improvement in quality due to the enormous distances parts had to travel. In an early attempt to rectify this problem, a small number of press and welding machines were placed side-by-side. By 1984, the direction of change was further clarified following the plant manager's decision to attend a seminar on group technology being held in Adelaide. On the basis of further reading and discussion, the local management team became familiar with the language and concepts of group technology which, combined with their initial experiments, formed the framework from which a plan of action was formulated. Discussions were held with the CSIRO's Division of Manufacturing Technology, a plan was formulated, and formal agreements of collaboration between the CSIRO and GMHAL were signed (see Chapter 9).

Although the local management team and the CSIRO collaborators were by this time convinced (largely through their own efforts) of the feasibility of introducing modularized work arrangements, senior management and plant employees remained uncertain. As the plant manager indicated: 'There were a lot of sceptics and the worst sceptics were our management'. Clearly, without the support and financial backing of senior management, the project would never be implemented. Consequently, the local management team decided to set up an initial cell to demonstrate how such a change would both increase productivity and quality, and simultaneously improve staff morale and motivation. The cell comprised one spot welder and two presses; and it was staffed by two hand-picked operators who were trained to carry out all the tasks (such as die-set, material handling, quality checks, schedule interpretation) required to manufacture a comparatively simple component. The trial period lasted three months and major improvements were recorded. For example, productivity increased by 3%, material handling was reduced by 70%, scrap by 90% and rework by 50%. The operators welcomed the extra responsibility and became strong supporters and advocates of cell manufacture. The enthusiasm of the operators and the efficiency of cell manufacture demonstrated the viability of the proposed change programme. On the basis of these results, finance was made available to set up a larger cell which was planned to run for a period of twelve months.

This further development towards cellular manufacture indicated the importance of being able to substantiate practical benefits in order to gain further support and financial backing from senior management. The larger cell was set up to operate over two shifts. There were six operators (three female and three male), two presses and five welders. The workcell operated on 10 day runs and was able to produce 70 individual assemblies. During this time, continual improvements were made in response to problems identified by the operators, and there were regular meetings between plant management and CSIRO staff to tackle problems as and when they arose. In conjunction with these technical improvements, operators within the cell positively appraised this new form of work organization. As one of the initial operators recounted:

> The basic concept of the workcell was to teach, not only the guys to die-set in the presses and with the weld tools as well, but also to teach the women. That was the concept and people who showed initiative for this experimental workcell were put in there to run it themselves. There was no foreman, no leading hand, you had no superior people in there, you ran the whole thing yourself. I went in there and that's exactly what I did. I learnt how to die-set, I learnt how to material handle, I did as we all did. There was actually six of us there to start with, three guys and three girls, we all did the die-setting, we did our work, we had all our own job sheets, our scheduling sheets. Normally a leading hand or foreman would do this, we were doing it ourselves and that's how it originally started.
>
> (Shopfloor Interviews, 1989)

No longer were operators constrained by the functional layout of machines placed in a series of lines, where they would work continuously on a few simple operations with little opportunity for social contact or physical movement. Under the workcell system, staff were required to move between various machines in processing a given part and in co-ordinating their activities with other workcell operators. In addition, they were also given greater responsibility in the planning and pacing of work. There was an expectation that they would meet their production schedules, but how they achieved this was left to the individual operator. The operational cell showed a bottom-line improvement of 18% and provided a working example of the manufacturing feasibility of moving from the traditional machine-centred job-shop layout to a human-centred system of cellular manufacture. Moreover, on the basis of these results, the local management team submitted a proposal to senior management requesting the necessary financial support for the change programme. This proposal was rejected, with one senior manager suggesting that what was needed was not the rearrangement of old equipment but the purchasing of new machinery. In 1987, the plant was threatened with closure from the directors. Nevertheless, through persistence and with the help and support of other team members and the CSIRO, the plant manager submitted an amended proposal to senior management. A series of presentations was made and the local management team was able to convince the directors of the feasibility of cellular manufacture.

By the beginning of 1988, the first design for a set of cells was submitted by the CSIRO, and in July of that year the first cell was selected for installation and cut over to cellular manufacture. A project co-ordinator was appointed at GMHAL, with the task of co-ordinating the workcell build to completion by October 1990. During the following months, there was considerable refinement of the cells from the initial plan of 18 cells to 7 multi-assembly cells and 7 cells dedicated to single assemblies. In June 1989, cell one became fully operational, and over the following twelve months the physical restructuring of the plant was undertaken. As the project co-ordinator recalled:

> What we did with the relocation of the machinery, we put it down on a plan; we had a co-ordinated meeting and things like that. We cleared all the electrical drops and the floor was made good, and then we'd hit it all in one. So if we were going to bring the crane in we didn't bring it in on one day, then another, we'd bring in two or three (consecutive) days. It was just like a battalion going through the desert – bang! That was it!
> (Local Management Interviews, 1991)

Working in liaison with production, areas were cleared, floors were painted and presses were moved. In order to minimize disruption, the relocation of the larger presses (up to 350 tons in capacity) was mainly done over the weekends and during the Christmas shutdown. Whilst these changes generated some aggravation between shopfloor operators and the tradespeople responsible for the equipment relocation programme, this presented a challenge which the project co-ordinator used to stimulate enthusiasm among the change agents. Within the twelve months allowed, all the larger equipment had been moved to its new location. However, through emphasizing the importance of computer skills under the new work arrangements, the local management team did instigate employee concerns, particularly among the older leading hands. At this stage, the cell-based computer Scheduler was viewed as an essential component of the workcells:

> We never really had much trouble in convincing the people that it was going to be better. The older type leading hands, they were dubious because people, myself included, were putting a lot of emphasis on this computer Scheduler. Now, to start telling old leading hands they'll have to use computers and things of this nature, that was, in hindsight, not a good thing to do. We should have assured them that we would get the younger guys to do that for them. I don't think, in the early stages, we'd have had as much resistance from the older guys. They were frightened. We frightened them. I take the blame for that, if anything, because I was telling them what their duties would be and I was working the Scheduler up. And even to this day we're not using the Scheduler to a large extent, so once that fear was out we had no problems. But I learnt that when you come into something like computers or hi-tech and it's an older work force, you've got to be a little bit careful. I learnt that very quickly.
>
> (Local Management Interviews, 1990)

Employee concerns about the use of new technology never did eventuate within the workcells. Today, the main methods of production control are through a computerized Production Control System (see Chapter 9) and workcell Kanban techniques (the workcells use a card system to indicate material requirements, see also Chapter 7), whereas the workcell Scheduler is used to simulate changes off-line, in order to identify the feasibility of modifying and revising component manufacture (that is, through a series of 'what if' scenarios simulated changes can be made to components schedules within the cells).

In June 1992, the components automotive plant was operating at around 90% cellular manufacturing, and there remained only a few 'finishing touches' required within the plant. As the project co-ordinator noted, one of the major strengths of the workcell concept is that it is open to continual improvement and should never be 100% complete: 'You can never say that the workcell concept is going to be finished, because there's always room for improvement: it's an ongoing thing.'

In general, the shopfloor response to these changes has been positive. Working conditions have improved, noise levels have been reduced, the incidence of back injuries has declined significantly, and employees are able to learn new skills and rotate between jobs within the workcells. As reported elsewhere, this transformation represents a movement from a machine-centred work environment towards a more human-centred manufacturing operation (Dawson, 1991c).

Workplace change: teamwork and supervision

There are some work organization issues which this case raises which are relevant to the broader changes occurring within industry and the transition towards new wave manufacturing techniques (Buchanan and Preston, 1991:3). In particular, two inter-related concerns which have consistently arisen in discussions and interviews centre on the movement towards teamwork and the declining emphasis on direct supervision. According to Figure 3.1, this change represents a transition towards a new manufacturing philosophy of flexible manufacturing cells with an emphasis on teamwork, self-supervision and multi-skilling (quadrant C). This raises important questions about the possible emergence of a new theory of manufacturing and the consequent implications of these changes for employee attitudes to work. For example, does the evidence of increased operator responsibility and control indicate a reversal of the traditional division of labour, or do employees view these changes as reducing their quality of working life? The answers to these questions are clearly important in understanding the nature of these changes and the concerns of employees on the shopfloor.

Among the employees interviewed there was general agreement that the original workcell concept signalled a redirection in management philosophy towards a more human-oriented approach to technology and work organization. The view that the implementation of workcells was likely to radically improve the quality of working life of shopfloor employees was also held by senior VBU officials. For example, one VBU official noted that:

> When I first found out about workcells and went down there I thought the workcell was something to screw the unions and undermine the union movement. So that was my biggest issue when I went down to the plant . . . Management told us what was going on and I went to those areas and had a look at how the workcells were working. I thought to myself, for a person on the shopfloor this is great because a person could operate a 250-ton press and then stop it . . . So I went around talking to the workers about it and I could see that they were a lot happier and the atmosphere was a lot better. I said how's it going, and they said: 'this is great' . . . 'we can make our own decisions' . . . 'we can decide what part to put in here' and so on. That was the whole object of the workcells when they originally started and you probably would have already got the people telling you that.
>
> (Trade Union Interviews, 1990)

The strong support by union officials and shop stewards turned out to be instrumental in allaying the fears of shopfloor personnel and in supporting a positive vision of the consequences of adopting cellular manufacture. However, many of these evaluations did not reflect a commitment to the principles of this new form of work organization, but to the recognition of the benefits associated with further improvements in the conditions of work (in terms of refurbished machinery, painted floors, easy die transfers and noise reductions), and to a reduction in the number of supervisory personnel and directive supervisory practices. Moreover, the plant was also breaking new ground in redesigning work processes which would reduce physical injuries (particularly back strains) and counter the 'physical-strength' arguments against the employment of women as die-setters. The increased variety in the work and the principle of closure, in machining material from blank to finished component, was positively appraised by operators and supports the principles of good job design forwarded by QWL programmes (see Littler, 1985:20–6). As one employee explained in comparing the two systems:

> [Under the old system] you were just a process worker. You came in the morning and you clocked on, then you just stood in front of your press like a stunned mullet. I mean it is, it's a very monotonous job and it drives you nuts. You look for any excuse to go for a walk for five minutes and come back again. Whereas when I went into the workcell, I had this total independence where I didn't have to depend on anybody other than myself.
>
> (Shopfloor Interviews, 1989)

With the growth in the size of the workcells and under full implementation, there has been a movement away from the original concept of operator-regulated workgroups towards self-regulating workgroups. The former is taken to refer to a situation where there is employee independence within the workcell, whereas the latter refers to the independence of workgroups between workcells, the major difference being that, whilst formal supervisory responsibility is absent from the original concept, it has been incorporated into current workcell structures. Essentially, the formally defined first-line supervisor is concerned with the efficient and smooth operation of a number of workcells. The job involves requesting schedule changes to meet immediate demands, dealing with unforeseen events and contingencies, and responding to employee issues on the shopfloor. There is now a broader area of responsibility and, whilst less emphasis is placed on direct supervision, there is still a key co-ordinating role for the supervisor under this new form of work organization. Within the workcell, it is now the leading hand who plays a major role in the allocation of work and the control of daily operations. Whilst they do not have the discipline function of the staff supervisor, these leading hands do act as the first level of supervision. In short, whilst they may not be formally defined as holding a supervisory position, they can be identified as carrying out supervisory functions according to the criteria that, first, they are involved in the direct day-to-day control of production operations; and, secondly, authority has been invested in their position by management and/or the workforce (see Dawson, 1991e:40).

This change in the nature of shopfloor supervision was not anticipated by management, and in common with other industries, largely reflects a misconception of the function of supervision (Dawson, 1991d). As argued elsewhere, substantive shifts in shopfloor supervision indicate that there is a far broader range of policy options available in the development of supervisors who are neither 'industrial dinosaurs' nor 'lost managers', but key organizational players whose position should be realigned to meet current organizational needs (Dawson, 1991e:35–48). Nevertheless, whilst this confusion about supervision continues through an over-emphasis being placed on formal supervisory positions, local management did view leading hands as holding a supervisory relationship to production: 'They're wages people but we treat them as having a supervisory role'. However, because they are not organizationally defined as 'supervisors' only potential promotees received supervisory training. Consequently, the redefinition of the leading hands role was not fully appreciated and resulted in a number of initial problems:

> We did have a bit of a problem in the first instance in selecting the right leading hand level, which we didn't think we were going to. We thought we'd be able to just transfer a leading hand from what he was doing previously into taking over a workcell and it really wouldn't be very much different. But that certainly isn't the case. There are a lot of extra skills that a leading hand must have, and a lot more responsibility that he must take to make the cell work.
>
> (Local Management Interviews, 1989)

In conjunction with the incorporation of supervisory positions into workcell arrangements, there has been a reconceptualization of what constitutes the workcells. Currently, the workcell comprises a set of new teamwork principles which have been combined with a traditional management structure and superimposed over an enhanced supervisory function, (with the former also being marked by a decline in the number of supervisory personnel). Within this redefinition, teamwork and collaboration remain central principles around which the workcell operates. For some interviewees, this raised the concern about the increased pressure to perform to group norms, to develop and maintain social relations at work, and to the possible intensification of work with little financial remuneration. As one workcell operator stated:

> When you were on the line, your quotas would be more individually based; whereas in the cell, because you've got your raw materials coming in and this product coming out, then it's more teamwork. So if someone bludges or goes slow then it affects the whole group. So would someone who did go slow have pressure put on them by others in the group? I'd have to say yes.
>
> (Shopfloor Interviews, 1991)

This movement towards collaborative teamwork can also be seen as a form of cultural control in demanding acceptance of the philosophy and principles of workcell manufacture. Individual rejection or resistance to the change is highlighted by behaviour which is inconsistent with group behaviour. The group may, in turn, take action through peer group pressure or, more formally, through their supervisor, to enforce acceptance of teamwork practices. Alternatively, some of the developing workcells may further refine the existing workcell principles and compete and/or conflict with management's strategic intention behind its initial design. On this point, one of the local managers indicated his surprise that some employees did not want to learn new skills but, rather, would prefer to remain single machine operators:

> There were a few things that we'd have to say, from a negative point of view, that we said would work and they didn't work. When we developed the cell, the cell philosophy said that unless you can do all of the things the cell requires you are not suitable, and that was what we fully intended, to have everybody trained to be able to do their own die setting. Now we find that not everybody's able to do it and not everybody wants to do it . . . It frightened the hell out of some. They didn't want to do it and they'd never wanted to do it. All they wanted to do was to be a press operator. It's surprising. My opinion has always been that people must be sick and tired of just standing there pushing the button or whatever, but that's what a lot of people like to do.
>
> (Local Management Interview, 1991)

In tackling these issues, not all members of the cell are required to learn a new set of skills. Management has revised its initial intentions and the workcell leaders are now expected to accommodate both machine-oriented workers and those who prefer the new teamwork approach. In consequence, the character of the workcell, in being composed of a group of people working together as a team, has been modified by shopfloor employees during the period of initial operation. Whilst the first operational cells comprised enthusiastic employees who were keen to adopt the new teamwork arrangements, the remaining cells have been staffed by many who were never fully supportive of the changes. Accommodating to their needs poses an ongoing problem for leading hands who must co-ordinate and manage this potentially disruptive setup:

> I've got some people who work their little bums off; I've got other people who couldn't work in an iron lung; and you can't expect them to work as a team. You've got the best operator on the most important jobs and the one who works like a snail, you put him on the least important jobs – that's all I can do. You can't really change the way they work because they've been here for so many years. Whereas on the other shift he's got a lot of the young lads and he'd say, 'pull your finger out'. But with these older people I've got, no chance.
>
> (Supervisor Interviews, 1991)

At the supervisory level, there is a degree of rivalry between the workcells which largely stems from the supervisor's praise or criticism of the workcell allocation of labour. Typically, the first cells to change over to cellular manufacture are seen to have received special treatment, leaving the later workcells with little choice but to 'work with what remained'. This has resulted in a tendency to blame employees for problems of low productivity and/or staff absenteeism. Nevertheless, in an attempt to tackle these problems and strengthen the teamwork philosophy, management has introduced a programme which ensures that each cell has its own QWL group. All cell members are requested to attend an initial two-day workshop on group problem-solving. The group then meets on a two-weekly or monthly basis to identify, analyse and, hopefully, solve workcell problems. The intention is to encourage teamwork through both cellular work arrangements and the problem-solving groups. Although long-term membership of the groups is voluntary, employees are obliged to abide by any decisions made by their particular group. In short, the redefinition of supervision and the movement towards teamwork activities is part of the ongoing process of change within the plant, and is not something which is likely to be achieved overnight. Whilst there has been a general level of enthusiasm and support for the change, there have also been a number of unforeseen concerns which have resulted in revisions in the policy and practice of managing change at GM's automotive component manufacturing plant in South Australia.

Conclusion: flexible workcells, inflexible behaviour and shopfloor transition

There are a number of issues raised by the chapter concerning the process of transition from a conventional job-shop layout to cellular manufacture. These include the rationale for change; management strategy; employee participation; trade union concerns; workcell design and task allocation; training; supervision; and career structures and promotion opportunities. Whilst space precludes the possibility of covering each of these in detail (for a comprehensive analysis of workcell design see Chapter 9), there are three significant and related issues raised in the main body of the chapter which warrant further discussion. The first relates to the process of managing change and the value of programmes designed for the purpose of gaining employee and trade union support. The second concerns the consequence of change for workcell employees who are now required to operate as a team. The third centres on the question of supervisory re-adjustment and shop-floor control.

In the case examined here, the whole process, from the initial stages of becoming aware of the possibility of restructuring work in cellular form, through to final cut-over, has taken approximately ten years. In practice, it has been difficult to identify either the beginning or the end of this major change programme. For example, whilst the seeds for change were sown in 1981 with the arrival of a new plant manager, the origination of group technology within the plant has more than one history (reflecting the various reconstructions of history from the perspective of different key players). Within the life of the programme, the physical restructuring of the plant has been accomplished within a twelve-month period. This achievement illustrates the amount of additional time and effort required to initiate a project, gain employee, trade union and senior management support, develop a competent team, and implement the change within a tight financial budget.

Gaining employee commitment to a continual programme of change was a key feature of local management's strategy. Central to this was the five-year plan developed by the local management which set about improving the work environment, encouraging employee participation in production, and improving the climate of industrial relations. Each of these objectives was achieved and was a critical contextual factor which enabled local management to gain employee acceptance and participation in the transition from the traditional job-shop layout to cellular manufacture. Moreover, this change in employee attitudes, and the creation of a more collaborative, as opposed to adversarial pattern of industrial relations, did not happen overnight but required a long-term commitment to a management approach based on consultative decision-making and co-operative implementation. The latter was particularly important in demonstrating the value placed by local management on employee participation in problem-solving. Thus, through creating an environment in which employee involvement was the norm, the local management team dispelled many of the usual barriers associated with major change programmes (they were also successful in gaining senior management approval through the submission of a proposal which outlined the tangible benefits of cellular manufacture).

The case of hardware fabrication provides a good example of a successful programme which was initiated, planned, implemented and developed by plant employees ranging from the plant manager to a newly appointed press operator. A policy of open communication and early discussions with union representatives, combined with a co-operative programme of employee involvement, has enabled the relatively smooth transition to workcell manufacture. Local management success in achieving commitment from a range of differing vested interest groups has created the need for further change and highlighted how continual refinements and revisions to work organization are integral to the new manufacturing philosophy. For example, a significant implication of the change is the way in which there has been an 'attitude shift' among employees towards not only accepting change but also to anticipating and expecting change. This new and emergent culture of change places extra demands on plant management, who need to maintain the momentum of staff participation and sustain the enthusiasm to be involved, to tackle and to solve production problems of the 1990s. In conjunction with this need to fulfil a heightened level of employee expectation, there is also a need for structural flexibility to meet future developments in the external environment (market competition, government policy) and/or management strategy (rationalization, standardization of product) which is likely to have a significant effect on production requirements at plant level.

The second issue raised by the case is that group technology in the form of cellular manufacturing creates social units conducive to teamwork, which promotes the devolution of control responsibilities for daily work processes to workcell operators. In this case, material handling and die handling are performed by operators who also pack and label completed work before it is forwarded to the customer. Essentially, the whole process of product manufacture, from the delivery of materials through to packing the completed component is carried out within the workcell. In the case of GMHAL, Cell 1 has considerably reduced its inventory with material handling improvements reaching 80%; there have been no industrial problems or disputes;

there has been a die set-up saving of 65%; and the staff within the cells function as teams in accepting responsibility for group performance. In short, the benefits which have derived from restructuring work around cellular manufacture would appear to have combined productivity increases with an improvement in the QWL of workcell operators.

This transition to cellular manufacture has also brought about an increase in the demands placed on individual operators to conform to teamwork practices and to get involved in the work process. Traditional operating practices which enabled employees to 'distance' themselves from the work are no longer deemed 'acceptable'. In contrast to conventional functional layouts which were criticized for their alienating properties in constraining social interaction and task engagement, the new teamwork structures are based on group work and collaborative employee involvement. However, they also set clear parameters on what is to be regarded as acceptable employee behaviour under new production arrangements, only in this case the new teamwork structures can be criticized for preventing employee disengagement from the work process. Paradoxically, traditional model employees who continue to distance themselves from process involvement will now be engaging in behaviour defined as 'inappropriate' by management. Moreover, organizational evaluation of this behaviour takes no account of personal choice but, rather, explains employee deviancy in terms of an inability to adapt to change. Consequently, the 'solution' is perceived to be either through training programmes which realign deviant behaviours with this new set of working principles, or through job transfer, resignation, redundancy or early retirement. In short, whilst there has been an improvement in the working conditions on the shopfloor, the new working principles under which appropriate employee behaviour is evaluated remain tightly constrained and controlled by management.

The third major implication refers to the change in supervision as a result of work reorganization. Under the initial workcell system, operators had the autonomy to plan and organize their work in co-ordination with other workcell operators. A supervisory structure of control was not imposed on the workcell but, rather, operated as a co-ordinating and liaising boundary function outside the day-to-day practices of workcell operation. Today, this initial workcell design has been revised to accommodate a teamwork facilitator who holds a supervisory relationship to other workcell operators. Whilst the overall number of supervisory personnel has been reduced by over 50%, the control function of supervision has been enhanced to take on a broader area of responsibility. Supervisors are also concerned less with inspection and technical issues and more with employee relations, teamwork facilitation and planning. Thus, one of the implications for the newly emerging teamwork-based work reorganization schemes is that, whilst there may be a reduction in the quantity of supervisory staff, there may also be an enhancement of the supervisory function. This qualitative expansion in the job of the supervisor may also signal the need to move away from traditional conceptions of supervision. The change suggests a movement from an adversarial to a more collaborative system of employee relations, and a shift in the nature of the working relationship between operators, supervisors, shop stewards and plant management.

In the case of Pirelli, Hewlett Packard and General Motors there have been a number of significant operational changes following the introduction of new production and service arrangements. In all these companies, there were also a number of other related changes; for example, PCAL have recently embarked on a JIT programme at their Minto plant in New South Wales, HP have been involved in the introduction of new technology, and GM operated a Kanban manufacturing system and were engaged in various quality initiatives to reduce scrap rates and improve operational efficiencies. Although TQM, JIT and cellular manufacture represent some of the most prominent and large-scale operational change programmes in modern organizations, there are a number of other related schemes associated with the introduction of new technologies and techniques (for example, Activity-Based Management and Best Practice Programmes). As such, there is rarely one single scheme which predominates company change. More often, managing transitions in the 1990s is likely to be about managing a composite range of different initiatives. Nevertheless, linked to these 'eclectic transitions' are a number of common threads. As indicated in Chapter 6, these include elements such as the movement towards teamwork practices, the emphasis on employee commitment, and the tendency to devolve responsibility for quality control to shopfloor employees. In addition, the redefinition of supervision towards facilitation and co-ordination, the development of more open and long-term customer–supplier relations, and the movement from an adversarial to a more collaborative system of employee relations all signal a transition towards new organizational arrangements. Central to all these transitions has been the use of participative management techniques in encouraging employee involvement in change programmes and this, is the focus of the chapter that follows which examines the management of new technology at Central Linen Service.

8

NEW TECHNOLOGY AT CENTRAL LINEN SERVICE

Introduction

In the early 1980s Central Linen Service (CLS) was operating with unreliable and outdated machinery; it experienced major industrial conflicts; strategic decision-making was constrained by a bureaucratic committee of management; and low employee morale reflected the poor conditions of work and the future uncertainty of the company. Within this context, the Liberal Government employed a group of consultants to investigate the commercial viability of CLS. Their first report made a number of recommendations, one of which centred on re-equipping the factory with advanced technology. This option then became part of a series of political negotiations between senior union officials and Government officers. The election of a Labor Government heightened these discussions and, under trade union pressure, the recommendation to revitalize CLS through the adoption of new technology was approved.

This chapter examines the process of technological change at CLS, from the initial conception of a need to change through to shopfloor operation. Particular attention is given to the issue of participative management and employee involvement in the organizational adoption of new technology. The importance of developing a cohesive management team with an enthusiastic chief executive who actively supports programmes of employee involvement is emphasized. The case also highlights how a sharp decline in the organization's commercial viability, combined with a commonality of interest among the major political stakeholders, produced an environment conducive to change. But before embarking on this analysis, the chapter first examines some of the major debates which surround the introduction of new technology in the workplace.

Managing new technology

Questions concerning the management of new technology and the implications of change for the organization and control of work have stimulated considerable debate (Knights and Willmott, 1986). Much of the early work focused on the consequences of technological change for economic well-being and levels of unemployment (ACARD, 1979; Baron and Curnow, 1979, Hines and Searle, 1979). For example, Jenkins and Sherman claimed that the economic imperative for adopting new technology meant that the choice was between a high level of structural unemployment (through the use of outdated capital equipment which would result in competitive disadvantage), or a high level of technological unemployment (through the labour-displacing effects of new technology): 'Remain as we are, reject the new technologies and we face unemployment of up to 5.5. million by the end of the century. Embrace the new technologies, accept the challenge and we end up with unemployment of about 5 million' (Jenkins and Sherman, 1979:113).

The capacity for new technology to displace jobs stems from its broad area of application. The miniaturization of what may be termed the 'brain' of the computer (central processing unit) onto a single-piece chip of silicon (microprocessor) resulted in the development by M. E. Hoff of a computer on a chip (Francis, 1986:1). This technological breakthrough dramatically reduced the size and cost of computers and established the economic viability of microelectronics, as Peter Large (1980:9–10) writes: 'The chip's revolutionary impact stems from its size. It's cheap because it's small, it's fast because it's small . . . and it can be used in places were computers would not fit before'. For example, the Ferranti mark 1 Star (Europe's first commercial computer built in 1950) filled two bays 16 feet long, 8 feet high and 4 feet deep. It contained approximately six miles of wire, 4,000 valves and 100,000 soldered joints, and it needed 27 kilowatts of power to function. In contrast, the Ferranti F100 (which was the first European-developed microprocessor) was only a quarter of an inch square. It had approximately 100 times the computing capacity of the Star; it required 5 million times less power; it was more reliable and cost 1/5000 as much.

On the question of shopfloor automation, Gill (1985:63) suggests that all production processes consist of three different functional activities: 'the transformation of work-pieces, the transfer of work-pieces between work stations, and the co-ordination and control of this transformation and transfer'. He identifies three historical phases of automation, namely:

1. *Primary mechanization*: which involved the use of steam power to drive machinery to accomplish the transformation of raw materials into products.
2. *Secondary mechanization*: at this stage electricity was employed to drive machinery to accomplish the transfer of tasks and to run continuous-flow assembly lines.
3. *Tertiary mechanization*: this has involved the use of information technology to control and co-ordinate the transformation and transfer of tasks (see also McLoughlin and Clark, 1988: 6–7).

The relationship between labour displacement and the level of automation is more readily identified in case study analyses, and is often a key issue surrounding the introduction of new technology. For example, in a survey of workplace change, Daniel found that although changes which displaced jobs, reduced wages and/or deskilled work tended to increase the level of resistance, employees placed a greater emphasis on job satisfaction and earnings, compared with union officials who placed a high priority on the employment implications (Daniel, 1987:267–8). These findings would suggest that, in managing change, attention must be given to the response of trade unions and to the concerns of employees on the issue of earnings, employment and job redesign. This is particularly significant, given the capacity of the new technology to improve the control of operations through enabling the more effective capture, storage, manipulation and distribution of information (see Chapter 5). For our purposes, there are three significant characteristics of this control technology, namely:

1. *Convergence*: in enabling several functions to be incorporated into the one device, such as programming, machining and inspection into a machine tool.
2. *Integration*: in combining previously discrete stages of a manufacturing operation into a continuous process (this may create a need for new forms of work organization based on teamwork).
3. *Innovative potential*: the applicability, programmability, extendability and linkability of the technology facilitates ongoing development and experimentation with the new technology (Boddy and Buchanan, 1986:25–6).

According to Fleck (1991), of crucial importance to the effective management of these developments is the type of technology. He distinguished between discrete, system and configurational technologies. The first refers to products or processes which are ready for immediate use. System technologies is taken to refer to the arrangements of complexes of components which constrain and condition one another. Finally, the term configurational technologies is used to refer to the information-integration associated with tertiary automation, which underlies many of the changes currently taking place in industry (Fleck, 1991:2–9). Whilst there are similarities between configurational and system technologies, the former are seen to comprise looser and more open connections: 'Configurations may be made up in a very wide range of patterns; the mutually interacting (but not necessarily mutually constraining) components may be deployed in many ways to meet particular requirements' (Fleck, 1991:3). He goes on to explain how prime examples of configurational technologies are the large-scale company-wide computer installations (such as Central Linen Service), and how the implementation of these more advanced systems requires that considerable attention be given to the non-technical components in order to achieve successful operation. Failure to do so may result in what has been termed the 'productivity paradox' where, despite organizational adoption of microelectronic technology, there is a general decline in productivity (Fleck, 1991:1).

The enabling characteristics of these configurational technologies provide organizational practitioners with a number of options in the way technology is introduced and used within companies. Whilst this would support the view that technology does not determine outcomes (the technological determinist perspective), some commentators have indicated that care should be taken not to throw the technology baby out with the determinist bath water (Clark *et al*, 1988:9–15). They suggest that electronic technology does have an independent influence and may reduce or eliminate tasks requiring manual skills, and generate complex tasks requiring interpretive and problem-solving skills; although they note that the tendency in managing change has been to ignore the new task and skills requirements and therefore undermine the effective use of new technology through reducing reliance on skilled human intervention (McLoughlin and Clark, 1988:118–41).

The importance of management's approach to the process of technological change is also highlighted by Boddy and Buchanan (1986) who distinguish between the 'distancing' and 'complementing' effects of new technology. The former is taken to refer to the consequences of introducing new working arrangements which replace significant human skills; and the latter where work is restructured for the purpose of complementing human skills and enabling people to enhance their contribution and performance (Boddy and Buchanan, 1986:84–112). They identify the main consequences of distancing as being an unwillingness to take responsibility, an inability to deal with unplanned changes, and feelings of alienation and boredom. These responses may, in turn, confirm management's assumption that employees require tighter systems of control (McLoughlin, 1991:297–8). The process by which this self-fulfilling prophecy occurs has been referred to as a 'vicious circle of controls', where new technology is introduced to meet a managerially defined need for control; jobs are designed to reduce the range of tasks and to limit the ability of operators to influence the pace or pattern of work; the resultant lack of employee commitment is evidenced by an increase in workplace conflict and resistance; this in turn confirms management's perception that employee behaviour requires direct control (Clegg and Dunkerley, 1980:364–5). In short, the consequence of introducing microelectronic configurational technologies for the organization of work is determined by a range of factors during the process of transformational change. Although the characteristics of the new technology (the substance of change) may enable and constrain the number of options available, the assumptions of management and the context in which the change takes place (the context of change), as well as the competing and conflicting interests of a range of internal and external stakeholders (the politics of change), are all determinants of the process and outcomes of technological change (see Figure 3.2).

In the study which follows, an examination is made of the process of change from secondary to tertiary mechanization in an Australian laundry facility. The organizational issues surrounding the introduction of a new configurational technology are detailed, and the significance of a participative approach to change is discussed.

Central Linen Service

Central Linen Service (CLS) is a government-owned commercial enterprise which was created in 1962 by the South Australian Government's Hospitals Department (now the Health Commission) to service the hospital and health care areas. CLS produces approximately 300 tonnes of finished laundry a week, has annual sales in excess of $16 million (as at June 1990) and has the highest productivity (measured in kilograms produced per hour) compared with any other laundry handling a comparable product range (for example, in 1983 production per operator hour was 25 kilograms and by 1989 this had risen to 46 kilograms). 1989 was also the year in which CLS created a new world record for the greatest amount of laundry washed, ironed and folded in a nine-hour period. Today, CLS operates one of the world's largest laundry production facilities and is recognized as an international leader in the application of high technology. It employs over 300 staff and services 360 clients over a geographical area of 150,000 square kilometres. A vehicle fleet is maintained in order to service 85% of the South Australian Government's hospitals and health care areas.

The context of change

In the year 1977–78, CLS provided 10,700 tonnes of linen and laundering services. This initial peak in production declined over the following five years and by 1982 there was a 55% increase in the cost per processed tonne (partially attributable to a 20% increase in wages and salaries), which combined with a decline in productivity of 23%. This lowering of performance led to a complete review of CLS operations by Touche Ross Services Pty on behalf of the South Australian Health Commission (SAHC). The first of two reports was submitted in September 1982, outlining a number of possible options for organizational restructuring, from which the government decided that CLS should:

1. Improve the structure and quality of management.
2. Adopt a more appropriate financing arrangement.
3. Introduce new technology into the workplace.

In following the first of these objectives, a new General Manager was appointed. Prior to this appointment, the senior management function was being undertaken by a Committee of Management appointed by the SAHC. This committee, which was also responsible for a state-owned frozen food factory located next to CLS, was a rather unwieldy and bureaucratic mechanism. In the regular transferral of money from CLS to the food factory, the commercial viability of both operations was being called into question. Touche Ross identified the need for an independent chief executive with the authority to make strategic decisions, and the consequent need to abolish the Committee of Management. However, due to a change of government, there was a delay in Cabinet decision-making which resulted in considerable 'behind-the-scenes' negotiations. For example, senior trade union officials arranged early meetings with the new Minister for Health in the newly elected Labor Government, and argued the case for the injection of funds into CLS to prevent closure of the factory. The support given by the Minister was later used to negotiate with the Australian Government Workers Union (AGWU) in ensuring that the newly appointed General Manager would be given union co-operation in restructuring work and introducing new technology. In addition, the Committee of Management was abolished and an Interim Board of Management established. The board members were to support and direct the new General Manager in the implementation of the recommendations of the Touche Ross report.

The champion of change

The main priority of the newly appointed General Manager was to create a climate conducive to technological change, and then to manage the process of organizational transformation. For the first three years, the General Manager was given considerable autonomy. Gone were the traditional bureaucratic layers of government-owned enterprise; there were no formal Boards of Management but, rather, an Interim Board which actively supported the decisions of the comparatively autonomous General Manager. Within this context, the General Manager set about improving employee relations and setting an agenda for change. At the outset, this involved an open and participatory approach to management, which encouraged the free flow of information between management and shopfloor operatives. For example, in an attempt to overcome some of the structural barriers to participation, the General Manager circumvented the conventional communication channels through supervisory management, and instead disseminated information directly to union representatives and plant operators. Initially, this was viewed by some managers as a pro-union and anti-management stance, and the later reconstitution of management did result in some conflict and resentment among a small number of supervisory staff. However, the main objective of the General Manager was to ensure that accurate information on the future direction of the plant was made available to every employee, who would then be in a position to make his or her own judgement. This philosophy of open communication and employee involvement was combined with a strong belief in the prerogative of management to lead employees and a commitment to making CLS a commercial operation. Some of the elements of this management approach are captured in the following quote, where the General Manager is describing the initial stages of gaining employee commitment to the revitalization of CLS:

> Before anything happened at all I asked that I should be able to speak to the entire factory personnel in the canteen, which was arranged. I told them that their performance was, without any doubt whatever, the lowest of any laundry – institutional or private sector – in Australia, and probably the world. They were probably the laziest bunch of layabouts

> it had ever been my misfortune to come across, and I had no intention whatever of coming across to take over unless I had an assurance from them that they wanted and would accept change, and change would be of a great and large magnitude.
>
> (Senior Management Interviews, 1990)

The main intentions of the General Manager were to build a cohesive management team, to develop good union–management relations, to gain employee support and commitment to change, and then to sustain this culture of change throughout the major re-equipment programme. The means for achieving this 'attitude shift' were through the deliberate communication of management's strategic plan for the future direction of the laundry. The General Manager made it clear that, unless there was a commitment to stemming the loss-making trend of linen operations, there was nothing that anybody could do to prevent job displacement. However, if they facilitated the planned programme of change, the General Manager could ensure them greater job security and a sense of pride in turning around a public liability into a self-funding and successful commercial enterprise. This theme was the bedrock of the General Manager's approach to change:

> There is no doubt that the most significant aspect of human interaction is communication. Generally, it is the lack of goals, the lack of direction, and the absence of communication that upsets the people on the shop-floor, and encourages them to precipitate unthinking action . . . It is essential that a bond of trust be established between management and worker, and building up a feeling of confidence in each other has been a prime concern.
>
> (Senior Management Interviews, 1990)

In referring to the personality of the General Manager, trade union officials, managers, supervisors and operators consistently described him as a great enthusiast who was able to engage others with his optimism and vision for the future. This ability to motivate and encourage others to believe in themselves, to believe in the abilities of management as leaders of change, and to engender trust in the General Manager, was a critical factor in bringing about a change in employee attitudes.

In conjunction with this programme of direct and open communication, the General Manager set up a Combined Unions Council to encourage worker participation and to build stronger links between shop stewards and managers. The intention was to improve industrial relations and to create an organizational climate conducive to change:

> Bob [The General Manager] set up what we call a Combined Unions Council very soon after he came here. He got all the unions together, because he used the union as his communication link with the floor; he couldn't trust the management in the factory. So he set up a Combined Unions Council. He wrote out a charter for them, organized for them to have meetings, provided a room down the back of the canteen for them.

> They would have their meetings regularly, and within 24 hours they could meet with Bob and raise any problems, and things would be fixed. And I guess part of his motive in doing that was to try and deal with people here rather than deal with the union organizers from the head office of the union, who would come in with maybe a distorted view or not all the information that was required . . . He really tried to develop a relationship with the people here. And that worked for two or three years, and then it outlived its usefulness. And we now deal direct with the shop stewards and have very little problem at all.
>
> (Senior Management Interviews, 1990)

The Combined Unions Council was created to promote unity among the shop stewards of the various unions represented in the CLS, and to provide a forum in which the council could work with management in formulating company policy. It was also used to resolve disputation internally without the need to bring external union officials into discussions. Essentially, the procedural arrangement was that the council should meet once a month. The General Manager would commence the meeting by advising members of any new developments and encouraging discussion. He would then leave and the council would discuss matters further, and if anything required resolution the Executive Committee were to attend a meeting with the General Manager within five days. Thus, the main purpose of the Council was to resolve industrial disputes internally and to act as a communication link between management and shopfloor employees.

Whilst the Combined Unions Council played a significant part in the earlier stages of change, it was later disbanded and does not currently exist. The major problem with the Council from a management perspective was that it began to be used as a forum for agitation rather than resolution and, from the union perspective, the Council posed a threat in ignoring external union officials. Nevertheless, in conjunction with the AGWU Shop Stewards Committee (which convened monthly to discuss member issues), the Council did prove instrumental in resolving many change issues without recourse to 'outside' negotiation.

Reconstituting management

The Touche Ross report had indicated that one of the major problems at CLS centred on the poor quality of management staff. This fitted well with the philosophy of the General Manager, who set about reconstituting management into a more cohesive and less fragmented and conflictorial group. This took place in parallel with the shopfloor employee involvement programmes, and was achieved through a series of psychological tests and close face-to-face discussions:

> The first thing I insisted on was that every senior manager should go through a complete battery of psychological appraisals. I also told them that, from my observations in the first week that I was there, and from my reading of the report, some of them would feel decidedly unhappy

> about working for me, and I suggested that those who in their hearts knew that, should start to look for other jobs in the department or to let me know and I would help them do it. They would do it with style and dignity and a position of similar status would be found for them.
>
> (Senior Management Interviews, 1990)

Only one of the senior management group was relocated elsewhere and a replacement was found. As a result of further discussions with the General Manager, the senior management began to see themselves as a team and became committed to the planned programme of change. In particular, the finance manager was able to assist in determining critical funding formulae for the new equipment. Whilst the General Manager did not instigate any regular participative management meetings, he did maintain a close relationship with every senior manager, and acted as the keystone which bound the management group together and gave them a common sense of purpose. Whilst senior managers were accountable for their actions, they were given freedom to exercise their responsibilities as they deemed appropriate.

At the middle managerial and supervisory levels, there was a lot of dissatisfaction and conflict. This supervisory 'problem' initially stemmed from the attitude of supervisors towards senior management. In part, this can be explained by the fact that, prior to the appointment of the General Manager, promotion from the shopfloor was based on seniority rather than merit. The General Manager changed this 'tradition' and encouraged any employee to apply for supervisory positions. He also instituted a comprehensive series of training programmes for all CLS supervisory staff. However, two dimensions of the supervisory 'problem' remained. First, there was a mixture of different supervisory approaches which resulted in considerable employee and inter-supervisory conflict. Secondly, the long-serving supervisors did not see themselves as being part of management:

> The next step came with the realization that the charge hands and leading hands simply had no idea that they were management people. They thought that they had been given their blue coats or their yellow coats, which was their sign of authority, because they had been there for a good many years.
>
> (Senior Management Interviews, 1990)

In an attempt to tackle this problem, the General Manager called all his supervisory staff and the union shop stewards to a meeting in the canteen. Once gathered, the General Manager gave a brief speech on the responsibilities for supervisors, such as discipline, staff appraisal, accountability, and so forth. The intention was to stress that supervisors are a part of management and, as such, are expected to hold a management perspective in the work in which they are engaged. The General Manager then asked the senior shop stewards and union officials to go down to the other end of the canteen, and asked those remaining to choose the side they felt represented their interests and viewpoint:

> I said those of you on the management side who don't feel you can handle my requirements I would like you to go down with the shop

stewards and the union people. You will not lose your salary levels but you will certainly lose your position of authority. But you'll do it with grace and you'll do it with dignity . . . Some of the ones who decided that they couldn't handle the management side of things really astonished me. But at least everybody who was left understood exactly what was required, and it was all to do with leadership and personal accountability, and that was where we started from.

(Senior Management Interviews, 1990)

The General Manager then set about rectifying this situation by replacing some of the traditional supervisors and, at the same time, recruiting new supervisory personnel. He also arranged for all supervisors to attend internal training programmes on the management of people, leadership skills and communication. In parallel to these changes to supervisory staff, a programme of training for shopfloor employees was also undertaken. The latter comprised a series of training programmes for groups of ten or twelve factory operators who attended 'in-house' courses organized by the CLS personnel manager at the Health Commission's training centre at Eden Park. In the morning, the General Manager would welcome them to the course, and then the production and personnel manager would discuss the importance of setting and achieving goals. After lunch, course attendees would be given the chance to discuss openly their problems, frustrations and worries about working for CLS.

The course was an important vehicle for achieving a greater commitment and loyalty of shopfloor employees to the proposed change programme, and within six months every person from the shopfloor had attended the course. Thus, the reconstitution of management, the practice of open communication and shop steward involvement, and the provision of in-house operator and supervisory training courses all contributed to a shift in attitudes and the creation of a culture of change. Other practices which reinforced this trend were the arrangement of iced cordial for employees on hot days and the encouragement of Management By Walking Around (MBWA) by all senior managers. Perhaps one of the key turning points was when the General Manager was able to get the 38-hour day for employees months before other public service organizations, and on the condition that productivity would increase. This event was particularly significant as it was a union objective which became a management deliverable. In other words, it provided a strong signal that the General Manager was in control and able to deliver on promised agreements. Consequently, even before the major re-equipment programme significant improvements in productivity were achieved, and served as tangible measures of the success of the General Manager's new management approach and his success in changing attitudes and creating a climate of trust and tolerance.

The re-equipment programme

In August 1983, Touche Ross submitted a second report outlining a management plan for the introduction of new technology. They identified the three main priority areas as being:

1. To develop master plans for laundry layout and equipment acquisition.
2. To improve productivity.
3. To develop marketing strategies to regain lost clients and to increase sales of profitable services.

On the basis of these recommendations, and with the provision of the necessary capital funds for equipment upgrading, the senior engineering manager set out a preliminary design. He was given free reign to set the specifications, call for tenders and decide on the appropriate machinery for plant installation:

> Now, we're talking about a programme worth millions and normally, to do that sort of thing, you have a team. You understand that you have a consultant group with subcommittees and working parties and the rest of it. But I guess there's a sense of pride in that at this place, because of the freedom a guy like [the General Manager] gives you, I was able to sit down and do all the drawings, write all the specifications (because I'd been involved in that in other places), then call the tenders and be involved in the tender appraisal . . . It meant travelling around the world with a stop watch and a set of scales, metaphorically speaking, really analysing what people said machines could do and what they couldn't; none of this, if you like, salesmen's nonsense.
>
> (Senior Management Interviews, 1990)

On the basis of this work, a report was written recommending certain tenderers. The South Australian Health Commission (SAHC) was reluctant to commit itself to such a major project without substantial supporting evidence, and arranged for two highly qualified engineers to evaluate CLS's appraisal. The two external engineers ratified the initial recommendations and the CLS set about arranging contracts for equipment purchase and delivery. Nevertheless, whilst the investment had been agreed and a contract set up, on 25 January 1985 the Health Commission queried the financial arrangements and requested further submissions. This resulted in a delay of twelve months, during which the CLS had to make up their own video-tapes and arrange a special interview with the SAHC commissioners:

> We had a group of commissioners around the table, and we had to deliver a presentation with video and pictures around the wall, and totally convince them to sign the cheques.
>
> (Senior Management Interviews, 1990)

A number of attempts were made by the commissioners to reduce the size of the investment, through questioning the need for three automated washing machines. Eventually, CLS management convinced the SAHC of the commercial viability of the re-equipment programme, although the delay of a year is reckoned to have added over $1 million to the total purchasing cost, due to adverse changes in the exchange rate.

In 1986, the CLS embarked on a major change programme which it hoped would take it to the leading edge of international laundry systems and make it one of the most technically advanced laundries in the world:

> We were going to create something which didn't exist anywhere else in the world, and this was a systemized laundry. It was no longer going to be a collection of this machine here and that machine there and another machine somewhere else. Furthermore, it was going to be a system which was going to be computer controlled.
>
> (Senior Management Interviews, 1990)

The factory design was drawn up by the engineering manager on an 8 foot by 4 foot board, which was put up on the wall in the canteen. Comments were invited from employees on the proposed layout of the new machinery. This draft was placed alongside a drawing of the existing plant to provide a greater understanding of the implications of change for work organization. At the same time, management were talking to employees on a face-to-face basis. They described the planned programme of change and discussed the consequence for employee jobs and responsibilities. As it turned out, there were only a few responses to management's request for employee comments, and this, in part, may be explained by the high level of discussion encouraged and promoted by management on the plant re-equipment programme. Once the period of preparing employees for change had been completed, the senior management team set about implementing the new machinery. The equipment included:

1. Milnor washing systems and dryers from the USA;
2. Dunnewolt batch handling transport systems from Holland;
3. Jensen feeders and folders from Denmark;
4. Kannegeisser steam finishing tunnels from West Germany; and
5. Spencer rotary presses from the UK.

These separate pieces of machinery are linked together by a series of computer programmes which are controlled from a central computer room within the laundry. Essentially, once the incoming linen has been sorted by hand, it is automatically tracked and processed along the overhead handling transport system through the Milnor washing systems and dryers and, finally, to the ironers, folders and dispatch. Consequently, once the soiled linen has been sorted into the appropriate soiled linen bag, there is no further contact with operators until the clean linen reaches the appropriate finishing station. At this stage, the linen is then stored or sorted for final distribution to CLS customers.

On the shopfloor: implementation and initial operation

On the shopfloor, employees were informed from the outset that there would be some changes in work arrangements which might require operators to relocate (through developing other avenues of business CLS was able to absorb displaced labour) into other departments. During this process of staff relocation, the management team focused their attention on communicating the proposed changes, both verbally and in writing:

> We took groups of people off the shopfloor away for a day to talk to them about change and organization, team work and how the new system was going to be totally integrated, computer controlled, and would be much more of a flow process than it was before, where it was sort of a stop/start operation before. We had to get them used to having bags of linen going around the ceiling, rather than trolleys of linen going on the floor, and all of these sorts of things that we felt were likely to affect people, together with the need for substantial overtime, substantial disruption to their work day – because the new machinery had to be introduced, the old taken out and production maintained. And, in fact, increased production was introduced at that time. We took on another thirty tonnes of work a week at the same time as we were introducing this new washing machine, so it put some enormous strains on a whole lot of people, not the least of whom were the people who were operating the machine and actually doing the work.
>
> (Senior Management Interviews, 1990)

One critical player during the implementation phase was the production manager who, in this case, was new to the laundry operating environment. This absence of a detailed operating knowledge meant that the production manager was unable to actively participate in the planning process, and yet had to deal directly with the disruptions imposed by change. At times, this created a degree of cynicism and conflict, particularly when the physical placement of new equipment was occurring. Over a period of six months, the production manager was continually firefighting in an 'impossible' attempt to meet customer demands. Although considerable pressure to maintain productivity was put on production from transport, the dispatch department and senior management, production continued to fall and considerable friction resulted at middle managerial and supervisory level. This interpersonal agitation was further exacerbated by the problems experienced with the new technology. As the Production Manager illustrated:

> We were washing the Stork nappies at the time, and Stork nappies are bloody awful things to wash. Under the old system we could get them clean, but with the new washing machine there were some nights here when we washed them five times to get them clean; because we ran out of chemicals or the rinse water wasn't going out right; or there wasn't enough steam being injected to get the temperature right, and all of these sorts of things. Of course, this was all supposed to happen automatically. This was the new whizz-bang computer-controlled thing where you pressed a button and it knew what to do. So we believed that when we were being told about this and, of course, it doesn't always work that way, at least initially. So we had the lady from Stork down here, and we were actually walking along the washing machine and we were saying, 'There're your nappies: see how they're going through', and then they'd come out grey or yellow at the other end, or something stupid like that. And we'd have to go back and wash them again. They're the sort of traumas we went through.
>
> (Management Interviews, 1990)

A number of technical problems also emerged during the initial operation of the new technology. They were difficult to resolve, largely due to an absence of any detailed local knowledge of how the new systems worked. When the automated systems were initially put into place, a technician (from the American suppliers) was made available to instruct CLS personnel on basic maintenance and operational techniques. Although under the initial plan the intention was to send two engineers to be trained in America, this became politically unacceptable and, consequently, a significant period of 'trial-and-error' elapsed before the engineers became fully conversant with the system (for example, nobody was sure how to tackle the first washer blockage). Operating under the old mechanical machinery required a high degree of mechanical skill to tackle the regular breakdowns, which often necessitated major repairs. As one maintenance technician recalled:

> The image before the change, when you had this very old technology, very old machinery with major breakdowns, you had to continually do serious maintenance, but patching up because the machinery could never totally be refurbished. It was always a bit of a patch job and you actually had to make some parts yourself. I should say we were more the grunt and groan brigade: typical chewing gum and bootlace type maintenance. When the new machinery came there was a chap who came from Milnor to assist with the information. He had the technical expertise for setting the machines up and getting them running. He gave our chaps guidance on how to make certain electrical connections, programming for the microprocessor systems. So we got a basic knowledge from him, and a lot of what he taught us we had to embellish on as we found different problems ourselves. We've had very good communication with the manufacturers over in the States. They've always been very willing to answer our requests so our knowledge has grown very quickly. In fact, our chaps, I would say, are very knowledgeable in their field now: so much so that we get called on from time to time for assistance from the agents for the machines.
>
> (Maintenance Interviews, 1990)

Whilst the responsibilities of the maintenance engineers continued to be the running, modification and maintenance of machinery, a new set of skills was required following the introduction of automated electronic technology. For example, far greater emphasis was placed on electronic maintenance tasks, and far more time was spent monitoring the system rather than dealing with basic repairs. Through working with the equipment and maintaining regular contact with their American suppliers, the maintenance engineers eventually adapted to the new technology, and are now sometimes called upon to visit other Australian laundries to assist with maintenance tasks. There was general agreement in the maintenance technician interviews that, whilst there was concern over the change, this was largely outweighed by an overall enthusiasm for getting new machinery. Furthermore, the change programme generated a lot of extra work and, as one technician described:

It's something not many people get the opportunity to do, which is rip a factory to pieces and rebuild it again. It's a very unique situation and something most tradesmen will never ever have the opportunity of doing. It was a big tactical task for the maintenance staff on their side, for the amount of work that was going to be involved; new services to be laid; air, steam, electrical. I reckon the electricians must have laid enough wire to go to the moon and back. It was that type of exercise. Like I say, we were all learning new skills so, in itself, that feeds you when you're interested in that. It gives you that enthusiasm.

(Shopfloor Interviews, 1990)

Through being involved in the implementation and ongoing maintenance and modification of the system, the engineers now view the equipment as 'theirs'. The previous technology is referred to as 'inherited machinery' and there are now better relations with production and a teamwork approach to maintenance tasks. This ownership of the machinery is seen to stem from their detailed involvement during implementation, and their consequent achievement in learning new skills without recourse to any formal training programme. This knowledge has been further developed in making changes to the configurational technology to meet the changing needs of CLS.

On the shopfloor, the implementation of change was further complicated by a large parcel of health and related laundry business from a major competitor (International Linen Service) being taken over by CLS. This occurred following a brief discussion with the Minister for Health, and CLS's decision to buy out the health sector business of International Linen Service (this was largely private hospitals and nursing homes). As a result, the process of change was occurring in the context of an expanding client base and declining productivity. This created a degree of tension between shopfloor employees and supervisors, who were anxious to maintain or even increase production. However, the marketing manager was able to reduce some of the external pressure from CLS's new client group by inviting them to the factory to witness the transfer from a mechanical to a semi-electronic washing facility. These occasions were also used to highlight the longer-term advantages in quality and reliability which would result from adopting the new technology:

One of the main things that we were doing was bringing them down here to visit the laundry, and showing them what was happening. And when they could see what was happening they were far more understanding of any difficulties that occurred and, by developing good relationships, they tended to overlook any problem area. But we offered a much wider range of services than they'd been used to and that made them happy. So it was a very challenging time.

(Senior Management Interviews, 1990)

In alleviating some of these external pressures, and preparing operators for the changes which were going to occur, there was general support for the movement from an outdated laundry operation, which was threatened with closure, to an automated linen service which could compete with private enterprise. Regular meetings were set up with all staff, showing videos of the new equipment and describing the period of adjustment required. As a result, there was a very high level of acceptance of change. As one operator described:

> They actually had this really big fork lift working there, turning and driving in and out all the time. There'd be exhaust fumes and everything, but there was no other way of doing it. And people had the table just next to it, working folding linen and all that sort of thing, and no one ever complained. We never had any problem. Everybody actually helped. If that fellow would have dropped a hammer or something like that, somebody would rush and give it back to him: 'Come on, keep on going'.
>
> (Shopfloor Interviews, 1990)

The commitment, enthusiasm and regular contact with senior management were critical factors which facilitated employee support for the change programme. This was particularly noticeable in situations were the changes were bringing about a major reduction in the number of staff required. As a senior shop steward noted:

> They made the sewing room a third of the size it was before. The sewing room used to have about 50 people in there at one stage. Now we're down to 10. And that was a big thing: the people were very worried about why it was being made smaller. But they didn't sack anyone; it's just that as people were retiring they never replaced them.
>
> (Shopfloor Interviews, 1990)

Apart from the displacement effects of introducing the new technology, there were also significant changes to the nature of work. Under the old system of operation, there was a lot of heavy lifting and physical manoeuvring of large linen bags. For example, it use to be necessary to both load and unload the machines by hand, and now this is all fully automatic. As a result, there has been a decline in the number of industrial injuries previously associated with 'pulling and pushing' laundry. In the view of one operator:

> It's made life easier, because with the machines we've got we can get through our work a lot easier, a lot quicker, and the work looks 100% better. That's made life a lot easier, for sure. You've still got a certain amount of work to do and you end up so exhausted at the end of the day because it is physical-type work. But the work is much easier.
>
> (Shopfloor Interviews, 1990)

Although not all the changes were appreciated by employees, there was an absence of any formal resistance to the new operating practices. In part, this can be explained by the general enthusiasm for change by management and employees who, through trade union support, were able to displace, deflect or ignore individual employee objections. As a shop steward recounted:

> I'd fight for anyone for anything, but I wouldn't fight for anyone if they didn't do their job. There was one lady – at one time we were supposed

> to sweep the sewing room. They cut the cleaners down, so they said would each section just sweep up once a day. We'd all have turns in the sewing room: one person sweeps one day. There are only a few rags and that's all it is in there, when you're cutting off your pieces. And this one girl, she just would not sweep. She said, 'Can I refuse?' I said, 'Well, you can't refuse the job: it's the job.' So she left. She'd been here for 12 years and she left because she had to sweep up the sewing room one day a week. That's how some people just won't take change.
>
> (Shopfloor Interviews, 1990)

The general acceptance of the need for change reduced the level of tolerance for individual objections to altered operating practice. The creation of a culture of change which anticipated and embraced the challenges of new work arrangements proved to be the dominant belief system which rejected any notion of 'reasonable resistance'. The unacceptability of alternative views may have masked the level of shopfloor concern and, yet, it also provided the cohesion which led to the successful and harmonious introduction of new technology at CLS.

Conclusion: unemployment, participation and change

Within the literature, considerable attention has been given to the employment effects of new technology, the tendency for work to be deskilled or enhanced, and the commercial necessity of adopting advanced automated equipment in order to maintain competitive advantage. In the case reported here, the threat of plant closure and unemployment was a significant factor which facilitated shopfloor acceptance of change. The survival of CLS was perceived to rest on the adoption of new practices and automated equipment, and the question of employment centred on either forced redundancy through plant closure or a decline in overall employment through natural attrition and the adoption of new technology. In identifying the need to replace existing machinery, the choice of the new systems rested largely with the senior engineering manager who was excited by the prospect of turning CLS into the most advanced laundry facility in the world. The availability of technology during the task of search and assessment enabled and constrained the options available in the redesign of plant operations. Whilst attempts were made to go beyond existing techniques, these changes have taken considerable time and the system continues to be modified to incorporate more advanced technical developments. As a configurational control technology, the new computerized laundry facility has raised unique problems requiring the local innovation and diffusion of new ideas and solutions (what Fleck, 1991, calls 'innofusion'). Through a process of experimentation and development, considerable knowledge has been gained, and new combinations of systems tested to tackle the particular and yet changing requirements of CLS. The high level of user-participation (in terms of the engineering function) and employee involvement (in terms of work restructuring) has resulted in a realization of some of the potential productivity gains of adopting new technology. In this case, it was not simply the technology which determined the system's design and implementation, but it was the interplay between the context in which change was taking place, the politics of negotiating routes to recovery, and the characteristics of the available technology for the design of an integrated laundry facility.

The agreement between the major political parties on the need to re-equip CLS proved instrumental in smoothing over potential shopfloor resistance to the transformation of factory operations. As it turned out, the open and participative approach of a newly formed management team was able to capture the support of shop stewards and operators on the shopfloor. A key figure in the process of improving employee relations and reducing industrial conflict was the General Manager. He quickly identified a problem with supervisory management and, through a series of meetings, observation of shopfloor activities, and discussion with other managers, set about recruiting new supervisory staff and displacing antagonistic supervisory personnel. In short, the functional divide between management and shopfloor operators was clarified (on the basis of responsibilities rather than on the formal authority accredited to positions within a defined organizational structure), and no attempt was made to make CLS a single status employer. The General Manager, through a programme of employee involvement and through exuding an enthusiasm for change and a willingness to talk over concerns with employees, was consistently cited as a major contributing factor to the successful management of change.

Once the climate for change had been set and the management team formalized, there was an unexpected delay brought about by a request to readdress the SAHC of the need to fund the project. Following a period of some twelve months, when a considerable amount of effort was put into presentations and debate on the re-equipment programme, a decision to fund the change was finally approved by SAHC. Installing the equipment was carried out with the assistance of an engineer from America, and during this time CLS bought the customer base of a major competitor. The disruption caused by the installation of the new equipment resulted in a downturn in productivity at the same time that customer demand was increasing. This placed considerable strain on staff, and particularly the production manager, who had to deal directly with the problems associated with maintaining productivity whilst undergoing shopfloor transition.

Although there were minor grievances and concerns by the employees, these were dealt with directly by the management without recourse to outside union involvement. For example, the Federated Miscellaneous Workers Union (previously the AGWU) adopted a 'hands-off' approach and had very little involvement throughout the change programme. Whilst they remained in contact with what was happening on the shopfloor, they did not directly influence the outcomes of change. Moreover, the local enthusiasm of the shop stewards later posed itself as a problem for the union, which had to request that a senior shop steward stand down because she had become 'too close to management'. Employee involvement in the management of change was realized at CLS, and perhaps was most noticeable among the maintenance engineers who felt a sense of pride in mastering the technical problem of installing automated continuous batch washers. This has resulted in the engineers taking ownership of the new technology, which they have continued to modify and develop to fit the operating requirements of CLS. In short, whilst the introduction of new technology has reduced the number of employees required to run the factory, it has also been central to the revitalization of CLS into a commercial business. In this case, the technology has not simply 'impacted' upon the organization but, rather, has been implemented and developed in response to contextual factors, the nature of the technology itself, and the political dynamics of managing large-scale organizational change in a government-owned commercial enterprise. As with the GM case, the recognition by employees of the need to change and the support of union officials were enabling factors which were further developed by an open and participative approach by management.

— 9 —

DEVELOPING SOFTWARE FOR ORGANIZATIONAL CHANGE: THE ALVEY AND CSIRO PROJECTS

Introduction

Systems design can restrict the choices available in the management of change (Noble, 1979:18–50; Wilkinson, 1983:35–7), in setting what John Bessant terms the 'design space' or options for organizational restructuring around the new technology (Bessant, 1983:14–30). For example, Maryellan Kelly, in a study of programmable automation (which refers to the use of computers to direct and control the operation of machines), found that automation resulted in neither a simple erosion nor enhancement of worker control, but that outcomes were the result of 'a combination of organizational, institutional and technical factors which act as a set of restraining influences inhibiting (or promoting) the degree of centralization or decentralization of control over programming responsibilities' (Kelly, 1989:246).

Concern over the organizational implications of adopting technology has resulted in an upsurge of interest in designing human-centred systems which take into account the 'informating' as well as 'automating' aspects of new technologies (Zuboff, 1988); where automation is used to refer to the displacement and deskilling aspects of technology and the 'informating' capacity of new technology is taken to refer to the generation of information on operational processes which can be used to enhance, develop and increase the level of skill and operational jurisdiction of employees. For example, Badham (1990) has discussed the design of human-centred systems in European manufacture and suggests that there is a move towards more collaborative systems of design which goes beyond software ergonomics. This involves the design of technology which collaborates with the skills, judgement and experience of the user for the purpose of increasing employee potential to perform (Kidd, 1990:422–3). Thus, whilst Appelbaum and Albin's (1989:247–65) claim that computer technology allows for greater managerial discretion (in choosing among alternatives) may be justified, design remains an important stage in which certain assumptions may be built into the technology, which later constrains the number of options available in the transformation of work: 'Designers frequently ignore the human factor implications of their work by failing to take into account the needs of individual users and the organizational contexts in which the equipment is to be used . . . These assumptions are often not openly examined and challenged and become irreversible features of equipment design' (Boddy and Buchanan, 1986:28).

The extent to which the organizational dimensions are incorporated in the design of computer systems and the factors which shape design decisions are the focus of the following two sections. The first examines the main factors influencing the research and development of a computer-based benefit advice system for use by the general public (see Dawson *et al*, 1990). The development of an expert system for use by non-experts took place within a government-sponsored five-year collaborative project between industry and academia (Oakley and Owen, 1989:87–91). The section highlights the problems associated with multi-disciplinary research groups and examines the context in which these developments took place. The case demonstrates how a purely developmental project with no explicit commercial objectives still finds it difficult to break away from a conventional systems development approach and recognize the significance of contextual and sociological contributions to computer design. The second case analyses the development of software for cellular plant restructuring and the commercial design of a shopfloor scheduling system. Unlike the Alvey project, system designers focused on the development and organizational application of computer technology. A project team was set up with the remit of gaining industrial collaboration and designing systems which would improve the commercial performance of Australian industry. Once again, an examination is made of the context in which the design of the system occurred. In this case, far greater significance was placed on the importance of organizational issues, and modifications were made to the system on the basis of budgetary restrictions and the feedback from managers and employees in the participating organization.

Expert systems: the Alvey DHSS Demonstrator Project

The term 'expert system' means different things to different people. For our purposes, an expert system is defined as a computer system which uses inference to apply knowledge to perform a task (DTI, 1982:32). To design such a system, it is necessary to have both formal knowledge representation and inferential problem-solving techniques. Whilst many of the early expert systems were *ad hoc* affairs, many of the current systems are driven by rules in the form:

IF<conditions>THEN<conclusion>

An example of such a rule is: 'IF the child is resident in Great Britain and the claimant is responsible for the care of the child and the child is under 16 or in school level education THEN the claimant is entitled to child benefit for that child'. (Dawson *et al*, 1990:47). Other rules within the program would establish whether the various criteria within this IF/THEN statement are met. The attractiveness of these programs is that the knowledge base is specified entirely in the rules themselves. This makes it possible to present a simplified version of the rules to the user in order to explain the reasoning behind computer-output, and it makes it easier to update the knowledge base following a change in rules and procedures. In an attempt to show how decision support systems could be used to advantage within large organizations, the Alvey DHSS Demonstrator Project was set up (Gilbert, 1985:28).

The project stemmed from the British government's decision to back the recommendations of John Alvey, and support research and development in the use of artificial intelligence (AI) in the development of expert systems (Oakley and Owen, 1989). The report of the Alvey Committee identified four important areas associated with advanced information technology which were in need of further research and development (DTI, 1982). These comprised software engineering; man-machine interface; very large-scale integration; and Intelligent Knowledge-Based Systems (IKBS). The programme had a budget exceeding £350 million over five years, with the industrial collaborators being 50% funded by Alvey and the academics being supported by the Science and Engineering Research Council (SERC). Within the Alvey programme, four application-oriented large 'Demonstrator' projects were set up to demonstrate the practical utility of advanced information technology. These consisted of a Department of Health and Social Security (DHSS) Demonstrator; mobile terminals; design to product; and a speech-driven word processor Demonstrator. The first of these resulted in a five-year collaborative research programme between universities and industry. The programme, known as the Alvey DHSS Demonstrator Project, was spread over nine different sites (with over 100 different people associated with the project during its lifetime), had a budget of about $7 million, and involved over 35 person-years of effort towards the design of large knowledge-based systems (Bench-Capon, 1991:199).

The validity of organizational issues?

Although these demonstrators have been described as being application led, their foremost objective was to learn general lessons about the way to develop advanced software and to provide demonstrations of useful systems based on AI techniques (Gilbert, 1985:28). This resulted in a tendency to overlook the longer-term organizational implications of large knowledge-based computer systems (on the basis that the design process was concerned with the development of innovative demonstrator systems). However, as Gill (1985) has argued:

> It is important to recognize that the effects of new technology on the workplace cannot be analysed in isolation from the political context of

> the design process itself . . . In all probability, many engineers and designers are usually unaware that social choices have already been made in the design process itself, largely because it is often carried out in isolation from the particular point of application, without reference to payment systems, skill hierarchies, established working practices and the politics of the workplace.
>
> (Gill, 1985:180)

Although it is not possible to predict the widespread organizational effects of introducing IKBS, comments can be made about the potential organizational issues that may arise following the tendency for computer scientists to down-play contextual factors and over-emphasize the technical aspects of design (see also Azani, 1990:154; Taylor, Elger and Fairbrother, 1991:309–28). For example, the development of decision-support systems for use by managers and other professional occupational groups could result in three potential challenges (Dawson, 1988). First, knowledge-based decision-support systems could be developed and introduced into organizations in a way that undermined the abilities and confidence of managers. This could occur in a number of ways and, in part, would clearly depend on the systems design. For example, if managers found that their decisions were being continually questioned by the system, then they could lose confidence in their ability to make good off-the-cuff decisions. Alternatively, if the system was designed to always recommend the most appropriate strategy for solving any given management problem, then in time the traditional decision-making skills of the manager could be displaced or simply eroded through lack of use. Finally, if the design of the system became clouded with mystique and the technology viewed as a type of magical black box with logical explanatory powers, then users may feel their skill superiority undermined and perceive the system more as an enigma and less as a decision-support tool.

Secondly, such systems could be used to redefine standard working relationships and control responsibilities of various professional occupational groups. This could happen to informal working practices both on a temporary basis, through the need to modify work patterns to accommodate the introduction of IKBS technology, and in a more permanent way, through the daily managerial use of the new technology which could necessitate considerable adjustments to the frequency, nature and type of contact managers have with other staff. The establishment of new patterns of working relationships and the organizational relocation of expertise could also result from the implementation of formal work reorganization schemes which, for example, could require the adjustment of skill hierarchies to facilitate a devolution of control responsibilities to the next level in the managerial decision-making command structure.

Thirdly, the introduction and use of IKBS technology could generate conflict and distrust between user and non-user management groups, as well as staff within the same department who may be required to implement the decisions made by managers using these new decision-support systems. Consequently, whilst these systems may have the potential for improving the consistency and quality of managerial decision-making, they could also jeopardize employee and interdepartmental relations and manufacture discontent and operating inefficiencies.

These potential outcomes highlight the importance of accounting for organizational issues during the process of software development. An opportunity for doing this arose as part of the Alvey DHSS Demonstrator Project. The author was initially involved in the development of a longitudinal qualitative field research programme to support the development of a supplementary benefit assessment system. Working in collaboration with geographically dispersed DHSS officials and computer scientists, the importance and significance of organizational based research was rejected by other members of the group. Instead, systems design was based on formal procedures, legislation and domain experts, with little account being given to occupational and employee concerns and to existing patterns of working arrangements. This insensitive approach to the attitudes of DHSS employees resulted in further union opposition to the project, as Oakley and Owen (1989:151) point out: 'All the large demonstrators had their problems. Union opposition to the DHSS project, for example, obstructed the task of obtaining relevant local-office information'.

One system which did attempt to incorporate social science research into system design was the development of a knowledge-based welfare benefit advice system. The aim of the system was to provide members of the general public with expert advice on social security administration and their entitlement to welfare benefits (Dawson *et al*, 1990). Within the broader DHSS Demonstrator programme, the multi-disciplinary team based at the University of Surrey acted as a semi-autonomous unit in the development and design of a benefit advice system, and was also the only group which incorporated sociological analysis into the design phase.

The value of sociological research: collaborative obstacles

The Surrey team was originally composed of a project manager, two sociologists who specialized in qualitative research, a psychologist concerned with human–computer interaction, two computer scientists, and a social scientist who specialized in quantitative analyses. The team had secretarial support and began their research using Xerox 1108 work stations running an Interlisp-D development environment. Whilst the intention was to ensure close collaboration between systems analysts and social scientists, in practice there were a number of problems which constrained open interaction. First, the timescale of the project. Although it was a five-year programme which sought to 'demonstrate' how things could be done (rather than develop commercially proven systems), there was an expectation that technical results would be achieved through 'rapid prototyping' (that is, building a prototype, evaluating, revising and then rebuilding). In principal, the ideal of rapid prototyping is effective in allowing for flexible development; in practice, however, the group expectations of incremental development, preset timeframes for project deliverables, and the context of past achievements all militate against design options which disregard foundation specifications. To learn from past efforts and start afresh is fine in theory, but when your achievements are being appraised by other collaborators the pressure to 'produce' improved systems can severely constrain design decisions.

A related timeframe problem stemmed from the longitudinal qualitative research which was carried out to support systems design. The research focused on the problems and practice of households claiming welfare benefits. Between July and November 1985, fifty households were interviewed in the first phase of a longitudinal, three-phase study. An inner-city (London) and town and country area (South-East England) were chosen for the study. These two sites were further sub-divided into inner-city council housing and inner-city private rented, and rural-countryside and urban-town. At all dwellings selected, a filter interview was carried out with an 'informant' (usually the person who answered the door) in order to identify individuals within households who:

1. had recently claimed welfare benefits;
2. felt that they were potentially eligible to claim benefits; and
3. were having difficulties in 'making ends meet'.

Once this data had been collected, a similar procedure was adopted for the second phase of the study (as it turned out, personnel and time constraints prevented the possibility of a third phase being carried out). However, the timescale involved in this longitudinal piece of research resulted in a mismatch between the setting up of the research, data collection and final analysis, and the data requirements for systems design. Although the team at Surrey was aware of the claiming model being developed by the social scientists and was supportive of the work being carried out, there were problems in communicating the significance of these findings to the design of a welfare benefit advice system. For example, as early as 1985 the evidence from the study was suggesting that household claiming behaviour was not the result of a simple choice between whether or not to claim a particular benefit but, rather, derived from a range of different decisions during the process of claiming one or a number of benefits. These decisions were identified as being influenced by a complex range of social factors at each event in the life history of a claim. We suggested that, in order to understand this, the claiming process had to be seen as a time-sensitive sequence of events, which is comprised of a series of claims each in a number of possible states, and concerned not just with the actions of individual claimants but with the claiming behaviour of households taken as a whole (Buckland and Dawson, 1989). Translating these findings into systems design was not an easy task, and this was made more difficult by, first, having to convince project members of the significance of these findings and, secondly, having to justify their relevance to software development.

This raises the second main inhibitor to collaborative work, namely, the predominance of a 'scientific' paradigm and the 'culture' of the Alvey collaboration. As the Project Manager notes in describing the culture of the DHSS Demonstrator:

> In an industrial or a civil service context staff tend to operate in groups with leaders or managers who guide the activities of the unit and are able to commit the resources that they command within the constraints of their delegated authority. This model did not apply to the academic partners whose staff were more nearly equal partners with considerable personal control over their own activities, the 'principal investigator' did not have the ability to direct their work.
>
> (Portman, 1991:202)

Another important dimension not mentioned by Portman (1991), was the difference in values, beliefs and perspectives of the different disciplines. This was most notable at the twice-yearly workshops where all project members were encouraged to present their work. At these events, attempts were made to bridge the discipline divide. This was typically based on a common recognition of the value of 'hard' scientific research, which ultimately devalued and marginalized the contribution of 'soft' qualitative sociological research to systems design. Although there was a recognition of the problems of language and, in particular, subjective interpretation of ill-defined terms such as 'virtually unable to walk', there was little interest shown in organizational issues such as occupational and employee concerns, or in the context in which individual and groups make decisions about claiming welfare benefits (see Dawson and Buckland, 1986). In contrast, procedural and psychological data collected from laboratory type 'scientific' experiments were accorded far more weight and relevance in systems design.

This leaves the problem of communication across separate discipline languages as the final main inhibitor to multi-disciplinary collaboration. In the untypical instance where a member of a group was familiar and active in both disciplines, this was not a problem. In general, however, there was a need for some common ground in order to begin the process of communication. This was often in the form of social interests or informal lunch discussions, which provided neutral ground for communication on which individuals rooted in particular disciplines could converse.

The presence of these three inhibitors significantly reduced the influence of sociological research on the development of expert systems. Whilst some elements of the research and, in particular, the model of household claiming behaviour was incorporated into the initial requirements specification for the advice system (Buckland *et al*, 1987), this achievement was restricted to the University of Surrey site. In part, this can be explained by the composition and relative isolation of the team at Surrey and the development of harmonious interpersonal relations between the computer and social scientists. As Portman has indicated, whilst this resulted in the lack of common use of ideas and methods and poor inter-team communication, it did allow for greater intra-team communication (Portman, 1991:201).

Outcomes from the project

The final demonstrations from the project were held in April, 1989 at the Department of Trade and Industry, Kingsgate House, London. Although it is unlikely that there will be sufficient political or economic incentives to further develop benefit advice systems and make them readily available to the public, the potential for applying knowledge engineering techniques to the design of socially useful systems for non-experts raises a number of interesting implications for the nature of work and client relations in service industries. For example, one important consequence of designing systems to aid non-experts in dealing with large complex bureaucratic organizations could be a redefinition of the power relationship between bureaucrat and client. By enabling a greater dissemination of knowledge to the public about formal administrative processes, the majority of enquiries and discussions of the future need not centre on the clarification of simple bureaucratic procedures, such as guidance on how to register a change of address. Consequently, the job tasks of staff who deal with members of the public could change from one of procedural adviser, information gatekeeper and layperson translator, to one which is modelled far more on that of an informed client seeking advice from a public servant. Moreover, through distributing knowledge to the public rather than containing knowledge within the boundaries of the organization, such systems could perform an educative as well as an advisory function, and help demystify the vagaries of bureaucracies while improving the service provided to the public.

In practice, however, the computerized advice system and other potential developments have not been taken up by the government or the Department of Social Security (DSS). The decision to go beyond the bounds of traditional expert systems, which are usually built for use by professionals, seriously questioned the organizational utility and commercial viability of the system designed. Moreover, the possibility of developing these ideas into a full-blown contextualist approach to systems design is highly improbable, given the academic and industrial political arenas in which these changes would have to take place. Finally, it is perhaps worth emphasizing that, whether or not there is a longer-term increase in users' participation in system design, the way in which organizations adapt to new technology will not solely be determined by the design process but also by non-technology factors during other periods during the process of technological change.

Cellular design and shopfloor scheduling: the CSIRO project

In contrast to the Alvey programme, the Commonwealth Scientific and Industrial Research Organization (CSIRO) scheduling system focused on the development of software for industrial application. The aim of the project was to develop a cell-build program for allocating groups of parts and equipment to specified work areas, and to design a shopfloor Scheduler which could be used by leading hands in the daily co-ordination of resources for product manufacture. Another important difference was the size of the project. Whilst the DHSS Demonstrator Project was geographically dispersed and attempted to accommodate a disparate range of academics and scientists, the CSIRO project was based in only two locations and involved the development of innovative techniques within a more conventional research arrangement. Moreover, one of the major strengths of this project was the direct involvement of employee groups and an early recognition of the need to account for issues surrounding the process of organizational change during systems design.

The initial idea and conceptualization of the need for a software research and development project can be traced back to 1981, when an industrial engineer (AS) from General Motors (GM) met an employee from the CSIRO outside of work. From this social contact, AS was introduced to another member of CSIRO, who had a common interest in home computers. As AS recounts:

> All this happened outside of work but, as usually happens, we got talking about work problems as well, and we discussed at length a need for a scheduling system to suit the manufacturing industry . . . So we talked about developing a user-friendly PC-based smart system that would learn from experience. In the first instance, the operator would make all the decisions about the plan. Gradually, as the operator got more confidence in the system's ability to cope with his decisions and understand the rules, he would pass the rules over to the system and the system would make more of the decisions and simply ask for a confirmation.
>
> (Interview, 1990)

On the basis of these discussions, a meeting was set up with senior members of the CSIRO. At this stage, the question of who should finance the project raised difficulties. The CSIRO stated that they were unable to fund the research and suggested that the estimated cost of $60,000 (plus the allocation of two full-time staff to collaborate on the project) should be met by GM. The team from GM also had funding problems, and as a result the project was shelved: 'If it had not been for subsequent events, that would have been the end of the collaboration between Holden's and CSIRO in the scheduling area. Then in 1985 (I was now at Elizabeth, managing an industrial engineering group), an idea arose for developing the hardware plant on a group technology basis' (Interview, 1990).

At this time, the hardware plant was manufacturing approximately two thousand different parts through eight operations, such as press shop operations, milling, grinding, drilling, turning, and other typical metal operations. It was set up as the first Holden's plant in the Elizabeth area on a work centre principle, in which all like operations were grouped together. For example, all the press operations were in one area; all the finishing operations were in another area; and all the intermediate operations (plating, drilling, milling, tapping) had their own groups of machines. Consequently, if a part had to go through ten operations it had to be moved ten times, and that often meant a move of three or four hundred metres (for example, from the press area down to milling, back to the plating area and over to packing). As a result, the whole plant revolved around a very costly material handling concept based on electric trains. Typically, parts went into bins at the press line; they were then loaded onto electric trains which shunted them around the plant to their next operation. Once this operation was completed, they were then placed back into bins and transported by train to the next sequential operation. Whilst this production system made sense with the high volume output required to produce a thousand cars a day, with current production running at approximately four or five hundred cars a day it no longer makes commercial sense to operate under these principles. The options identified by senior management were to either outsource component manufacture and close the plant down, or to restructure the plant and make it into a commercially viable option. (The process of transforming the hardware fabrication plant from a conventional job-shop layout to cellular manufacture is discussed in detail in Chapter 7.)

Plant restructuring and the problem of scheduling

The new plant manager (BM) initiated the idea that the local management team should set about restructuring the hardware plant into cellular form. Under this arrangement, parts which have similar processing requirements are grouped together. These groups are then assigned to pieces of equipment needed to produce them, and then this combination of parts and equipment are located in a specified area or cell (the equipment is not used for any other parts and the parts are not made anywhere else). The final element is to create a work team that has its own operators, its own leading hand, its own tool setter and maintenance personnel. The responsibility of the work group is to run the cell and to schedule parts to ensure they meet vehicle requirements.

The new teamwork arrangements required of this system create a scheduling problem, as the system no longer has the flexibility of being able to transfer the manufacture of parts across locations and equipment. For example, if a cell has only one type of a particular press, the sequence in which the parts are made becomes critical. Furthermore, because much of the equipment in plant one was relatively unreliable and old, the scheduling system had to be capable of responding very quickly to breakdowns and other equipment contingencies. As a result, the decision to move towards cellular manufacture, combined with the previous discussion and connections between GM and CSIRO, meant that two major problems were identified: first, the question of cellular design and how to select and categorize parts into cells. For example, if you have a thousand part numbers, how do you divide them into groups which form workable cells? Secondly, how do you devolve control for the scheduling of operations to the local work group and still meet the global requirements set by the production scheduling system?

In addressing the first of these issues, GM looked towards America for an already tried and tested system. A company in the business of merchandizing systems to support the cell philosophy was identified, and an approach made for purchase of the system. However, at a cost of a million dollars, it was deemed too expensive so GM began to investigate the possibility of a locally developed system:

> It was then we turned back to CSIRO, remembering the discussions we had with them in 1982 and how fruitful that had appeared at the time. We restarted discussions with the Woodville manufacturing group . . . RL [CSIRO employee] did the system work for the cell analysis. He took all the routings for all of the parts that were going through the hardware plant and did what you call a cluster analysis . . . The analysis he did proved to us that it was worthwhile proceeding. Part and parcel of that involved the next stage of preparing a scheduling system to allow the scheduling of one cell, which was the initial phase that we contracted for: creation of one cell and a system to schedule that one cell on the shop floor, and that gave rise to the mark one scheduling system, of which we saw the merchandisable product last week.
>
> (Interview, 1990)

Through the previous contacts with CSIRO and the need to restructure hardware fabrication, a meeting was set up in which the main protagonists discussed the options available. During this period, the CSIRO had a complementary objective of trying to strengthen the Adelaide manufacturing group. The chief of the CSIRO had appointed WG (CSIRO employee) in July 1981, in order to develop a new group called Integrated Engineering Manufacture which was based in Melbourne. This group continued to grow throughout the 1980s and, at the same time, another branch of the CSIRO was working closely with the GM press shop at Woodville in the development of a strain detection system for depressed sheet metal. Before a new leader of the integrated manufacturing activity in Adelaide was appointed, discussions between the mathematics and statistics group of CSIRO and GM took place (on what was then perceived as a mathematical problem). At this time, part of the CSIRO operation and the GM press shop were located on the same complex at Woodville (the rest of the GM manufacturing facilities were located some 16 kilometres away at Elizabeth). During a period of two or three meetings, a GM manager (who was also one of the founding members of the Computer Society in Adelaide) perceived that it should be possible, given the current state of technology, to produce an annotated screen where the shopfloor supervisor could look at a representation of operations and simulate a modification to evaluate possible changes and outcomes. At the same time, the manager of hardware fabrication was still looking for the means of rebuilding and revitalizing a 1950s style plant into a 1990s style of operation.

The GM and CSIRO agreement

In April 1985, the first formal meeting took place at General Motors–Holden's Automotive Limited (GMHAL). Shortly after, it was agreed that the CSIRO's Division of Manufacturing Technology (DMT) would provide a confidential proposal on the benefits of collaborative work. A three-way collaboration was agreed (the mathematics and statistics group later withdrew following the transfer of a key employee to the manufacturing division). By the end of the month, a draft proposal had been submitted for a preliminary study on the feasibility of tackling a project on plant cellularization. A sum of approximately $40,000 was requested and, although there was a significant delay before gaining acceptance (it was not until December that GM committed itself to the collaborative agreement, and then it took another seven months before any action was taken), the CSIRO continued with its research in anticipation that the results could be used elsewhere if the GM collaboration did not eventuate.

During the familiarization of the manufacturing operations at GM, three CSIRO staff spent considerable time at GM observing and analysing operations. In February 1986 they submitted a summary proposal for the integration of the hardware facilities at GM. The four phases identified comprised:

1. analysis of current manufacturing operations (three months);
2. design and development of an improved manufacturing system (6 months);
3. development and installation of integrated production management system (12 months); and
4. detailed hardware design and installation of new systems (12 months).

The objective of phase I was to examine all the plant's manufacturing data and to use these for a feasibility study on the implementation of a cellular approach. At this time, phase II was centred on the complete development and design of a workable cellular manufacturing system. Phase III was to involve the implementation of the cell design in collaboration with GM personnel. The CSIRO would support, advise and guide implementation, but the actual restructuring would be carried out by GM. The final phase was to be a review of the whole system, with the aim of suggesting ways of integrating the system with their Production Control System (GM's MRPII equivalent):

> The collaborative arrangement was set up between Manufacture and Technology (CSIRO) and General Motors/Holden Automotive (who have changed their name several times in the process of the project). To my knowledge there were four phases. One to prove that cellular layout would be an effective solution, to provide tools for achieving that purpose, and then to build designs which, at least theoretically, could be proved by simulation that the whole thing was going to work. So we had, prior to that Phase Two proposal, a requirement to be able to demonstrate to the management of Holdens that within the limits of our modelling the thing was going to work. That is why the simulation type exercise of the scheduling process was done in-house, it was the support information needed by BM (plant manager) to be able to take the case for funding to (senior management).
>
> (CSIRO Interview, 1989)

On 19 February 1986 the collaborative agreement was signed and a number of new CSIRO personnel were appointed to the project.

The problem of inconsistent shopfloor data

During the initial data collection phase, it soon became apparent that a valid database was a necessary prerequisite to any Group Technology project. The preliminary studies highlighted major problems with shopfloor information, and considerable time was spent going through various forms of data and agreeing on a formula for a combined data set. As a member of the CSIRO team noted: 'There were enormous numbers of mis-matches in data and the mis-matches between the files were quite separate from the mis-matches between the manufacturing data and the floor actualities'.

The data matching and verification exercise was further complicated by the fact that the recording of welder functions and functionalities was being held on a desktop PC which had been initiated and programmed separately by the maintenance manager. The time-consuming process of manually cross-checking files and then returning inconsistencies for rectification by GM eventually initiated concern at plant level, which was tackled by the introduction of GM's production control system (the combined data set on which everything that used to be scattered around the place is now located).

The problem of consistent and verifiable data was raised at one of the early collaborative meetings between the CSIRO and GM. Two GM personnel worked closely with the CSIRO in sorting the computer files. Essentially, the materials data (what parts and how many are used to make product X) which specified the tree relationships between all the components and sub-components were in one computer database, and the manufacturing information (to make this part you need five different operations, this amount of time, and this type of operator) which provided routing data and detailed manufacturing information was in a separate file. The major problem was that the files did not match and, as a result, it was possible to have manufacturing routing information for parts which had not been made for five years. In tackling this problem, the CSIRO developed software which was able to carry out consistency checks between the two files and highlight errors that could be returned to GM so that the appropriate actions could be taken. The time delay caused by mismatching data bases 'stretched our objective project time incredibly, because it took us literally years to get it right – to get it good enough to use. In the early sets, any mis-matches we stripped them out and went on with what we had. We had to have something to do to be able to develop our software' (CSIRO interview, 1989).

On the basis of this information, members of the CSIRO team set about developing software for cellular design. The approach taken, Process Flow Analysis (PFA), was to identify the key elements which needed to be satisfied in order to obtain a solution. These key elements (or defining sets) were used to build algorithms and display mechanisms to enable the 'interactive' use of the computer in the building of cells (out of 1,500 parts from the original data, CSIRO identified 80 defining sets). Combinations of these defining sets were used to build cells. These designs were then forwarded to GM for comment, modified, and forwarded on an iterative basis.

The PC Scheduler

In addition to a cell designer, attention was also given to the development of simulation software to evaluate the operational use of potential cell designs. This resulted in the development of two related versions of the PC Scheduler (PCS). The first simulates a design of a cell and provides various statistics on how good the design would be in meeting various load requirements. This was also the first Scheduler to be built. Basically, through using a time-line and a series of computer requests for things to be scheduled, the system starts at the current time and looks at what jobs have got a minimum amount of time between now and the time that they are due, and orders them in priority: 'What it does is it moves forward in time, taking things out of the bin of requests according to some priority and plugs them into the time slots until it gets to the end of the list of things to be done, and sometimes that turns out to be four shifts overall' (CSIRO interview, 1989).

The second comprised a shopfloor PC version for actual operational use. Although this was not part of the original proposal (and was never fully developed at GM), it has become the main commercial product designed by CSIRO which has come out of the collaborative project. The initial shopfloor Scheduler was an enhancement of the simulation based Scheduler for use in the demonstration cell. As such, it is not particularly 'user-friendly', and as the CSIRO project leader commented:

> It was adequate for the demonstration cell with several machines, and it does the job for cell one. But, because of the complexities involved in cell one, it suffers from more hiccups than the demonstration cell did. The Scheduler in its present form really doesn't lend itself sufficiently well to frequent rescheduling – it becomes a pain – particularly in setting up what the existing conditions of the cell are so that you can schedule onwards.
>
> (CSIRO Interview, 1990)

Whilst the idea of a shopfloor Scheduler, which allowed a leading hand to reschedule work within a cell to meet changing conditions and the needs of staff, was accepted by GM, it was never fully developed as part of the collaboration. In part, this can be explained by the strategic objectives of CSIRO, which sought to develop the product into a commercial item, and by the information management problems present at GM. One of the keys to the success of the PC Scheduler was its ability to interface with the larger Production Control System. This system was designed and installed by Electronic Data Systems (EDS), a company bought by GM in 1984 to standardize data processes across all divisions (essentially, the system schedules material requirements). In the context of the workcell, however, the system was too broadly based to be of any major use in daily scheduling. As an EDS employee noted:

> PSC creates a global type demand: in other words, of part X in this cycle, please give me two thousand five hundred. But PSC does not recognize the specifics of the cell. It just says, hey, here's the demand on these parts. According to the rules you've given me, this is when I want them. The function of the cell Scheduler then becomes, hey guys, to satisfy this demand this is how I believe you should be running your parts. Start this one first and after you've produced five hundred stop it, start the next part and then bring the first part back. In other words, it is the management of the demand against the availability of resources and facilities, whether it be people or tooling or whatever.
>
> (EDS Interview, 1991)

However, there is no effective electronic data interchange between PSC and the shopfloor Scheduler. It is therefore necessary to take a hard copy and manually input the data into the PC. Furthermore, because of the cost of developing an integrated system it was generally claimed that it would be unlikely for this particular change to take place. Apart from the demonstration cell, the shopfloor Scheduler never evolved in the context of the design, development and implementation of workcells at GM's hardware fabrication plant. As the leader of the CSIRO project described:

> We went into the project regarding it as a loss leader. The property rights to the software reside with CSIRO, although Holden's have the right to use the cell Scheduler and the facility design software in their Australian operations. But we also have the rights to exploit and capitalize on the development on those two pieces of software . . . The Scheduler has been extended way beyond what we delivered to Holden's. They are aware of and interested in the enhanced Scheduler, but their acquisition of that will be outside of the scope of this particular agreement.
>
> (CSIRO Interview, 1990)

Design constraints: critical decisions and workplace issues

During the course of the project, there were a number of changes in emphasis. For example, at an early phase of the project GM put considerable pressure on CSIRO to produce 'tangible' results. GM's decision to support the project meant that they wanted to see some practical changes early on. Consequently, rather than prepare a total design prior to implementation, it was decided that implementation should take place parallel with cell design (this was also partially due to the financial constraints imposed by GM, and their reluctance to wait eighteen months for cell design).

The main consequence of planning, implementing and operating a pilot cell parallel with the development of the cell-build software, was that the CSIRO team was put under pressure to produce workable fragments of the design before they felt they were completely ready. This revision in the collaborative strategy lends support to the non-linear and dynamic processes of change illustrated in Figure 3.2. In this case, the original proposal had set out a series of sequential stages from the identification of the type of change through to initial operation. However, due to the organizational politics of funding the project, and the comparatively junior managerial positions of the GM personnel directly involved, it was necessary for local plant management to show some initial returns on investment. Senior management had to be convinced (and later re-convinced) of the value of the change programme. The need for local management to justify the investment led them to put pressure on the CSIRO to provide a meaningful cell design which they could implement swiftly. Furthermore, at this stage in the design process neither the integrity of the GM data nor the sophistication of the CSIRO software would have allowed for a total design. Thus, by a partial match between a sub-group of parts identified by GM, with a sub-group of parts being analysed by the CSIRO, the pilot cell came into being:

> We finally reached an agreed sub-set of parts that required a sub-set of machines, and that was going to be the pilot cell. All the disciples of the idea were convinced it was going to work, and they had done all the little bits of cigarette packet calculating and everything else. But there were those doubters, particularly from on high, who were saying, you can't convince me that just by shifting that stuff around you're going to get that much more improvement. I don't believe you. So it had to be demonstrated, and that was the reason for the pilot cell.
>
> (CSIRO Interview, 1990)

During the process of design, there were a considerable number of collaborative group discussions and cross communications. One interesting aspect which arose during these meetings was that, although two pieces of machinery may be theoretically identical, in practice, they were not. This instigated the plant manager to initiate a large internal programme of machine standardization. Whilst a lot of the idiosyncrasies of the equipment did not pose themselves as a problem under the traditional way of working, under a group technology environment this was not the case. The standardization of shopfloor machinery also highlighted the objective of multi-skilling. For example, historically, the only person allowed to set up the electrical side of the welder was a fully qualified electrician, whereas the person required to ensure that the tooling worked in the welder was the tool maker; and, finally, the person required to ensure that all of the conditions on the welder were set properly was the leading hand. In other words, three people were required to set up a welder (it was necessary to turn an electrical switch to change the settings, and if you were not a qualified electrician you were not allowed to open the cabinet containing the switch). Consequently, there was a whole series of engineering changes which were required so that an operator only had to press a button to re-set the machine, and to ensure that tools were interchangeable and could be easily replaced. However, even with all these changes the first job in the pilot cell resulted in a broken tool:

So you can imagine how that went down with everybody, because it was a big tool, nearly as big as this table, and it did an enormous amount of damage. The tool was built to have a – I forget – let's say a nine-inch clearance hole in the middle of the machine to allow a piece of the tool to move out the bottom as the operation occurred, and this particular piece was the only one that had a six-inch hole. Now, this nine-inch diameter thing won't go down a six-inch hole without a lot of noise! . . . I mean, Murphy's law: it's inevitable that it's going to happen, but it again underlines the importance of being meticulous in the preparation.

(CSIRO Interview, 1990)

Following the pilot cell design, the CSIRO team applied their process flow analysis software to plant data, and regrouped the equipment into isolated sets that could exist in their own right. Whilst other software on the market could do a similar exercise, the CSIRO software was able to consider the total number of steps required to manufacture a finished part, no matter how many sub-parts it went through. Nevertheless, in using the cell-build software there were also a number of design 'constraints' which they had to consider. These consisted of the following requests:

1. There should be no more than fifteen to eighteen machines in a cell.
2. There should be no more than a hundred parts in any one cell.
3. There should be no more than ten to twelve people in a cell.

These constraints were specified by the plant manager, who argued that groups larger than twelve in a workcell setup would be difficult to manage and would require direct supervision. This would destroy the objective of increasing operative autonomy and replacing supervisory direction with group supervision. Similarly, a limitation was placed on the number of parts to ensure that effective control could be maintained by a team of employees within the workcell.

Working within these design constraints, the CSIRO presented a first-cut of plant cellularization to local management, and requested their guidance on how the cells should be re-arranged to take into account the detailed workings of the shopfloor. Plant personnel were then required to closely examine current manufacturing operations in the light of the proposed design. Once they had made amendments to the design it was returned to the CSIRO, which then presented another blueprint. This cycle of events continued for nearly twelve months and a number of significant changes occurred. For example, this was the period in which a separation was made between the smaller specialized cells (such as handbrake assembly, rocker covers, and so forth) and the larger multi-purpose cells. The decision to create specialized cells arose because in some cases high-volume output was required of a small number of parts requiring a small number of machines. In these situations, it did not make sense to place the equipment in multi-purpose cells but, rather, to create smaller sets of dedicated units.

The final process of refining cell design

Once all these factors had been taken into account and the equipment re-celled through applying the process flow analysis, the final cell design finished up with eighteen cells. However, under this layout there were not enough machines, so over a period of prolonged discussion between the collaborators a smaller number of cells was identified:

> We spent many, not terribly happy, days in this office here with scrawl all over that board, with me working at some terminal with about twenty-seven windows on it with all the different data files, arguing out how we were going to resolve this problem of not having enough machines. 'This is currently planned on the so-and-so machine: can we shift it to something-or-other else?' 'That will mean re-building the tooling.' 'What does that involve?' 'Oh, that's no problem we can do it' . . . I reckon there would have been, out of the final count of six hundred parts, there would've been two or three hundred of them that were re-planned in this office. But that, to my mind, was what the collaborative exercise was about, because if I'd sat here as a consultant and said: 'Well it will work if you do that', and they look at it and say: 'You can't do that. No way. Forget it. Goodbye.' But because we worked together on the thing and resolved all these difficulties one at a time over a very, very long period, it worked.
>
> (CSIRO Interview, 1990)

There was considerable refinement of the cells from the initial plan of eighteen cells to 7 multi-assembly cells and 7 cells dedicated to single assemblies. The process of redesigning the cells and the decision to increase their size and complexity is captured in the following quotation:

> The cells grew in size because of Holden's desire to process their parts according to the Total Process Prove-out (TPP) strategy, where all the steps of the process are set up simultaneously and the total process is proved-out with several parts, so you know you are going to get a good end item before you start production. This implies that, if you are going to process a part from start to finish, you need at least as many machines as there are steps in that process chain to be able to do this TPP bit; Some of the parts require up to 17 process steps, most of them require somewhere around three to five. If you start combining machines so that a subset of your machines can process one part and another subset can process another part, the total machines required in a cell expands beyond the five or six you might require to around fifteen. By making cells that big, we got TPP ability on all but some 15 to 20 parts by the time they had done a little bit of reprocessing of some parts. I thought that was an exceptional result. Out of some 600 parts, we could do all but 20 or so in the desired method, but the cells do have to be some 15 machines . . . We are now running nine or ten operators on 15 machines per shift, as opposed to three operators on seven machines. So there is a significant increase in complexity, and that is why the cells are the size they are.
>
> (CSIRO Interview, 1990)

In May 1986 data collection was stopped and, following an analysis of the material, two possible areas for the location of manufacturing cells were identified. The establishment cost for cell 1 was $18,000 and for cell 2 $35,000. At this time, GM were concerned about the costs involved and requested that CSIRO concentrate on lower cost alternatives. In late June a new cell option was submitted to GM and later Arthur Anderson [Consulting] confirmed that savings of up to $2 million per annum could be achieved by undergoing the suggested changes. During July and August, there was considerable discussion and consultation between the CSIRO and GM on cell design and the appropriate complement of parts. By September, a workcell was approved and became the focus for factory installation and complementary computer modelling.

Workcell 3.6 (the demonstration cell) was installed adjacent to the axle line, and comprised five welding machines and two presses. In practice, the machine layout was a compromise between the cost of installation and location of optimum work flow. By mid-October, cell 3.6 had been physically implemented, but it was not due to go into full operation until after the Christmas break. This became the first operational workcell and in January 1987, the CSIRO formally reported on the conclusion of phase I of the project. In short, CSIRO had developed software to simulate cell design; they had been instrumental in the setting up and operation of a demonstration cell; and they had documented the financial justification for GM in adopting cellular manufacture.

In November 1988 the plant locations of the cells were decided by GMHAL, and the cells were renumbered to match the sequence of installation. Revisions and refinements to the workcell layout continued into 1989. By February 1989 the cell designs were deemed acceptable by the plant manager, and in March 1989 cell 1 became fully operational. Over the following twelve months, the physical restructuring of the plant was completed. This involved clearing areas, painting floors, moving large presses and upgrading tools and equipment (see Chapter 7).

A reappraisal of data management and accounting measures

From this discussion of the collaboration between CSIRO and GM, there are two issues worth discussing further. First, the disparity between corporate data and the way things are actually done on the shopfloor. Whilst it may be difficult to identify information inconsistencies between the shopfloor and data processing departments, it can cause major problems and result in considerable delays. As one CSIRO employee recalled: 'A lot of the delay time in getting designs from our end has been because they have not been able to provide good data at the time when they said they were going to.' In order to facilitate change, it is important to maintain and verify that corporate data accord with shopfloor operations. This is becoming increasingly necessary and strategically significant with the rapid expansion in the introduction and use of computer information systems. Consequently, information management remains an undervalued and yet an integral part of management.

The second major issue centres on the methodologies being used in accounting circles for the justification of the adoption of new manufacturing technology. For example, accounting measures such as pay-back-periods and benefit-cost-ratios are often being used in an inappropriate fashion. The question of whether these accounting conventions impeded the adoption of new technology was highlighted by a member of the CSIRO team who stated that:

> If you look at the whole project, they have paid us $150,000. They have spent approximately $880,000 making changes in the plant, depending on who you believe, whether you believe Holden's numbers, Arthur Anderson's numbers, or our numbers. The saving is somewhere between 1.2 and 2.1 million dollars per annum for an outlay of something like one million when it is all added up. Whatever way you want to work it out, the return (excluding the usual things like staff turnover, staff skill, flexibility and all the other things that you can not put clean numbers on) in sheer accounting terms makes it seem so stupid that it took so long to convince them. We had to cool our heels on many occasions in the process to do other things. We did not have the data or they did not have money to proceed.
>
> (CSIRO Interview, 1991)

This focus on cost justification can impede the adoption of new techniques and new technologies. Although it is clearly necessary to ensure that a project has the potential to recoup costs, and that higher returns are likely, an over-emphasis on the financial aspect without due regard to the strategic importance or the longer-term consequences can inhibit innovation and change at work. This is particularly noticeable in the case reported here, where the change was initiated by local management through extra-organizational contacts and collaboration.

Conclusion: the political process of design collaboration

In examining the relationship between collaborative research projects and the organizational adoption of new techniques and new technologies, this chapter has illustrated the processual nature of technical advance, the influence of non-technology variables, some of the practical consequences of information processing technologies for work, and the potential of knowledge engineering technologies for the relocation of expertise and the establishment of new patterns of working relationships. It has been shown how the management of change is likely to depend not only on technology but also on the way in which governments, organizations, political and occupational groups, employers and employees, academic researchers, systems designers, and even members of the public, respond to and participate in the process of innovation and change. This is particularly evident during the conceptual period of change when organizations may be responding to external and/or internal pressures. As shown in the CSIRO example, early decisions on the viability of change projects are also influenced by the development of relationships within, between and outside organizations.

The importance of the politics of change was illustrated in both examples. In the case of the CSIRO collaboration, the need for local GM management to justify corporate investment led them to put pressure on the CSIRO team to produce a workable single cell design which could be implemented and then used to substantiate their claim for corporate funding. The CSIRO's willingness to compromise was influenced by their objective of using the GM project as a springboard to further collaborations (the CSIRO's loss leader approach). Both parties had other complementary agendas which influenced negotiations and served to reconcile differences. The innovative nature of the change programme (the substance of change) also made it possible to break new ground and experiment in new methods of operation. Management's acceptance of the need to tackle existing problems on the shopfloor, and the CSIRO's recognition of the need to modify computer generated cell designs to accommodate the 'practicalities' of plant operations, were critical ingredients to successful project collaboration. In the case of the PC Scheduler, this was never perceived as a central feature by local GM management, nor was it developed by CSIRO as a one-off exercise for GM. Although GM has continued to publicly support the Scheduler, this is not through a recognition of its value to their shopfloor operations but, rather, in response to the success of the collaboration in helping restructure hardware fabrication into a profitable small components manufacturing plant. Again, the political dimension is crucial to understanding actions and events during the process of change. The PC Scheduler is currently being used in a number of organizations in Australia, and the CSIRO is hoping to market the product worldwide.

In the case of the DHSS Demonstrator Project, the political dimension has been no less important. However, in this example a failure to address organizational issues during the design phase has resulted in the development of systems which would significantly constrain the options open to organizational practitioners in the management of change. This was oddly surprising, given that some of the application areas centred on demonstrating the usefulness of IKBS technology as decision-support tools for policy-makers, administrators and operations managers within business organizations. Undue reliance on formal procedures, legislation and domain experts outside of the organizational context in which such systems would be expected to operate (or demonstrate their potential), does present a longer-term obstacle to organizational adoption. In particular, the absence of a detailed examination of the working practices of potential users of such systems could result in resistance to change among professional groups and managers, as well as questioning the applicability of new computer systems to the work environment. As I have discussed elsewhere, organizational users of computers often seek to actively accommodate and adapt their position to change, and rarely act as passive recipients (Dawson, 1987). Similarly with IKBS technology, users are likely to play an important part in establishing new patterns of relationships and new working practices. Moreover, if expert systems were made available for public use, then this could result in the restructuring of unequal power relationships between the organizational provider of goods and services and the public consumer. This again highlights the political nature of such decisions: 'Whether such systems are in fact adopted is a political issue, an opportunity exists for computer systems to help non-experts in dealing with the complexities of large legislation based service organizations like the DHSS. Their potential seems to be clearly appreciated by the public these systems would serve' (Dawson, Buckland and Gilbert: 1990:52).

In conclusion, the development of software for organizational use is an important and under-researched area of technological change. The conventional divisions between research and development functions and manufacturing operations are increasingly being called into question. The breaking down of organizational barriers; the growing focus on designs which are manufacturable under existing conditions; and the quest for human-centred systems; all signal the significance of technology design for organizational change. In this way, the outcome of operational change is not solely determined by the process of organizational transition but, also, by decisions made during the research and development of new technologies and techniques. Finally, it is perhaps worth noting that even within the wider world economy, the national and international political dimension is particularly significant in directing research programmes and in providing or withholding support for the exploitation of non-productive socially useful technology, and in evaluating existing technology policies (see also DITC, 1988; Oakley and Owen, 1989; Zegveld, 1987).

In the chapter which follows, all the case studies reported in this book are used to construct a number of practical guidelines on the management of change. Questions concerned the blurring of organizational boundaries are raised and the movement towards more collaborative inter-organizational arrangements are discussed. The inclusion of the design process into change models and the problem of compartmentalizing change issues, remain important areas which require further research and investigation. What this chapter has attempted to do is to highlight the need to go beyond self-contained organizational explanations in search of extra-organizational processes which may not only influence the process of managing change, but also challenge existing organizational arrangements.

10

CONCLUSION: MANAGING TRANSITIONS IN MODERN ORGANIZATIONS

Introduction

Managing transitions in modern organizations is about managing an unfolding, non-linear, dynamic process in which players and actions are never clearly defined. During this process there are likely to be a number of unforeseen contingencies which may necessitate a modification of intended pathways and stated objectives of achieving future planned states. The need to revise strategies to meet the demands of unpredictable events may form part of a predefined task of evaluation and appraisal, or it may result from the response of individuals or groups to problems arising from the transition process. Whether these tasks are part of a blueprint for change or evolve over time, their management is critical to the 'successful' establishment of new organizational arrangements. Their significance centres on the ability of key players to maintain an overview of the multiple and changing routes to organizational transition and their actions in creating, displacing, redefining and directing the ongoing development of change programmes. Consequently, unlike the management of short self-contained changes which may happen over a period of weeks or months, the dynamics of large-scale change are of a qualitatively different nature and may require a high degree of understanding and stamina on the part of change agents who have to deal directly with the messy, and at times painful and unsettling task of managing this type of transition. In part, the complexity and untidy nature of large-scale organizational transitions stem from the timeframe associated with these changes (in the case of General Motors the process of cellularization took approximately ten years from initial conception through to operation of the new work arrangements) and highlight the importance of management in steering the process towards long-term objectives.

Apart from the importance of tasks which maintain some form of continuity in steering the process towards some token end point (which in practice, is often continually redefined throughout the change process), there will also be a number of tasks associated with minor transitions within larger organizational change initiatives. As such, the management of major change programmes is likely to involve a diverse range of transitional tasks, activities, and decisions which in some cases may appear as discrete and small-scale change activities within a broader and more loosely coupled framework of change. This may add further to the sense of confusion and chaos, particularly during the 'middle' periods of change when the disruption to production or service operations may be at its height. At this time there may be: an increase in senior management concern brought about by a decline in productivity; feelings of frustration and anxiety among management unable to see the end to change; dissatisfaction and low morale among operative staff who are expected to perform their normal duties under transitional arrangements; and high levels of stress and resistance among supervisory personnel who may be experiencing criticisms both from management and the workforce. The organizational reality of multiple stakeholder groups (the power and politics of change) is clearly in evidence and the initial vision of change may be seriously called into question. A major problem facing the organization is how to maintain the momentum of change and yet also allay the fears and frustrations of different employee groups.

When the process of managing change is reaching completion and the hurdles, disruptions and conflicts become anecdotes and legends, then a period of comparative stability may occur and act to constrain further developments. Managers may feel that their tasks have been completed and their vision achieved, employees may find that less attention is paid to their views as a period of operating under the new work arrangements becomes a part of their daily routines. For many employees, the long-term process of major transitions may have created an expectation that change is the norm (a culture of change) and the formal completion of change may be seen to mark an end to management commitment.

Although the range of issues and problems which arise during the process of organizational change make it difficult to provide comprehensive explanations which can also be used to formulate practical guidelines, longitudinal in-depth case study research does provide a comparatively robust methodology for cross-referencing and checking data validity and furthering our knowledge of the change process. In the sections which follow, the organizational implications of adopting new production and service concepts are discussed; the key elements of a processual approach to managing change are summarized; and some practical guidelines for the management of change are outlined. The chapter concludes by re-emphasizing the theoretical and practical benefits of adopting a processual approach to the study and management of organizational transitions.

The challenge of new organizational arrangements

There are a number of challenges presented by the emergence of new organizational arrangements. Lansbury, for example, suggests that 'an important element in learning to change involves rethinking traditional concepts of job functions, organization hierarchies and even the nature of work itself' (Lansbury, 1992:27). Within the studies reported here the common threads include: the movement from an adversarial to a more collaborative system of employee relations, an emphasis on employee commitment, the tendency to devolve responsibility for quality control to shopfloor employees, the redefinition of production and supervisory management, and the gradual replacement of single operator tasks with teamwork activities. At the workplace, these transitions can be located along three continua (the first two of which are represented in Figure 3.1) consisting of the following dimensions:

1. *Work organization*: which ranges along a continuum from individual-based tasks to group work.
2. *Workplace control*: which ranges along a continuum from tight transparent control mechanisms (direct control) to autonomous self-directing systems (responsible autonomy).
3. *Workplace relations*: which ranges along a continuum from adversarial to collaborative systems of employee relations.

The challenge of new organizational arrangements centres on the successful management of change from a system based on a detailed division of labour, where employees are closely observed and directed by supervisors and an adversarial and combative system of employee relations is the norm, to one where individual tasks are being replaced by group activities (although in some cases reliance on existing plant and equipment has severely constrained group work), and where employees are taking on control responsibilities previously carried out by higher ranking personnel and a more harmonious system of employee relations is being encouraged through participative management. However, as the experiences reported in this book have highlighted, these changes can also create a number of new problems and issues for employees; for example, the stress associated with the issue of 'non-work' and the pressures of conformity associated with teamwork structures which prevent employee disengagement. Consequently, the challenge of change also incorporates a need for critical appraisal and for an ability to recognize and accommodate ongoing contingencies and unexpected outcomes.

In addition to these internal changes, there has also been a shift along the relational continuum of external customer–supplier relations. This transition mirrors the change in management practices which are being used to improve internal employee relations and can also be represented by a continuum which ranges from adversarial to more collaborative systems. As described in Chapter 5, more conventional adversarial customer–supplier relations based on contract formulation are being replaced with a collaborative approach based on trust, joint participation and the objective of mutual benefits and rewards. In this sense, managing these transitions is not only about meeting the intra-organizational challenges, but also about managing new collaborative inter-organizational arrangements with major supplier and customer firms. This movement towards a more collaborative system of contract relationships highlights the increasing reliance organizations are placing on good customer–supplier relations, in order to respond to competitive pressures resultant of the internationalization and globalization of markets.

The success of Japanese MNCs has also turned attention towards the qualitative aspects of business operations which have previously largely been ignored through an unquestioning acceptance of the logic and importance of quantitative measures. Today, statistical measures are used to support decisions and evaluate process changes, but they are no longer heralded as the primary mechanism for regulating employee behaviours or governing customer–supplier relations. Far greater emphasis is being placed on quality and continuous process improvement through developing the commitment and involvement of suppliers, employees and customers. The importance of developing a network of relations within organizations, across departmental and operational divisions or sites (particularly with MNCs) and between the immediate customers and suppliers of a local operating unit or firm, signal the emergence of *collaborative organizational networks*. For the most part, organizations are still under transition and have not fully developed the collaborative relational and qualitative aspects of their operation. In the process of changing, organizations are having to create different types of structures and apparatus to locate and manage the new production and service concepts. As highlighted in both the Hewlett Packard and Pirelli cases, the movement towards a collaborative approach has resulted in the adoption of a problem-solving model of contracting, based on the creation of trust between partners and joint participation, with the objective of mutual benefits and rewards. It has involved the establishment of structures to facilitate exchange of information between the customer and the supplier about user needs and problems in implementation and use. The development of the partnership is based on reciprocity and a shared belief that low cost and high quality are mutually compatible. Contractual arrangements are seen to be more flexible, although collaboration necessitates a longer-term mutual commitment. It is not simply about developing networks based on mutual trust and reciprocity, but also about maintaining and managing change within a less clearly defined unit of operation. As a result, the successful management of change will, in future, require negotiation and consultation beyond the company in which change is taking place. It is change within the collaborative network of organizations which will pose new challenges for management and will ultimately shape the development of competitive strategies for companies operating in the global market place.

This movement towards collaborative organizational networks signals a re-evaluation of the qualitative elements of organizations and an attempt to adopt more responsive and flexible patterns of structural arrangements, combined with co-operative operational relationships. Within organizations, the emphasis is on teamwork, joint worker–management consultative committees, and the development of a culture of commitment and employee involvement. For example, in the case of GM, the shift from a conventional flow-line manufacturing system, with a detailed division of labour and a well-defined system of supervisory management, to a new production arrangement which facilitates collaborative teamwork and responsible autonomy represents a major attitudinal shift at all levels within the organization. Managers are now expected to collaborate and communicate workplace issues as a part of the participative decision-making process, and operators are expected to learn new skills, work collaboratively, and commit themselves to continuous process improvement. The emergence of this new form of work organization is based on the incorporation of indirect elements of control into co-operative teamwork arrangements and does not signal a reversal in the division of labour towards a historically suspect era of autonomous craft work. In this sense, workgroups do have greater autonomy and discretion in their ability to stop work to deal with process problems and to allocate tasks; although the monitoring and evaluation of performance remains the concern of supervisory and managerial staff.

Operating within these new patterns of work organization, staff are not only required to be more adaptable and responsive to daily demands, but also to internalize new working practices which are the antithesis of traditional methods (such as building up buffer stocks) for coping with unexpected orders. Consequently, traditional operating practices previously deemed 'acceptable' (enabling employees to 'distance' themselves from the work in which they were employed) are now viewed as 'unacceptable'. Thus, just as structures which prevent employee engagement can be criticized for their alienating properties, so can structures which prevent employee disengagement be criticized for their failure to accommodate an individual's choice to remain 'independent' from the work process. In this sense, these new organizational arrangements still act to constrain operator choice within predefined working practices, only in this case the principles centre on employee involvement and teamwork collaboration. Furthermore, whilst these trends indicate a movement away from machine-paced work and the detailed division of labour associated with Taylorite systems of production, there is still considerable managerial resistance towards industrial strategies which aim to devolve policy decisions to joint consultative committees. Although employees may have greater autonomy over the pace and pattern of their work, they do not have any control over corporate policies and are expected to continually adapt to ongoing programmes of change. They are also expected to identify process problems, intervene in production to rectify them and suggest changes in the organization of production to prevent their recurrence. Far from simply improving the quality of working life, this widening of responsibility creates extra stress and makes the experience of work 'more precarious', as employees live on the edge of perpetual stops in production or service operations. The need for managers, engineers and production workers to respond quickly to production problems has also threatened conventional workplace status relations. In accordance with the new philosophy of teamwork and problem-solving, engineers and managers have to reveal to production staff when they do not have the answers to process problems. The resultant breaking of traditional barriers between functions has undermined the confidence of some junior and middle managers. This has been particularly noticeable at the supervisory level, where a process of redefinition is occurring in response to the introduction of new technologies and new techniques.

Traditional supervisory control responsibilities embedded in prior structural arrangements are no longer appropriate under team-based work arrangements (especially in those cases where the allocation and co-ordination of tasks has been devolved upon the workgroup). In many cases these changes to supervision have simply been ignored, and it has been left to supervisors to redefine their position. Typically, there has been a shift in task emphasis away from inspection functions and technical issues and towards elements of employee relations, teamwork facilitation and planning. These changes have also been marked by an increase in the control responsibilities of supervisors and the emergence of workgroup leaders. These informal workgroup leaders, or teamwork facilitators, hold a supervisory relationship to other operators in the control and co-ordination of workgroup activities. This suggests that the function of supervision remains central, even if it is no longer being carried out by formally defined first-line supervisors. Essentially, there has been a quantitative reduction in the number of organizationally defined supervisors and a qualitative expansion in the function of supervision. Consequently, supervision is undergoing a complex redefinition in which the characteristics of the newly emerging supervisory positions remain unclear and ill-defined.

The nature and character of the new organizational arrangements reported here signal a movement away from the traditional adversarial approach to managing contract relationships and towards the development of collaborative customer–supplier relationships based on reciprocity and high-trust, long-term partnerships. This indicates how major product and process change may, in the future, require adaptation by a local network of organizations. The successful management of organizational transition may no longer be contained within the structural arrangements of a single organization, but require a series of changes within a number of different organizations which combine together for the purpose of forming collaborative organizational networks to meet the dynamic and competitive markets of a global economy. Whilst these changes may not signify a paradigmatic shift but, rather, a movement along existing work organization, control and relational dimensions, they do reflect real organizational innovations. The successful management of these changes is part of the new organizational challenge which confronts future practitioners of industry and commerce.

A processual approach to understanding change

Throughout this book it has been argued that the temporal and processual nature of transformational change makes it difficult to analyse and understand. For example, the occurrence of conflicting histories of change at different points in time, and at the same point in time among different groups, calls testimony to the complex and political nature of these processes and to the problems of data analysis which seeks to construct pathways of organizational change. In many studies, the tendency has been to either generalize from snap-shots of change or to focus on a particular activity, such as the problems and practice of implementing change. In contrast, the research reported in this book has been based on a series of longitudinal, in-depth case studies. This approach has supported processual analysis, and demonstrated how critical events during the process of change may serve to impede, hasten or redirect the route to change. Furthermore, it has been shown how a processual approach provides a useful methodology for the systematic analysis of qualitative, longitudinal data. The approach developed in Chapter 3 draws on the temporal nature of large-scale operational change and is based on the view that, first, there is a period in time in which an idea or a conception about the need to change will arise, and a decision will be made on whether or not to invest in a major change programme; second, there is a timeframe over which equipment will be purchased or consultants hired and the change option implemented; and, third, there is a stage in which new operating practices will become the norm within the context of other ongoing processes of change. In this sense, there is a temporal history of large-scale change programmes and there will be a number of tasks which organizations will engage in during the process of managing these organizational transitions.

It was also argued that, whilst there may be an organizationally defined beginning and end point to major change programmes, what happens in the intervening period is often muddled, confused and difficult to understand. This complex period in the management of transitions does not centre on managing logical sequences of events which phase models can often suggest but, rather, on managing a composite and non-linear series of transitional tasks composed of decision-making and non-decision-making activities and historical events. For example, a number of categories for locating and analysing data can be defined for the purpose of increasing our understanding of the 'black box' process of establishing new production or service concepts. Data located within these categories can later be recombined to construct a more detailed and contextual understanding of the process of organizational change. Whilst there is an historical dimension to the unfolding of a change programme the 'black box' process of change may move backwards and forwards between various tasks and be involved in a number of different activities simultaneously. It is therefore important to stress that, whilst it is useful to identify categories of tasks for analytical purposes, these should not be treated as representing a rational, sequential series of steps in the process of managing transitions but, rather, as providing a useful analytical technique for uncovering and making sense of the dynamic process of large-scale change.

In Chapter 3, a processual approach to studying organizational change was developed and then employed in the case study chapters. The first case study, of British Rail, was used to illustrate the processual nature of organizational change, and the need to account for the substance of change, the political decision-making processes which may influence and shape the direction and speed of transition, and the context in which changes takes place. The later studies covered a range of contemporary business concerns, such as the strategic advantage of adopting a TQM programme, the implications of JIT for low-volume operations, the effects of introducing automated technology, and the benefits of cellular work arrangements for component manufacturers. Although the case chapters focused on different change initiatives (there has been considerable variation in the substance of change) they all demonstrate the utility of a processual framework for locating data and making sense of the factors which shape the process of change.

In examining these factors, the major determinants of change were classified into three broad categories. The first centred on the context of change and included external contextual factors (such as level of international competition and government legislation) and internal contextual factors (such as administrative structures and history and culture). The substance of change was identified as the second major determinant. This was used to refer to the nature, type and scale of organizational change. In this book, the focus of attention has been with large-scale operational change and the introduction of new technologies and techniques. The third category of determinants was defined as the politics of change, and was taken to refer to all political activity (both internal and external) which serves to influence the process and outcomes of organizational change. By combining the data categories for analysing change with this threefold classification of determinants of change, a processual framework was presented (see Figure 3.2).

Whilst this approach was principally developed for the purpose of furthering our understanding of the complex process of managing organizational transitions, it is also important to take into account the effects of design and development processes on the establishment of new organizational arrangements. In the studies reported, Chapter 9 was used to highlight some of the practical and conceptual issues which surround the design and development of software products prior to their organizational adoption. The comparative examples of the Commonwealth and Scientific Research Organization and the Alvey DHSS Demonstrator Project were also used to illustrate the importance of the politics and context of change during the design process. This period in the development of new technologies and/or management techniques is often overlooked in accounts which focus on the effects of change on existing organizational arrangements. Although the design task is often treated as an independent activity to the management of organizational transitions, the significance of design decisions should no longer be dealt with as a separate issue. Increasingly, the links between design decisions and the organization and control of work are being emphasized by practitioners and academics (see for example, Badham, 1991; Havn, 1991, and Salzman, 1991) and the design task, rather than being a distinct stage, may in practice overlap with the process of managing transitions. For example, in the case of the CSIRO project the design task straddled the two general timeframes of conception and transition, whereas in the Alvey project design was defined as a separate research activity from which products could be later exploited for commercial purposes. In short, the grounded case studies presented in the empirical chapters have been used to highlight how previously discrete areas (such as research and development) are forming closer ties with the production/operations function (through such schemes and design for manufacturability) and how the dynamic and 'black box' process of change should not be viewed as progressing through a rational linear path of organizational transition.

The processual approach has also been used in the case study chapters to demonstrate how changes in business market activity, management strategy, occupational and employee response and the nature of the operating system, in addition to various other internal and external determinants of change, do not have equal explanatory significance throughout the process of organizational transition. For example, the decision to change and the choice and design of new techniques or technologies will generally be influenced by management's strategic objectives, the state of the business market, and the availability and applicability of alternative systems and philosophies to particular operating environments. During the implementation of change, business market considerations are likely to decline in significance, whereas occupational and employee concerns are likely to increase in importance and influence the outcome of management's strategic intentions. Following the emergence and operation of new organizational arrangements, occupational and employee responses will further serve to shape the operational use made of the new system(s). During this period, employees and occupational groups will finally adapt to change and, in the process, they are likely to redefine the consequence of change for their positions within the new organization structures and operating practices imposed by management during the initial operation of the new operating system. Finally, it is worth restating that, although it is possible to generalize about the relative importance of a range of variables in shaping the process of organizational transitions, these variables need to be examined empirically in order to evaluate their significance in redefining particular types of work organization and systems of management control in different operating environments.

Practical guidelines on the management of change

One of the main conclusions which can be drawn from a processual analysis of change is that there can be no simple prescriptions for managing organizational transitions successfully. What may prove successful in one context and in one time may not prove appropriate to comparative companies operating from different locations at some future point in time. Consequently, it would neither be appropriate nor feasible to produce either 'tablets of stone' or exhaustive lists of the key ingredients to successful change. Although this position may seem to indicate a return to a chaos theory of managing transitions, this is not the stance adopted here, as the grounded case studies do provide material from which lessons on the management of transition can be extracted (the final cases chosen for inclusion all represent examples of the successful management of large-scale operational change). Although these lessons do not provide a blueprint for successful change management, they can be used to formulate a series of fifteen guidelines which should be seriously considered by organizational practitioners about to embark on a programme of large-scale organizational change.

The guidelines presented are located within and derive from a processual framework which emphasizes the importance of ongoing timeframes and the interconnected dynamics between the substance, context and politics of change. Unlike contingency models, this processual perspective does not advocate or identify a single emergent homogenous structure which can be prescribed as an appropriate design for a 'changed' organization. Change is viewed as an ongoing process which is both progressive and regressive, is planned and unplanned, and incorporates intended and unintended innovations from the initial conception of the need to change through to the emergence of new work arrangements. Furthermore, unlike situational (or contingency) approaches which (whilst recognizing the importance of context) tend to use snap-shot models and assume that context is singular and unproblematic, the processual perspective sensitizes the researcher and practitioner to the importance of the interplay between organizational governance and politics, and the history and culture of organizations and change programmes. For example, processual research is able to identify competing histories of change and show how organizational stories may be rewritten to lend support to the claims of differing vested interest groups and, thereby, reflect the political agendas of powerful decision-makers rather than representing some 'objective' reconstruction of past events.

One of the most important lessons which can be learned from this approach is that large-scale operational change is a non-linear dynamic process which should not be characterized as a rational series of decision-making activities and events. In practice, organizational transitions cannot be predicted as they unfold over time and comprise management omissions and revisions as well as unforeseen employee responses, technical problems and contingencies. In short, the processual approach views change as a dynamic and *ongoing* process from which two practical pieces of advice can be outlined.

First, it is important to be aware and to maintain an overview of the dynamic and long-term process of change (managing organizational transition does not occur overnight but takes time). This, of course, refers to major change programmes, such as the re-equipping of an entire laundry facility. In this case, change occurred over a period of five years, from the initial conception of the need to change through to the final modifications of the system and the emergence of new work practices and procedures. In fact, in all the cases studied the large-scale operational change programmes took a number of years and required considerable planning and preparation. Consequently, the strategic significance of these transitions and the enormity of the implementation task should be recognized from the outset. Change should not be defined as a one-off process but seen as a long-term, continuing dynamic composed of various critical events and activities which are likely to influence the design and implementation of future policies aimed at changing organizational arrangements.

The second lesson is that the management of organizational transition is unlikely to be marked by a line of continual improvement from beginning to end. In the case of Central Linen Service, this was illustrated during the re-equipment phase when there was a downturn in productivity at the time of major disruption. This is also the time when there is likely to be an increase in agitation and complaints from employees and customers, a potential wavering of management commitment, and a possible loss of faith and growing uncertainty among outside stakeholders. In the case of Pirelli Cables, this period also highlighted the importance of developing appropriate reward and recognition systems, and the inappropriateness of evaluating the 'success' of change in terms of monetary benefits without regard to the strategically significant attitudinal changes which may accompany major change programmes. However, once this period is over and the quantitative and qualitative benefits of change become visible, this downside is soon forgotten and often absent in reconstructed histories of change.

With respect to the *context* of change, there are also a number of practical issues to consider. In the case of British Rail, the context was of a declining business market due to competition from road haulage and the decline of the industries which were the railway's principal source of freight revenue (coal, iron and steel); in conjunction with an identification of inefficiencies in freight operations stemming from inaccurate and out-of-date information about the whereabouts of freight resources. Within this context, a computerized system of freight information control was seen to offer the potential solution to the problem of external business market competition and internal operating inefficiencies. Furthermore, British Rail's freight plan had unequivocally recommended computerization, so corporate management set about the task of identifying an appropriate system. The context of change was also important in determining the types of systems available and their applicability to railway freight operations; for example, the TOPS computer system was chosen due to the absence elsewhere of any similar system at the same stage of development or with the same capabilities.

Apart from the external context, an awareness of the internal context is also important for the successful management of change. This includes technology, human resources, administrative structures and the history and culture of an organization. For example, the values postulated by, and implicit in, the proposed change must be congruent with the values and assumptions that comprise the organization's culture. Where there is conflict between the two, the change is likely to be resisted. The responsiveness of an organization's culture to change can therefore be a crucial determinant of the process and outcomes of organizational change. Thus, the contextual dimension raises a host of issues which should be accommodated in the planning and management of change programmes and highlights a third general lesson; namely, the need to be aware of and understand the context in which change is due to take place.

A fourth and related observation centres on the importance of ensuring that change strategies are culturally sensitive and appreciate the significance and potential tenacity of existing cultures. For example, in the case of the large bureaucratic organization of British Rail an assessment was made of the most appropriate means for cutting across traditional divisional structures and occupational boundaries. The potential lack of responsiveness of the existing sub-cultures and groups associated with freight operations was identified as a possible barrier to change. Consequently, the implementation team was deliberately constructed along cross-functional lines, incorporating under the overall control of one project manager operating computing and telecommunication specialists. This form of project organization proved useful in overcoming inter-departmental rivalries and procedural delays and highlights how within certain contexts it may prove beneficial to set up a cross-functional implementation team which is not tied to particular vested interests or perspectives.

A fifth consideration is the value of having a champion of change who is identified with the change programme and is able to maintain the direction and consistency of change. Although this may not serve as a general lesson (in that it is rarely possible to predict who one should appoint to act as a champion of change), the cases do clearly illustrate the value of having a champion of change who is able to manage the context (or atmosphere) within which changes takes place. In General Motors, for example, the local plant manager took on this role and maintained a high level of commitment and enthusiasm among local managers and employees. He was not only able to converse in open and frank discussions with trade union representatives, shopfloor personnel and supervisory staff, but also to engage employees in his 'vision' of the future. Employee acceptance of change was further supported by the early delivery of practical benefits to staff in terms of improved operating conditions and the opening of opportunities for skill development and increased remuneration. The time and effort spent communicating management's rationale for change served to create a climate which was conducive to change and provided the bedrock from which change took place. In this way, the champion of change was used as an agent for highlighting changing contexts (past, present and future) and routes to achieving comparatively 'better' working conditions.

Questions concerning the *substance* of change also raise a number of practical concerns over how to successfully manage organizational transitions. The two elements of content which were most clearly illustrated by the case material centre on understanding substance during the choice and selection of the change (for example, what are the main constituents of the new technology or management technique) and, also, ensuring that employees who have to adopt to new working practices (the changing context) are adequately trained in the use of new equipment, techniques or procedures.

Thus, the sixth major guideline which can be distilled from the case studies is the need to fully understand the substance of change. Considerable time and attention needs to be given to the substance of change in terms of the technical, financial and human implications of change for the organization. This includes the need to appraise technical requirements against existing techniques and technologies, and the development of appropriate implementation and training programmes within the financial constraints set by the company. This should involve discussions and decisions on work organization, on who are going to be the major implementors, and how the process is going to be managed. In the case of Pirelli Cables, attention was paid to gaining employee involvement in the early stages in order to clarify the substance of change and to ensure that planning was not done in isolation from the people whose jobs were to be affected.

Misunderstanding, delay and conflict can result from inappropriate perceptions of the type and nature of change. For example, in the case of Hewlett Packard, there was considerable uncertainty about what constituted JIT. This resulted in some initial confusion over what were the main factors which needed to be addressed during the process of change. In order to make appropriate decisions, practitioners must first clarify what a change programme (the substance) means for a particular organization (the context). In other words, be wary of banner definitions which may mask the contextual requirements of successful organizational transition.

The seventh guideline centres on the need to train staff in the use of new equipment, techniques or procedures. In British Rail, the decision was made to combine the task of training with that of implementation. This provided staff with the opportunity to put their new skills into immediate use, and proved particularly effective. Furthermore, it is important that all staff receive training and that supervisors are not overlooked. Again, a major obstacle to change occurred in cases where supervisors, or those holding a supervisory relationship to production, were not accounted for in designing training programmes and implementing change. Training can also be used as a vehicle for informing employees of the nature, consequences and opportunities afforded by change, in order to minimize disruption during initial operation.

In considering the *politics* of change, six practical lessons are drawn from the case material. The central argument is that it is important to try and obtain the support of senior management, local management, supervisors, trade unions and workplace employees. Whilst it is clearly beneficial (although rarely achievable) to try and gain the support of all employees, some of the main obstacles which arise during processes of change are not due to an inability to gain total employee support but, rather, result from the lack of involvement of particular key groups (most noticeable at the supervisory level).

The eighth lesson highlighted by the case material centres on the mobilization of senior management commitment and support. In the case of Central

Linen Service, the strong support and commitment of the Interim Board of Management was critical to the successful management of change in providing a clear, unfettered, encouraging environment for the General Manager and the senior management team. Similarly in Pirelli Cables, the support and backing of the managing director and senior executives was critical to the successful management of change.

A ninth and related factor is to develop a committed and cohesive local management team. This is especially important when implementing large-scale changes which are likely to be disruptive and take considerable time to complete. In Central Linen Service, the General Manager's reconstitution of management into a more cohesive and enthusiastic local team provided a cross-functional resource which facilitated change. For example, the finance manager was able to assist in determining critical funding formulae for the new equipment. Whilst the General Manager did not instigate any regular participative management meetings, he did maintain a close relationship with every senior manager, and acted as the keystone which bound the management group together and gave them a common sense of purpose. Working within the team, managers were accountable for their own area of control responsibility and became fully committed to the planned programme of change.

Ensuring that supervisors and line managers are part of major change programmes is the tenth guideline which emerged from the case studies. In many of the cases, the job of the supervisor was being redefined and the numbers of supervisory staff were being reduced. These changes threatened the position of supervisors and resulted in conflict and resistance to 'imposed' implementation strategies. Change was also impeded by the general failure to recognize the central function of supervision under changed systems of operation and the role of the supervisor as a potential change catalyst.

The eleventh major lesson is to gain trade union support. This refers to both the external, full-time trade union officials and the internal union representatives. In the case of British Rail, formal support from the major unions representing freight operations staff enabled management to tackle emerging industrial relations issues directly with the shop stewards. Moreover, official trade union support for the programme proved instrumental in allowing the defusion of potentially sensitive issues. Open communication and shop steward involvement in local implementation teams set the scene for a good industrial relations climate in which problems could be solved without recourse to industrial action.

A twelfth and related lesson raised by the case studies is the need to spend time developing good employee relations. In all the organizations studied, communication was central to bringing about a shift in employee attitudes, towards the management and change. In General Motors for example, the local management team set about improving employee relations prior to the introduction of change. They developed two major strands to their plan. The first centred on improving the work environment, whereby the shopfloor was transformed from a grey and greasy workplace to a newly painted and clean work environment. The second major thrust of the plan was based on improving the climate of industrial relations through the practice of greater communication between management and shop stewards. The central aim was to achieve full union involvement and co-operation, and to develop and maintain a relationship of trust between local management and union officials. At the outset, there was considerable conflict between the plant manager and shop stewards. However, following the provision of accurate information and a more open management approach, there evolved a far more harmonious climate of employee relations. This set the context in which the successful management of change could more easily be achieved.

The thirteenth element which was deemed central to gaining and maintaining good employee relations was to clearly communicate the intentions of a change programme to employees. In Central Linen Service, the factory design was drawn up by the engineering manager on an 8 foot by 4 foot board which was put up on the wall in the canteen, and comments were invited from employees on the proposed layout of the new machinery. This draft was placed alongside a drawing of the existing plant to provide a greater understanding of the implications of change for work organization. At the same time, management was talking to staff, both individually and in groups. They described the planned programme of change and discussed the consequence for employee jobs and responsibilities. Furthermore, because they were concerned about employee responses to the introduction of an overhead system of linen transportation, the management team constructed a mock system and asked employees to respond. All this was carried out months before the actual installation of the new equipment, in order to inform employees and identify potential problems.

The two final lessons which can be drawn from the case material relate to funding arrangements and the need to take a total organizational approach to managing transitions. The importance of ensuring that appropriate funds are allocated to major change programmes is the fourteenth suggestion. Without the appropriate funding, it is highly unlikely that the objectives of change will be achieved. This may be a major hurdle to programmes where the potential benefits cannot be easily quantified, or where the proposed changes are initiated by local management. In General Motors for example, the local management team submitted a proposal to senior management on the basis of a series of results from the running of a pilot cell, which showed a bottom-line improvement of 18%. The request for financial support was rejected, with one senior manager suggesting that what was needed was not the rearrangement of old equipment but the purchasing of new machinery. Nevertheless, through persistence and with the help and support of other team members and the Commonwealth and Scientific Research Organization, the plant manager submitted an amended proposal to senior management. A series of presentations was made and the plant manager was able to convince the directors of the feasibility of cellular manufacture. However, the justification for investing in change was based on conventional accounting methods which sought to identify the 'real' financial returns and economic incentives for supporting the proposed transition. Whilst this method for assessing the viability of a change programme is generally accepted, with the increasing focus on the qualitative dimension of production, it is questionable whether conventional accounting procedures will suffice in the future. In this case, it was the financial pay-back on investment which secured senior management support.

The fifteenth piece of practical advice is that implementation strategies should not confine themselves to a specific area of operation or section of the company but, rather, should take a total organizational approach. In the case of Pirelli Cables, the programme was not simply about product delivery but about a total approach to quality right across the organization. This is perhaps self-evident in programmes of change which aim to transform existing organizational arrangements and systems of operation; however, a fragmented and localized approach can occur during implementation and prevent strategic intentions from being realized. In other words, whilst it is important to set clearly defined objectives and identify areas in which the immediate benefits of change can be achieved, care should be given to ensure that functional divisions do not occur and impede the change process.

These, then, are the major practical guidelines which can be drawn from a processual analysis of managing organizational transitions. To summarize, they are as follows:

1. Maintain an overview of the dynamic and long-term process of change, and appreciate that major change takes time.
2. Recognize that the transition process is unlikely to be marked by a line of continual improvement from beginning to end.
3. Be aware of and understand the context in which change takes place
4. Ensure that change strategies are culturally sensitive and do not underestimate the strength of existing cultures.
5. Consider the value of having a champion of change.
6. Affirm that the substance of change is fully understood.
7. Train staff in the use of new equipment, techniques or procedures.
8. Ensure senior management commitment and support.
9. Develop a committed and cohesive local management team.
10. Ensure that supervisors are part of major change programmes.
11. Gain trade union support.
12. Spend time developing good employee relations.
13. Clearly communicate the intentions of change to employees.
14. Provide appropriate funding arrangements.
15. Take a total organizational approach to managing transitions.

As indicated in the guidelines, the management of change does not happen overnight, it takes time and involves a range of political events, activities and actions by various stakeholders and key occupational groups. There is context and substance to change which continually influences key decision-makers and shapers of change at critical junctures during that process. In the case of British Rail, the major players and groups included the British Government and trade union officials, the Board of Directors, senior management, supervisors and shop stewards, and the employees at the various freight yards. In the case of Central Linen Service, a comparable range of stakeholders influenced the direction and pace of change. This resulted in the revitalization of CLS, which now operates as a commercially viable business with some of the most advanced technology in the world. That these results illustrate a good example of the successful management of change is not in doubt; however, whether CLS continues to maintain its competitive advantage throughout the 1990s will also depend on its ability to continually update and adjust operations to meet changing market conditions.

Conclusion

A major challenge facing modern organizations centres on their capacity to manage the ongoing processes of change associated with survival and success in turbulent and dynamic business markets. The management of these processes requires an acceptance of a need to change and a willingness to challenge many cherished assumptions about the nature of organizations. Work organization and the system of management control is undergoing transition; the boundaries of what constitutes an organization are being redefined; and the relationship between customers and suppliers is undergoing fundamental change. In managing these transitions practitioners need to be aware of: the importance of power politics within organizations as a determinant of the speed, direction and character of change; the enabling and constraining properties of the type and scale of change being introduced; and the influence of the internal and external context on the pathways and outcomes of change on new work arrangements. These elements – the politics, substance and context of change – all interconnect during the unfolding of large-scale operational change programmes. Consequently, a processual approach is the most appropriate framework for understanding and preparing for the temporal and non-linear nature of change. As Kanter, Stein and Jick (1992:391) have noted: 'Managing change today is actually managing a cascade of change; most people are bleary-eyed with their "change agendas" . . . Yet the more we have studied change, and the more we brush up against its effects, the more humble we have become about dictating the "best" way to do it'.

The complexity and confusion of managing transitions has also been highlighted by the case material presented in this book, which has been used to illustrate the broad range of factors which may serve to impede, hasten and shape organizational change. It has been shown how successful change programmes generally commence with some initial conception of the need to change which is followed by a period of transition in which management attempt to pilot the process towards certain specified change objectives. This is also the period in which the disruption and confusion of change is likely to be most marked and management may be faced with the problem of how to allay the concerns of various employee groups and yet also maintain some form of momentum and continuity in steering the transistion process. One potential way in which this problem can be tackled is through accepting and responding to the realities of change, and being prepared to accept unforeseen events during the process of transition management. The acceptance of the need to respond to and accommodate omissions and revisions to preset plans and objectives, compliments rather than replaces proactive management tactics and strategies. It is argued here that whilst the planning and formulation of strategies of change are important, these preplanned pathways should not be viewed as definitive or all encompassing but, rather, they should be seen as presenting a potential road map based on experience, contextual understanding and future expectations. In practice, it is impossible to predict all future scenarios or adapt to the unexpected consequences of political decision-making and power plays during the process of change. Contextual redefinition as change programmes unfold within organisations interconnect with the dynamics of organizational politics and substance issues to complicate and muddy the clear waters of preplanned schedules of change. For these reasons, strategies for managing transitions should take account of the need to assimilate and respond to contingencies and issues which are as yet, unforeseen. The approach to managing change should be flexible and responsive to unforeseen events and thereby accommodate diversity in the development and revision of change strategies. However as already indicated, the approach should also be able to maintain a longer-term objective whilst responding to some of the immediate needs and expectations of various disillusioned individuals and/or groups.

The second element of this approach relates to an understanding of the process of change in terms of timeframes and the more negative and frustrating elements associated with large-scale organizational transitions. For example, before embarking on major change programmes, it would be helpful if employees (including senior management) were educated about the reality of large-scale change. These types of transition take time and will normally involve a 'downside' (this may be in the form of a fall in productivity and/or an increase in levels of disruption, employee absenteeism and industrial disputes). An open recognition of these factors may help to alleviate some of the tensions when conditions worsen and the change process is in threat of being destabilized and disrupted.

In conclusion, transition management involves reactive and proactive elements, and requires a realistic understanding of the temporal and non-linear processes of change. For example, although planning and preparation are important ingredients to successful organizational transitions, the management of these changes can not be characterized as being composed of a linear series of phases, nor do the outcomes represent the results of objective rational decision-making on the part of managers. In practice, even when change programmes have reached an organizationally defined conclusion the process bedevils those who seek to construct rational linear and retrospective explanations of the organizational experience of large-scale transition. The existence of competing organizational histories of change are likely to complicate the most skeletal of explanations, and ongoing political agendas are likely to influence individual reconstructions. Hence, in the transitions reported here, it has been argued that the conventional view of refreezing operations at some end point of change is misdirected and would be an ill-advised strategy within modern organizations. Although it is important to recognize the completion of major change programmes, there may often be a number of other changes which have commenced or emerged during the process of organizational transition. No longer is it appropriate to talk of long-term stability followed by change followed by long-term stability but, rather, organizational transition should be viewed as an ongoing process which may develop from partial incremental commitments as well as by the formulation of corporate strategies for the wholescale introduction of new organizational arrangements. For these reasons, caution should be given to studies which present linear models in an attempt to construct commandments of change or to prescribe the best way to manage organizational change. In short, change needs to be managed as an ongoing and dynamic process and not as a single reaction to adverse contingent circumstance.

APPENDIX
RESEARCH STRATEGY AND METHODOLOGICAL ISSUES: THE CASE FOR LONGITUDINAL QUALITATIVE DATA

This appendix sets out to, first, examine the debate on the significance of qualitative longitudinal data for understanding the process of change; and secondly, to summarize the research strategies employed in the collection of the data used in the main body of the text. In presenting this material here, it should be noted that no methodological account is given within individual case chapters (further information can be obtained from the case references listed in the bibliography), and that a summary of the five supporting programmes of research is provided in Chapter 1.

The debate on the value of qualitative methodology over quantitative approaches for understanding the process of change is not new (see, for example, Bryman, 1988a and 1988b). Since the turn of the century, there has been a heightened awareness of the value of qualitative data for understanding the dynamics of social relations as 'career' promoters and inhibitors (Silverman, 1985:18). Howard Becker's well known work on becoming a marijuana user illustrates the value of this methodology for providing a detailed account of an individual's assimilation (or career passage) into alternative social groups (Becker, 1953). More recently, William Foote Whyte has produced his fieldwork autobiography which reports on some fifty years' experience of doing qualitative longitudinal research in a variety of social settings (Whyte, 1984). However, what is different about today's debate is, first, the greater confidence among qualitative researchers about the value of their studies (for example, Dawson, 1990b); and, secondly, a shift in attention towards the technical as opposed to epistemological issues which have dogged the qualitative/quantitative divide (Bryman, 1988a:93–126). On the first count, Gans (1982) demonstrates this change in attitude by making a deliberate reference to his originally published 1962 Appendix in *Urban Villages*, and stating that he would, given the opportunity, expunge its apologetic conclusion that the study was not scientific (Gans, 1982:409). This concern with 'scientific' validity is also described by Whyte, who currently derides the question of whether qualitative work is truly scientific as 'a foolish issue' (Whyte, 1984:263). In conjunction with the increasing confidence of qualitative researchers there has been a shift towards greater academic acceptance of the validity of qualitative research. This has resulted in the attempts of an increasing number of research methodologists to 'build bridges' between the traditional quantitative/qualitative divide (for example, Crompton and Jones, 1984; Whyte, 1984). On this count, Bryman (1988a:127–56) has specified the ways in which the methods associated with quantitative and qualitative research can be combined, and concludes that: 'Quantitative and qualitative research can frequently be found together in particular substantive areas in the social sciences . . . the two research traditions can be viewed as contributing to the understanding of different aspects of the phenomenon in question' (Bryman, 1988a:170).

Bryman uses the example of social mobility to substantiate his claim, arguing that quantitative studies contribute to our understanding of rates and patterns of social mobility, whereas in-depth qualitative research of particular institutions (for example, schools) would be needed to identify the processes associated with the perpetuation of the class system (Bryman, 1988a:170). We could thus apply this to various other areas of research, such as unemployment, where we may be concerned with both the rates and patterns of change (quantitative dimension) and what unemployment means for the unemployed and other household members (qualitative dimension).

On the basis of this discussion above, it may appear that there is no problem in bridging the gap between quantitative and qualitative research. However, this is not the case, and it is worth spending some time presenting some of the theoretical issues which militate against communication between practitioners of opposing epistemological camps.

According to Filstead (1979), the quantitative approach uses a fundamentally different framework to qualitative research for evaluating acceptable knowledge. The former follows the procedures of scientific inquiry, whereas the latter is more concerned with actors' interpretations of their situations. Consequently, quantitative data are often associated with 'science' and are seen to be systematically rigorous and reliable. They adopt an epistemological stance that true knowledge can only be obtained in the pursuit of science and, hence, automatically discredit and devalue research which actively engages in the subjective and non-scientific world of the actors' interpretation. From the qualitative camp, the main criticisms levelled against a quantitative approach to the study of society is that the research methods produce superficial data and may result in the complete physical separation of researchers from the field they are studying (Bryman, 1988a:104; Whyte, 1984:267). Moreover, whilst the quantitative analyses of existing survey data can be used to uncover changing relationships and stimulate healthy academic debate (see, for example, Dale 1986; McGlone and Pudney, 1986; and Taylor-Gooby, 1985 and 1986), this method can also be used as a way of achieving the 'fast-thesis', with little concern for the origination of the data or the research process. For example, with the recent developments in communication and information technologies, Whyte notes that the quantitative approach to original research is being discredited through increasing academic awareness of the popular modern method for doing doctoral theses, which is to get hold of some existing (computer readable) data, to devise some hypotheses, to test these with the use of some sophisticated statistical techniques, and then to write up the findings as a thesis (Whyte, 1984:267). In this example, the intention is not to devalue quantitative methodologies but to illustrate how the application of the scientific model does not by itself increase our stock of knowledge, and that it can be used as a means for masking poor research. Thus, it is not a question of which approach is adopted but of how it is used in practice.

In the battle-ground of hostilities, qualitative research has been described by quantitative theorists as subjective, unscientific, having limited generality and being 'soft'. Whilst qualitative researchers have not proven to be so vocal in their criticisms of quantitative methods, Whyte suggests that this may largely be a reflection of the powerful influence of physics as *the* model for social scientists to follow (Whyte, 1984:266). He describes his early research years as being a period of both guilt for violating scientific rules and pleasure for learning about social processes through transgression.

Today, these epistemological differences remain. What is different is that an increasing number of researchers are more interested in using the appropriate 'tools' to tackle a research problem, rather than with the maintenance of a preconceived set of assumptions about how the world operates. In this sense, there is a considerable amount of exploratory and innovative research being carried out which is more concerned with overcoming technical problems than winning epistemological points. For example, in a recent edited book on *Doing Research In Organizations*, which provides 'insider' accounts of the process of research, it is noted that:

> By and large, the broader epistemological issues of positivism versus phenomenology in the social sciences, which have underpinned many renditions of the debate about quantitative and qualitative research are absent in spite of various attempts to inject them into the study of organizations.
>
> (Bryman, 1988b:17)

Similarly, Silverman argues that it is not a choice between polar opposites, but rather a decision about balance and intellectual breadth and rigour (Silverman, 1985:17). Thus, the agenda appears set for greater communication and understanding of the value of quantitative and qualitative approaches to social research. Consequently, whilst the empirical data presented in this book are based on qualitative longitudinal research, they neither reject the use of quantitative methodologies (for example, a quantitative approach may be required for the purpose of identifying the diffusion of robotic technology in industrialized economies), nor the value and significance of qualitative methodologies for understanding the complex processes associated with change. Moreover, what is published in journals and what takes place in the field are often worlds apart, making it difficult for the new researcher to learn from published material. For the quantitative researcher, the world is more clearly defined and the methods well documented, the biggest problem being whether the issue lends itself to 'scientific' inquiry. For the qualitative researcher, everything is grey, ambiguous and at times 'spiritual', the biggest problem being how to make sense of the data and how to generalize from a small sample. There is, however, a very simple lesson to be learnt from each perspective, namely, that there is nothing intrinsically wrong with quantification nor with phenomena which cannot be explained quantitatively. As indicated at the outset, some topics such as the changing structure of employment lend themselves to a quantitative classificatory methodology; others, such as documenting the complex and dynamic processes associated with major organizational change programmes, require a more qualitative approach.

On the question of the timescale of the research, the term 'longitudinal' can be used to refer to a number of quite different types of study. For example, longitudinal designs are often proposed for quantitative studies which seek to identify the temporal relationship between two causally reciprocal variables. Alternatively, cohort studies may be carried out over a number of years in order to take a number of time-spaced sequential snapshots from which more general trends and explanations can be derived. This static snap-shot view of social life runs contrary to the primary characteristic of qualitative research, which seeks to explain the interconnected and dynamic processes inherent in everyday life. Through a concern with holistic and detailed descriptions of social settings and a commitment to reporting actors' interpretations of events, the final product is commonly a processual account of interaction and change. In contrast, qualitative studies which use semi-structured interviewing as their primary method of data collection are, according to Bryman, generally characterized by an absence of a sense of process compared to participant observer studies (Bryman, 1988a:115). However, whilst much of the qualitative research in which the author has been involved has relied heavily on this technique, a longitudinal element was built into the research design at the outset, enabling the collection of new empirical evidence on the process of change. For example, in the research work at Edinburgh University on innovation and change (which now forms part of a broader three-year study of new technology and the management of expertise in customer–supplier relations), time was spent at the workplace in order to become familiar with the activities and relationships between employees. The main research objective was to examine the transformation of work in changing from 'production for stock' to 'production to order' in two different operating units on a single site of a UK division of the US-owned multinational corporation, Hewlett Packard. One was starting as a totally new operation (as a greenfield unit), and the other was in the process of changing established methods of working to new production arrangements (as a brownfield unit). In examining these two processes of change, interviews were carried out with managers of the various functional areas in each operating unit. Some interviews were two hours in length and covered topics which included job history; experience of innovation and change; job tasks and responsibilities; and employer practice and philosophy. However, it was soon realized that because of time constraints it would not be possible to interview all employees, and that in order to get a broader picture as well as to make sense of the data collected, it was important to spend some time doing 'research-by-wandering-around'.

From a series of visits to the plant, it was possible to discuss some of the issues surrounding change with female assemblers, secretarial/clerical staff and male test engineers (in addition, taped interviews were carried out with some of the supervisory staff in one of the operating units). These informal group and individual discussions, and the writing of observational notes after leaving the plant, were central to a later analysis of the interview data. The workplace layout was open plan with no internal dividing walls or enclosed offices. There were low, movable partitions which could be moved around to meet the current needs of staff. The uniformity of design and facilities for managers, technicians, clerical workers and production staff made it difficult to identify status relationships and the general workflow of the plant. Thus, it was only through non-participant observation of plant operations that it became possible to identify working relationships and the sequences of events associated with the daily operation of the plant. In this case, the observational research was used both to enable the work process and staff relationships to be understood, and to tackle the real problem of time constraint, so common in qualitative research (see also, Dawson and Webb, 1989; Webb and Dawson, 1991).

In the work of the New Technology Research Group at Southampton University, although the timespan of the research was far longer, the time constraints were no less pressing as a consequence of the size of the projects undertaken. In short, three longitudinal case studies were conducted by an interdisciplinary research group which sought to examine the introduction of new electronic and computer technologies at the level of the individual workplace. The first of these case studies was concerned with exchange modernization in British Telecom (Clark *et al*, 1988); the second with the introduction of a computerized system of freight information control in British Rail (Dawson, 1986); and the third with the introduction of Electronic News Gathering (ENG) in Southern Television (Jacobs, 1983). The longitudinal case study method was chosen for the purpose of achieving the group's principal objective to examine the processes associated with technological change at the workplace. This included the nature of technological innovation and engineering decision-making in the economic and social context of business organization; the bearing of organizational structures on the capacity of managers to generate methods and mechanisms for the introduction and control of new technology; the consequences of technological change for the nature of work and occupations; and the effectiveness of industrial relations procedures in handling new technology issues. The case study settings were chosen to cover organizations in different stages of economic and technological development.

British Telecom (BT) provided an example of an organization operating in a rapidly expanding and changing market. By contrast, British Rail (BR) operated in a far more constrained market environment, and thus marked a critical case concerned with the introduction of a very new technology in a rather conservative organization. The ENG case study was of value in that it involved just one technological change, which took place over a short period of time and within a relatively small organization. In each of the case studies, a variety of methods were used centring on the use of documentary data, observations and interviews over periods of up to two-and-a-half years. However, because of the timescales involved in major change programmes, only parts of the change process could be covered 'as-it-happened' in BR and BT. In the latter case, some of the fieldwork involved observing the switchover from electro-mechanical Strowger exchanges to a semi-electronic telephone exchange system known as 'TXE4' (see Clark *et al*, 1988). In the former case, the study comprised a retrospective analysis of management strategy and industrial relations issues around the process of change, and an examination of workplace activities under routine operation (see Chapter 5).

In BR the examination of routine operation over a period of eighteen months meant that observational methods and repeat interviews became critical methods to establishing the process of change under so-called 'stable' conditions. Voluminous observation notes were taken during months of observation of the work of yard staff in BR marshalling yards. Typically, the author would arrive at a marshalling yard just prior to a shift changeover, and then leave just after the next shift changeover. All shifts were observed in each yard studied. Ironically, the timetabling of BR passenger services to these large marshalling yards sometimes left the author for periods of twelve hours or more trying to fight off fatigue and to remain personable and interested in the work, issues and problems of yard staff. However, the time spent at the yards proved instrumental in establishing good relationships, building up rapport and eventually being seen as another member of the organization. By the end of the study, the author was invited to a number of outside social events, he was attending informal group discussions in the local pub and, in the absence of a passenger service, would be accommodated by an outbound freight train to return to his lodging accommodation. This proximity to the people being studied, and familiarization with their work routines, produced very rich and detailed data. The observation notes collected during the study were used to validate much of the data collected during the semi-structured interviews. The procedure adopted was to transcribe the interviews, develop from them a series of themes (BR management, BR unions) and sub-themes (conflict at work, direct supervision of staff), and then write them up as annotated 'summaries'. The evidence and findings contained in the summaries were subsequently cross-checked and validated with the material contained in the observation notes prior to being used for publication (see Dawson, 1986).

A passage from the observation notes made during the period of research is presented below to illustrate the information recorded by using this method:

> At the shift changeover, Courtney and Bob had already left before either Ron or Jim had arrived. Consequently, there was no talk through, even though the importance of 'handing-over' was stressed in their interviews. However, notes had been left for both of them.
>
> Ron (Assistant Yard Manager) arrived at 1400 and spent the first 20 minutes reading through Courtney's notes and the 22 messages. He informed me that the afternoon shift is really busy and that he wouldn't have time to sit down and be interviewed, but that if I wanted to follow him around the yard that was fine.

In the example above the observation notes provide an account of what happened chronologically during the shift. Notes were also made on issues of specific concern, such as the type of contingencies yard supervisors had to deal with (see Dawson, 1987:55), and 'deviant' events (often the source from which the great railway anecdotes are created and embellished).

In the longitudinal study of General Motors-Holden's Automotive Limited (GMHAL), data were collected between October 1989 and July 1992, and comprised three main elements: a two-phase shopfloor interview programme; a key player interview programme; and a one-off series of operational workcell interviews. The two-phase shopfloor interview programme consisted of pre-change and post-change interviews with ten plant employees. The first phase interviewing was completed in 1989 and the repeat interviews were concluded in March 1991. The major objective was to get descriptions of current work practices prior to change and an in-depth discussion of their primary concerns about change, and to then compare these with their actual experience and concerns under routine operation. Other areas covered in the interview schedule included job content; work organization; working and personal relationships with other operators, shop stewards, supervisors and managers; career history; training; job satisfaction; cellular manufacture; management and industrial relations; and perceptions and attitudes towards change. The supporting programme of observation and discussion has involved regular visits to the plant in order to observe changes and to validate much of the data collected during the semi-structured interviews. The main point of contact at the plant has been with the project implementation manager who, as a part of management, works on the morning shift (shopfloor employees rotate between the morning and afternoon shifts). The focus on the morning shift has been necessary because most of the collaborative decisions on work re-organization have been made during this period, (it is also the shift in which most of the changes have occurred). However, the author has also spent a period on the afternoon and night shift, observing and informally discussing work with plant operators (although it should be noted that, due to the current recession in the automotive industry, the night shift no longer exists).

In examining the process of change from job-shop layout to cellular manufacture, interviews have been conducted with over thirty key players involved in the planning, implementation, operation and evaluation of workcells (the key player interview programme). This included plant management and project team members, staff at the CSIRO, union representatives involved in the process of change, ex-Holden and CSIRO personnel, and senior management. Interviewing this broad range of people who were part of the change programme has involved considerable travel within Australia. Each interview has been tailored to the proposed interviewee on the basis of information collected from previous interviews. Although the initial number of key players identified was less than 20, this number has increased as more information has been collected. Each interview has lasted between 1–3 hours comprising approximately 30 minutes' structured interviewing. A further element in this part of the research programme has been a search of files and documents held by the CSIRO's Division of Manufacturing Technology (DMT). This has involved two major visits to their Adelaide branch for documentary analysis and a number of other visits for discussions, observation and formal interviews at the South Australian Centre for Manufacturing and CSIRO offices in Melbourne and Adelaide.

The final dimension to the research (the operational workcell interviews) involved a series of interviews with shopfloor operators, supervisors, managers and shop stewards, who have been working under a fully operational workcell system for some time. These interviews commenced in October 1989 and were completed by August 1990 (see Dawson, 1991c). A typical interview lasted an hour and covered topics such as job history; job tasks and responsibilities; experience of change; problems, expectations and worries; involvement in change; views on management and union representation; and consequences of change for work. Data from these interviews have been supplemented by informal individual and group discussions, observation of work routines and plant layout, and documentary analysis.

In practice, the actual design of the research, the data collection techniques employed, and the analysis of the data were all influenced by various 'opportunities' and 'constraints', such as funding, period of grant, staffing of project, and the geographical location of the principal investigators (see also Dawson, 1990a). Essentially, during data collection particular emphasis has been given to the importance of using a number of complementary techniques: for example, in-depth interviewing, observation, use of documentary material, informal individual and group discussions, attendance at social functions, and research by wandering around. In addition, whilst the write-up of material often relied heavily on interview data, the information collected through the use of these other complementary techniques was equally central to the final analysis. In particular, observation notes proved to be an important data source, providing a chronology of events; an account of routine and unforeseen activities and tasks; an awareness of the informal organization of work; and the non-linearity of processes of change. On this last point, it is perhaps worth stressing that between 1989 and 1992 (when the major GM fieldwork was undertaken) changes continued to occur, highlighting the weakness of studies which saw change as an event and not a process, and the value of qualitative longitudinal research which can compare and contrast changes in perceptions and expectations over time.

In conclusion, it is worth restating the importance of ending hostile debates on either the value of quantitative research over qualitative research or vice versa. The 'divide' between qualitative and quantitative longitudinal research for understanding the process of change should centre on the research question being posed, rather than with epistemological issues which serve to perpetuate hostilities between the two approaches. It is in the nature of these different research methodologies that one is more suited to a macro analysis of change (that is, identifying key trends and changes over time), and the other to a micro analysis of change (that is, identifying the details of a particular change over time). In this book, a qualitative approach has been adopted for the purpose of examining the complex and dynamic processes associated with managing organizational transitions.

BIBLIOGRAPHY

Abrahamson, E. (1991) Managerial Fads and Fashions: The Diffusion and Rejection of Innovations, *Academy Management Review*, 16(3):586–612.

Adams, G. B. and Ingersoll, V. H. (1990) Painting Over Old Works: The Cultures of Organization in an Age of Technical Rationality, in B. A. Turner (ed.) *Organizational Symbolism*, Berlin, Walter de Gruyter.

Advisory Council for Applied Research and Development (ACARD) (1979) *Technological Change: Threats and Opportunities for the United Kingdom*, London: HMSO.

Aldag R. J. and Stearns T. M. (1991) *Management*, Cincinnati: South-Western.

Aldrich, H. (1979) *Organizations and Environments*, Englewood Cliffs: Prentice-Hall.

Aldrich, H. (1988) Paradigm Warriors: Donaldson versus the Critics of Organization Theory, *Organization Studies*, 9(1):19–24.

Anderson, P. and Tushman, M. (1991) Technological Discontinuities and Dominant Design: A Cyclical Model of Technological Change, *Administrative Science Quarterly*, 35:604–33.

Ang, C. L. and Willey, P. C. (1984) A Comparative Study of the Performance of Pure and Hybrid Group Technology Manufacturing Systems Using Computer Simulation Techniques, *International Journal of Production Research*, 22(2)L, 193–233.

Appelbaum, E. and Albin, P. (1989) Computer Rationalization and the Transformation of Work: Lessons from the Insurance Industry, in S. Wood (ed.) *The Transformation of Work*, London: Unwin Hyman.

Argyris, C. (1988) Review Essay: First- and Second-order Errors in Managing Strategic Change: The Role of Organizational Defensive Routines, in A. M. Pettigrew (ed.) *The Management of Strategic Change*, Oxford: Blackwell.

Armstrong, P. (1988) Labour and Monopoly Capitalism, in R. Hyman and W. Streeck (eds.) *New Technology and Industrial Relations*, Oxford: Blackwell.

Arnott, R. (1979) *The Story of a British Railways Project*. London: British Railways Board.

Ashen, M. (1960) The Accessibility and The Black Box, *Harvard Business Review*, 38:85–92.

Ashton, J. E. and Cook, F. X. (1989) Time to Reform Job Shop Manufacturing, *Harvard Business Review*, 67:106–11.

Atkinson, J. (1985) The Changing Corporation, in D. Clutterbuck (ed.) *New Patterns of Work*, Aldershot: Gower.

Atkinson, J. and Meager, N. (1986) *New Forms of Work Organization*. Institute of Manpower Studies Report No.121, University of Sussex.

Azani, H. (1990) Managerial Issues in the Analysis, Design and Implementation of Computer Integrated Manufacturing Systems, in W. Karwowski and M. Rahimi (eds), *Ergonomics of Hybrid Automated Systems II*, Amsterdam: Elsevier.

Badham, R. (1990) Beyond One Dimensional Automation: Human Centred System Design in European Manufacture, in W. Karwowski and M. Rahimi (eds.) *Ergonomics of Hybrid Automated Systems II*. Amsterdam: Elsevier.

Badham, R. (1991) Guest Editorial – Technology, Work and Culture, *AI & Society*, 5(4):263–76.

Badham, R. and Mathews, J. (1989) New Production Systems Debate, *Labour and Industry*, 2(2):194–246.

Bagwell, P. S. (1982) *The Railwaymen Volume 2: The Beeching Era and After*, London: Allen & Unwin.

Bailey, J., Schermerhorn, J., Hunt, J. and Osborn R. (1991) *Managing Organizational Behaviour*, Brisbane: John Wiley.

Baird, L. S., Post J. E. and Mahon J. F. (1989) *Management: Functions and Responsibilities*, New York: Harper & Row.

Bamber, G. and Patrickson, M. (1994) *Strategic Management and Organisational Change: Case Studies*, Melbourne: Longman Cheshire.

Barnett, N. S. (1991) Management and Statistical Issues Affecting Quality Improvement in Australia, *International Journal of Quality & Reliability Management*, 8(5):9–13.

Barron, I. and Curnow, R. (1979) *The Future With Microelectronics*, London: Frances Pinter.

Batstone, E. *et al* (1987) *New Technology and the Process of Labour Regulation*, Oxford: Clarendon Press.

Becker, H. (1953) Becoming a Marihuana User, *American Journal of Sociology*, 59:235–42.

Beckhard, R. (1969) *Organization Development: Strategies and Models*, Reading, Mass: Addison-Wesley.

Bench-Capon, T. J. M. (ed.) (1991) *Knowledge-Based Systems and Legal Applications*, London: Harcourt Brace Jovanovich.

Benson, I. and Lloyd, J. (1983) *New Technology and Industrial Change*, London: Kogan Page.

Bessant, J. (1983) Management and Manufacturing Innovation: The Case of Information Technology, in G. Winch (ed.) *Information Technology in Manufacturing Process: Case Studies in Technological Change*, London: Rossendale.

Biddle, G. (1990) Group Technology and its Relevance to Australian Industry. Unpublished paper, Brisbane: University of Griffith.

Blackburn, P., Coombs, R. and Green K. (1985) *Technology, Economic Growth and the Labour Process*, London: Macmillan.

Blake R. and Mouton J. (1964) *The Managerial Grid*, Houston: Gulf.

Blakemore Consulting (1987) *TQM 12 Steps*, Parramatta: Blakemore Consulting.

Bloor, G. and Dawson, P. (1994) Understanding Professional Culture in Organizational Context, *Organization Studies*, 15(2).

Boddy, D. and Buchanan, D. (1986) *Managing New Technology*, Oxford: Blackwell.

Boeker, W. (1991) Organizational Strategy: An Ecological Perspective, *Academy of Management Journal*, 34(3):613–35.

Bratton, J. (1991) Japanization at Work: The Case of Engineering Plants in Leeds, *Work, Employment & Society*, 5(3):377–95.

Braverman, H. (1974) *Labor and Monopoly Capital*, New York: Monthly Review Press.

British Broadcasting Corporation (1989) *Production Management: Just In Time*, Training Videos. London: BBC Enterprises.

British Railways Board (1970) *The 1971/1975 Freight Plan*, London: British Railways Board.

Brocka, B. and Brocka M. (1992) *Quality Management: Implementing the Best Ideas of the Masters*, Illinios: Business One Irwin.

Bryman, A. (1988a) *Quantity and Quality in Social Research*, London: Unwin Hyman.

Bryman, A. (ed.) (1988b) *Doing Research in Organizations*, London: Routledge.

Buchanan, D. (1983) Technological Imperatives and Strategic Choice, in G. Winch (ed.) *Information Technology in Manufacturing Processes*, London: Rossendale.

Buchanan, D. and Boddy, D. (eds) (1983) *Organizations in the Computer Age: Technological Imperatives and Strategic Choice*, Aldershot: Gower.

Buchanan, D. and Boddy, D. (1992) *The Expertise of the Change Agent: Public Performance and Backstage Activity*, London: Prentice-Hall.

Buchanan, D. and Huczynski, A. (1985) *Organizational Behaviour*, London: Prentice-Hall.

Buchanan, D. and Preston, D. (1991) Life in the Cell: Teamwork and Supervision in a Manufacturing Engineering Environment. Working Paper. Loughborough University Business School, University of Technology.

Buckland, S., Cordingley, B., Frohlich, D., Gilbert, N. and Luff, P. (1987) Initial Requirement Specification for the Advice System, Guildford: Alvey DHSS Demonstrator Project.

Buckland, S. and Dawson, P. (1989) Household Claiming Behaviour, *Social Policy and Administration*, 23(1):60–71.

Burlingame, J. F. (1961) Information Technology and Decentralisation, *Harvard Business Review*, 39:121–6.

Burns, T. and Stalker, R. (1961) *The Management of Innovation*, London: Tavistock.

Campbell, B. and Davies, L. (1992) *Total Quality in Australia: A Resource Guide*, Sydney: Australian Institute of Management.

Campbell, I. (1989) New Production Concepts? The West German Debates on Restructuring, *Labour and Industry*, 2(2):247–80.

Carlson, J. (1989) *Moments of Truth*, Sydney: Harper & Row.

Carroll, G. R. (ed.) (1988) *Ecological Models of Organizations*. Cambridge, Mass: Ballinger.

Cavestro, W. (1989) Automation, New Technology and Work Content, in S. Wood (ed.) *The Transformation of Work*, London: Unwin Hyman.

Child, J. (1972) Organization Structure, Environment and Performance: the Role of Strategic Choice, *Sociology* 6(1):1–22.

Child, J. (1984) *Organization: A Guide to Problems and Practice*, (2nd edn), London: Paul Chapman.

Child, J. (1988) On Organizations in Their Sectors, *Organization Studies*, 9(1):13–18.

Child, T. and Smith, C. (1987) The Context and Process of Organizational Transformation, *Journal of Management Studies*, 24(6):565–93.

Clark, J. (forthcoming) Personnel Management in an Automated Factory: Self-Supervision and Total Flexibility in Practice, in J. Clark (ed.) *Personnel Management and Technical Change*, London: Sage.

Clark, J., McLoughlin, I., Rose H. and King, R. (1988) *The Process of Technological Change: New Technology and Social Choice in the Workplace*, Cambridge: Cambridge University Press.

Clegg, S. R. (1988) The Good, The Bad and The Ugly, *Organization Studies*, 9(1):7–12.

Clegg, S. R. (1990) *Modern Organizations: Organization Studies in the Postmodern World*, London: Sage.

Clegg, S. and Dunkerley, D. (1980) *Organization, Class and Control*, London: Routledge & Kegan Paul.

Clutterbuck, D. (1985) *New Patterns of Work*, Aldershot: Gower.

Cressey, P. (1984) Participation in The Electronics Sector: The Comco Case Study, Research Paper. Glasgow: Centre for Research into Industrial Democracy and Participation.

Crompton, R. and Jones, G. (1984) *White-Collar Proletariat: Deskilling and Gender in Clerical Work*, London: Macmillan.

Crowe, T. and Jones, J. (1978) *The Computer and Society*, London: Fabian Society.

Curzon, C. (ed.) (1986) *Flexible Patterns of Work*, London: Institute of Personnel Management.

Daft, R. L. (1986) *Organization Theory and Design*, New York: West.

Dale, A. (1986) Differences in Car Usage for Married Men and Married Women: A Further Note in Response to Taylor-Gooby, *Sociology*, (20)1:91–2.

Daniel, W. (1987) *Workplace Industrial Relations and Technical Change*, London: Frances Pinter.

Dankbaar, B. (1988) New Production Concepts, Management Strategies and the Quality of Work, *Work, Employment & Society*, 2(1):25–50.

Davies, L. E. and Taylor, J. C. (1976) Technology, Organization and Job Structure, in R. Dubin (ed.) *Handbook of Work, Organization and Society*, Chicago: Rand McNally.

Dawson, D. (1989) *Just In Time*, Training Notes. London: BBC Enterprises.

Dawson, P. (1987) Computer Technology and the Job of the First-Line Supervisor, *New Technology, Work and Employment*, 2(1):47–60.

Dawson, P. (1988) Intelligent Knowledge Based Systems (IKBS): Organizational Implications, *New Technology, Work and Employment*, 3(1):56–65.

Dawson, P. (1990a) The Changing Face of Line Management, in D. Wilson and R. Rosenfeld (eds.) *Managing Organizations: Text, Readings and Cases*, Maidenhead: McGraw-Hill.

Dawson, P. (1990b) The Importance of Qualitative Longitudinal Research for Understanding Innovation and Change at Work, paper presented at the Annual Conference of the British Sociological Association at the University of Surrey, Guildford.

Dawson, P. (1991a) The Successful Management of Change: The Case of Central Linen Service South Australia, in C. Selvarajah, S. Petzall, and Q. Willis (eds.) *Management Case Studies*, Melbourne: Longman Cheshire.

Dawson, P. (1991b) Cellular Manufacture in Hardware Fabrication: The Case of General Motors-Holden's Automotive Limited, in C. Selvarajah, S. Petzall, and Q. Willis (eds.) *Management Case Studies*, Melbourne: Longman Cheshire.

Dawson, P. (1991c) Machine-Centred to Human-Centred Manufacture, *International Journal of Human Factors in Manufacturing*, 1(4):327–38.

Dawson, P. (1991d) The Historical Emergence and Changing Role of the Industrial Supervisor, *Asia Pacific HRM*, 29(2):36–50.

Dawson, P. (1991e) Lost Managers or Industrial Dinosaurs? A Reappraisal of Front-Line Management, *Australian Journal of Management*, 16(1):35–48.

Dawson, P. (1991f) Flexible Workcells: Teamwork and Group Technology on the Shopfloor, paper presented at the 9th ASTON/UMIST Annual Labour Process Conference. UMIST, Manchester.

Dawson, P. (1994) Total Quality Management, in J. Storey (ed.) *New Wave Manufacturing Strategies: Organizational and Human Resource Management Dimensions*, London: Paul Chapman.

Dawson, P. and. Buckland, S. (1986) The Potential User Study: Interim Report, Research Paper, Alvey DHSS Demonstrator Project, University of Surrey.

Dawson, P., Buckland, S. and Gilbert G. (1990) Expert Systems and the Public Provision of Welfare Benefit Advice, *Policy and Politics*, 18(1):43–54.

Dawson, P. and McLoughlin, I. (1988) New Technology and the Problem of Supervision: Enter the Information Manager, in D. Boddy, D.Buchanan and J. McCalman (eds.) *The New Management Challenge: Information Systems for Improved Performance*, London: Croom Helm.

Dawson, P. and Palmer, G. (1993) Total Quality Management in Australian and New Zealand Companies: Some Emerging Themes and Issues, *International Journal of Employment Studies*, 1(1):115–136.

Dawson, P. and Palmer, G. (forthcoming) *Total Quality Management*, Melbourne: Longman Cheshire.

Dawson, P. and Webb, J. (1989) New Production Arrangements: The Totally Flexible Cage?, *Work, Employment & Society*, 3(2):221–38.

Dawson, P. and Webb, J. (1991) Information Technology and JIT: The Case of Silica Tele Test and Production Planning, in K. Legge, C. Clegg and N. Kemp (eds.) *Case in Information Technology*, Oxford, Basil Blackwell.

Dawson, S. (1986) *Analysing Organizations*, Basingstoke: Macmillan.

Delbridge, R., Turnbull, P. and Wilkinson, B. (1991) Pushing Back the Frontiers: Management Control and Work Intensification under JIT Factory Regimes, paper presented to the 9th ASTON/UMIST Annual Labour Process Conference. UMIST, England.

Department of Industry (1982) *A Programme for Advanced Information Technology: The Report of the Alvey Committee*, London: HMSO.

Department of Industry, Technology and Commerce (1988) *Innovation for the 1990s: New Challenges for Technology Policy and Strategy*, Canberra: Commonwealth of Australia.

DiMaggio, P. J. and Powell, W. W. (1983) The Iron Cage Revisted: Institutional Isomorphism and Collective Rationality in Organizational Fields, *American Sociology Review*, 48:147–56.

Dobyns, L. and Crawford-Mason, C. (1991) *Quality or Else: The Revolution in World Business*, Boston: Houghton Mifflin.

Donaldson, L. (1985) *In Defence of Organization Theory: A Response to the Critics*, Cambridge: Cambridge University Press.

Donaldson, L. (1986) Size and Bureaucracy in East and West: A Preliminary Meta Analysis, in S. R. Clegg, D. Dunphy, and S. G. Redding, (eds.) *The Enterprise and Management in East Asia*, Hong Kong: University of Hong Kong.

Donaldson, L. (1987) Strategy, Structural Adjustment to Regain Fit and Performance: In Defence of Contingency Theory, *Journal of Management Studies*, 24(2):1–24.

Donaldson, L. (1988) In Successful Defence of Organization Theory: A Routing of the Critics, *Organization Studies*, 9(1):28–32.

Doz, Y. and Prahalad, C. K. (1987) A Process Model of Strategic Redirection in Large Complex Firms: The Case of Multinational Corporations, in A. Pettigrew (ed.) *The Management of Strategic Change*, Oxford: Basil Blackwell.

Drucker, P. F. (1990) The Emerging Theory of Manufacturing, *Harvard Business Review*, 68(3):94–102.

Duncan, R. B. (1972) Characteristics of Perceived Environments and Perceived Environmental Uncertainty, *Administrative Science Quarterly*, 17(3):313–27.

Dunford, R. W. (1992) *Organizational Behaviour: An Organizational Analysis Perspective*, Sydney: Addison-Wesley.

Dunphy, D. and Stace, D. (1990) *Under New Management: Australian Organizations in Transition*, Sydney: McGraw-Hill.

Edwards, R. (1979) *Contested Terrain: The Transformation of the Workplace in the Twentieth Century*, London: Heinemann.

Elger, T. (1990) Technical Innovation and Work Reorganization in British Manufacturing in the 1980s: Continuity, Intensification or Transformation?, *Work, Employment & Society*, Special Issue May: 67–101.

Elger, T. and Fairbrother, P. (1990) Inflexible Flexibility: Case Study Evidence and Theoretical Considerations, paper presented to the British Sociological Association Annual Conference at the University of Surrey, Guildford.

Emery, F. E. and Trist, E. L. (1965) The Causal Texture of Organizational Environments, *Human Relations*, 18:21–31.

Feigenbaum, A. (1991) *Total Quality Control*: (Fortieth Anniversary edn), New York: McGraw-Hill.

Ferner, A., (1985) Political Constraints and Management Strategies: The Case of Working Practices in British Rail, *British Journal of Industrial Relations*, 23(1):47–70.

Filstead, W. J. (1979) Qualitative Methods: A Needed Perspective in Evaluation Research, in T. D. Cook and C. S. Reichardt (eds.) *Qualitative and Quantitative Methods in Evaluation Research*, California: Sage.

Fincham, R. and Rhodes P. (1988) *The Individual, Work and Organization: Behavioural Studies for Business and Management Students*, London: Weidenfeld & Nicolson.

Fleck, J. (1991) Information-Integration and Industry – A Digest of the Development of Information-Integration: Beyond CIM, PICT Policy Research Papers. Economics and Social Research Council.

Forester, T. (ed.) (1980) *The Microelectronics Revolution*, Oxford: Basil Blackwell.

Forester, T. (ed.) (1985) *The Information Technology Revolution*, Oxford: Basil Blackwell.

Forker, L. B. (1991) Quality: American, Japanese, and Soviet Perspectives, *The Executive*, 5(4):63–74.

Francis, A. (1986) *New Technology at Work*, Oxford: Oxford University Press.

French, W. (1969) Organization Development: Objectives, Assumptions and Strategies, *California Management Review*, 12:23–46.

French, W. and Bell, C. (1983) *Organization Development: Behavioral Science Interventions for Organization Improvement*, Englewood Cliffs: Prentice-Hall.

Friedman, A. (1977) *Industry and Labour: Class Struggle at Work and Monopoly Capitalism*, London: Macmillan.

Gabor, A. (1990) *The Man Who Discovered Quality: How W. Edwards Deming Brought the Quality Revolution to America – The Stories of Ford, Xerox, and GM*, New York: Times Books.

Gabor, S. C. and Petersen, P. B. (1991) When Giants Learn to Dance: Mastering the Challenges of Strategy, Management, and Careers in the 1990s, (Book Review), *Academy of Management Executive*, 5(1):97–9.

Gagliardi, P. (1986) The Creation and Change of Organizational Cultures: A Conceptual Framework, *Organization Studies*, 7(2):117–34.

Gaither, N. (1990) *Production and Operations Management: A Problem-Solving and Decision-Making Approach*, Chicago: Dryden Press.

Gallagher, C. (1980) The History of Batch Production and Functional Factory Layout, *The Chartered Mechanical Engineer*, April: 73–6.

Gallagher, C. and Knight, W. (1973) *Group Technology*, London: Butterworth.

Gans, H. J. (1982) *Urban Villages: Group and Class in the Life of Italian-Americans*, (Originally published 1962.) New York: Free Press.

Garraham, P. and Stewart, P. (1991) Flexible Systems and the International Automobile Industry: A Case of Lean or Mean Production?, paper presented to the 9th ASTON/UMIST Annual Labour Process Conference. UMIST, Manchester.

Gilbert, G. N. (1985) Decision Support in Large Organizations, *Data Processing*, 27(4):28–30.

Gill, C. (1985) *Work, Unemployment and the New Technology*, Cambridge: Polity Press.

Gordon, D. M. (1976) Capitalist Efficiency and Socialist Efficiency, *Monthly Review*, 3:19–39.

Gray, E. R. and Smeltzer, L. R. (1990) *Management: The Competitive Edge*, New York: Macmillan.

Gray, J. L. and Starke, F. A. (1988) *Organizational Behavior: Concepts and Applications*, Columbus: Merrill.

Greiner, L. E. (1972) Evolution and Revolution as Organizations Grow, *Harvard Business Review*, 50:37–46.

Guth, W. D. and MacMillan C. (1989) Strategy Implementation Versus Middle Management Self-interest, in D. Asch and C. Bowman (eds.) *Readings in Strategic Management*, London: Macmillan.

Ham, I., Hitomi, K. and Yoshida, T. (1985) *Group Technology: Applications to Production Management*, Boston: Kluwer-Nijhoff.

Havn, E. (1991) Joint Organizational and Technical Development of CIM-Systems: An Extension of the Classic Scandanavian Approach, *AI & Society*, 5(4):308–20.

Hewlett Packard (1989) Annual Report. Hewlett Packard.

Hewlett Packard (1990) Annual Report. Hewlett Packard.

Hill, R. C. and Freedman, S. M. (1992) Managing the Quality Process: Lessons from a Baldridge Award Winner. A Conversation with CEO John W. Wallace, *The Executive*, 6(1):76–88.

Hill, S. (1991a) Why Quality Circles Failed but Total Quality Management Might Succeed, *British Journal of Industrial Relations*, 29(4):541–568.

Hill, S. (1991b) How Do You Manage A Flexible Firm? The Total Quality Model, *Work, Employment & Society*, 5(3):397–415.

Hines, C. and Searle G. (1979) *Automatic Unemployment*, Sussex: Earth Resources Research.

Hinings, C. R. (1988) Defending Organization Theory: A British View from North America, *Organization Studies*, 9(1):2–6.

Hinings, C. R. and Greenwood, R. (1988) *The Tracks and Dynamics of Strategic Change*, Oxford: Blackwell.

Hirst, C. (1974) *The British Railways System*, Milton Keynes: Open University Press.

Hodgetts, R. M. (1991) *Organizational Behaviour: Theory and Practice*, New York: Macmillan.

Hoos, I. R. (1960) When The Computer Takes Over The Office, *Harvard Business Review*, 38:102–12.

Huse, E. F. (1982) *Management*, New York: West.

Jacobs, A. (1983) Film and Electronic Technologies in the Production of Television News: A Case Study in the Introduction of Electronic News Gathering in an ITV Company. Ph.D. Thesis, University of Southampton.

James, D. (1991) Business Lacks Commitment to Total Quality Management, *Business Review Weekly*, July 5:66–70.

Jenkins, C. and Sherman, B. (1979) *The Collapse of Work*, London: Eyre Methuen.

Johnson, G. (1987) Commentary on Chapter 1, in A. Pettigrew (ed.) *The Management of Strategic Change*, Oxford: Basil Blackwell.

Kanter, R. M. (1983) *The Change Masters*, New York: Simon & Schuster.

Kanter, R. M. (1990) *When Giants Learn to Dance: Mastering the Challenges of Strategy, Management, and Careers in the 1990s*, London: Unwin Hyman.

Kanter, R. M. (1991) Transcending Business Boundaries: 12,000 World Managers View Change, *Harvard Business Review*, May-June: 151–64.

Kanter, R. M., Stein, B. A. and Jick, T. D. (1992) *The Challenge of Organizational Change: How Companies Experience It And Leaders Guide It*. New York: Free Press.

Kantrow, A. (1987) *The Constraints of Corporate Tradition*, New York: Harper & Row.

Karpik, L. (1988) Misunderstandings and Theoretical Choices, *Organization Studies*, 9(1):25–8.

Kelly, D. and Amburgey, T. L. (1991) Organizational Inertia and Momentum: A Dynamic Model of Strategic Change, *Academy of Management Journal*, 34(3):591–612.

Kelly, M. R. (1989) Alternative Forms of Work Organization under Programmable Automation, in S. Wood (ed.) *The Transformation of Work*, London: Unwin Hyman.

Kidd, P. T. (1990) Information Technology: Design for Human Involvement or Human Intervention?, in W. Karwowski, and M. Rahimi (eds.) *Ergonomics of Hybrid Automated Systems II*, Amsterdam: Elsevier.

Knight, D. O. and Wall, M. L. (1989) Using Group Technology for Improving Communication and Co-ordination Among Teams of Workers in Manufacturing Cells, *Industrial Engineering*, 21(1):28–34.

Knights, D. and Willmott, H. (eds.), (1986) *Managing the Labour Process*, Aldershot: Gower.

Knowles, M. C. (1990) *Organizational Behaviour: Changing Concepts and Applications*, Sydney: Harper & Row.

Lane, C. (1988) Industrial Change in Europe: The Pursuit of Flexible Specialisation in Britain and West Germany, *Work, Employment & Society*, 2(2):141–68.

Lansbury, R. (1992) Managing Change in a Challenging Environment, *Asia Pacific Journal of Human Resources*, 30(1):16–28.

Large, P. (1980) *The Micro Revolution*, London: Fontana.

Laughlin, R. (1991) Environmental Disturbances and Organizational Transitions and Transformations: Some Alternative Models, *Organization Studies*, 12(2):209–32.

Lawler, E. and Mohrman, S. (1985) Quality Circles after the Fad, *Harvard Business Review*, 63(1):65–71.

Lawrence, P. and Lorsch J. (1967) *Organization and Environment*, Cambridge, Mass: Harvard University Press.

Leavitt, H. J. (1964) Applied Organizational Change in Industry: Structural, Technical and Human Approaches, in W. W. Cooper, H. J. Leavitt, and M. W. Shelly (eds.) *New Perspectives in Organizations Research*, New York: John Wiley.

Leavitt, H. and Whisler T. (1958) Management in the 80s, *Harvard Business Review*, 36:41–8.

Ledford, G. E., Mohrman, S. A., Mohrman, A. M., and Lawler, E. E. (1990) The Phenomenon of Large-Scale Organizational Change, in A. M. Mohrman, S. A. Mohram, G. E. Ledford, T. G. Cummings, and E. E. Lawler (eds.) *Large-Scale Organizational Change*. San Francisco: Jossey-Bass.

Lewin, K. (1947) Frontiers in Group Dynamics, *Human Relations*, 1:5–42.

Lewin, K. (1951) *Field Theory in Social Science*, New York: Harper & Row.

Lewin, K. (1952) Group Decision and Social Change, in G. E. Swanson, T. M. Newcomb, and E. L. Hartley (eds.) *Readings in Social Psychology*, New York: Holt, Rinehart and Winston.

Littler, C. and Quinlan, M. (1989) Debates Over New Technology, New Production Concepts and Restructuring: Editorial Introduction, *Labour & Industry*, 2(2):189–93.

Littler, C. R. (1985) Taylorism, Fordism and Job Design, in D. Knights, H. Willmott, and D. Collinson (eds.) *Job Redesign: Critical Perspectives on the Labour Process*, Aldershot: Gower.

Lovering, J. (1990) A Perfunctory Sort of Post-Fordism: Economic Restructuring and Labour Market Segmentation in Britain in the 1980s, *Work, Employment & Society*, Special Issue May: 9–28.

Lubben, R. T. (1988) *Just-In-Time Manufacturing*, New York: McGraw-Hill.

Majaro, S. (1988) *The Creative Gap: Managing Ideas for Profit*, Harlow: Longman.

Martin, J. and Siehl, C. (1983) Organizational Culture and Counterculture: An Uneasy Symbiosis, *Organizational Dynamics*, 12:52–64.

Mathews, J. (1989) *Tools of Change: New Technology and the Democratisation of Work*, Sydney: Pluto Press.

McGlone, A. M. and Pudney, S. (1986) Personal Consumption, Gender and Marital Status: A Comment on Taylor-Gooby, *Sociology*, (20)1:88–90.

McLoughlin, I. (1991) Human-Centred by Design? The Adoption of CAD in the UK, *AI & Society*, 5:296–397.

McLoughlin, I. and Clark, J. (1988) *Technological Change at Work*, Milton Keynes: Open University Press.

McLoughlin, I., Dawson, P. and Smith, J. (1983) *The Introduction of a Computerised System of Freight Information Control – TOPS*, University of Southampton: New Technology Research Group.

McLoughlin, I., Rose, H. and Clark, J. (1985) Managing the Introduction of New Technology, *Omega*, 13(4):251–62.

McLoughlin, I., Carr, R., Dawson, P. and Smith, J. (1982) *Origin, Operation and Utilisation of TOPS*, University of Southampton: New Technology Research Group.

McWhinney, W. (1990) Meta-Praxis: A Framework for Making Complex Changes, in A. M. Mohrman, S. A. Mohrmnan, G. E. Ledford, T. G. Cummings and E. E. Lawler (eds.) *Large-Scale Organizational Change*, San Francisco: Jossey-Bass.

Meyer, A. D. (1982) Adapting to Environmental Jolts, *Administrative Science Quarterly*, 27:515–37.

Mitroff, I. (1987) *Business Not as Usual: Rethinking Our Individual, Corporate, and Industrial Strategies for Global Competition*, San Francisco: Jossey-Bass.

Mitroff, I. and Mohrman, S. (1987) The Slack is Gone: How the United States Lost its Competitive Edge in the World Economy, *Academy of Management Executive*, 1:65–70.

Mohrman, S. A., Ledford, G. E., and Mohrman, A. M. (1990) Conclusion: What We Have Learned About Large-Scale Organizational Change, in A. M. Mohrman, S. A. Mohrman, G. E. Ledford, T. G. Cummings and E. E. Lawler (eds.) *Large-Scale Organizational Change*. San Francisco: Jossey-Bass.

Mohrman, S. A. and Mohrman, A. M. (1990) The Environment as an Agent of Change, in A. M. Mohrman, S. A. Mohrman, G. E. Ledford, T. G. Cummings and E. E. Lawler (eds.) *Large-Scale Organizational Change*. San Francisco: Jossey-Bass.

Monden, Y. (1981) Smooth Production Lets Toyota Adapt to Demand Changes and Reduce Inventory, *Industrial Engineer*, 1(9):22–31.

Morgan, G. (1986) *Images of Organization*, London: Sage.

Morgan, G. (1988) *Riding the Waves of Change: Developing Managerial Competencies for a Turbulent World*, London: Sage.

Mumford, E. and Banks, O. (1967) *The Computer and the Clerk*, London: Routledge & Keegan Paul.

Mumford, E. and Ward, T. (1965) How the Computer Changes Management, *New Society*, 6(156):6–9.

Myers, C. (1967) *The Impact of Computers on Management*, Massachusetts: MT Press.

National Economic Development Office (1986) *Changing Working Patterns: How Companies Achieve Flexibility to Meet New Needs*, London: National Economic Development Office.

Noble, T. (1979) Social Choice in Machine Design: the Case of Automatically Controlled Machine Tools, in A. Zimbalist (ed.) *Case Studies in the Labour Process*, New York: Monthly Review Press.

Oakland, J. (1989) *Total Quality Management*, Oxford: Heinemann.

Oakley, B. and Owen, K. (1989) *Alvey: Britain's Strategic Computing Initiative*, Massachusetts: MIT Press.

Oliver, N. and Wilkinson, B. (1988) *The Japanization of British Industry*, Oxford: Basil Blackwell.

Opitz, H. and Wiendahl, H. (1971) Group Technology and Manufacturing Systems for Small and Medium Quantity Production, *International Journal of Production Research*, 9(1):181–203.

Parnaby, J. (1987) Practical Just-In-Time: Inside and Outside the Factory, The Fifth F.T. Manufacturing Forum, London: Mimeo.

Perrow, C. (1970) *Organizational Analysis*, Belmont: Wadsworth.

Peters, T. (1987) *Thriving on Chaos*, Basingstoke: Macmillan.

Peters, T. and Waterman, R. (1982) *In Search of Excellence: Lessons from America's Best-Run Companies*, New York: Harper & Row.

Petrov, V. A. (1968), *Flowline Group Production Planning*, London: Business Publications.

Pettigrew, A. M. (1985a) *The Awakening Giant: Continuity and Change in Imperial Chemical Industries*, Oxford: Basil Blackwell.

Pettigrew, A. M. (1985b) Examining Change in the Long-Term Context of Culture and Politics, in J. M. Pennings (ed.) *Organizational Strategy and Change*, San Francisco: Jossey-Bass.

Pettigrew, A. (1987a) Context and Action in the Transformation of the Firm, *Journal of Management Studies*, 24(6):649–70.

Pettigrew, A. (ed.) (1987b) *The Management of Strategic Change*, Oxford: Basil Blackwell.

Pettigrew, A. (1990) Longitudinal Field Research on Change: Theory and Practice, *Organization Science*, 1(3):267–92.

Piore, M. and Sabel, C. (1984) *The Second Industrial Divide. Possibilities for Prosperity*, New York: Basic Books.

Pollert, A. (1988) The 'Flexible Firm': Fixation or Fact?, *Work, Employment & Society*, 2(3): 218–316.

Porter, L. W., Crampon W. J. and Smith F. J. (1976) Organizational Commitment and Managerial Turnover: A Longitudinal Study, *Organizational Behavior and Human Performance*, February: 87–98.

Portman, C. (1991) Managing a Large Collaborative Project, in T. J. M. Bench-Capon (ed.) *Knowledge-Based Systems and Legal Applications*, London: Harcourt Brace Jovanovich.

Pryke, R. (1971) *Public Enterprise in Practice*, London: McGibbon & Kee.

Pryke, R. (1981) *The Nationalised Industries: Policies and Performance since 1968*, London: Martin Robertson.

Pugh, D. S., Hickson, D. J., Hinnings, C. R. and Turner, C. (1969a) The Context of Organization Structures, *Administrative Science Quarterly*, 14:91–114.

Pugh, D. S., Hickson, D. J. and Hinnings, C. R. (1969b) An Empirical Taxonomy of Structures of Work Organization, *Administrative Science Quarterly*, 14:115–26.

Pugh, D. S. and Hickson, D. J. (1976) *Organizational Structure in its Context: The Aston Programme I*, London: Saxon House.

Quinn, J. B. (1980) *Strategies for Change: Logical Incrementalism*, Homewood, Ill.: Irwin.

Quinn, J. B. (1989) Managing Strategic Change, in D. Asch, and C. Bowman (eds.) *Readings in Strategic Management*, London: Macmillan.

Reid, E. and Allen, D. (1970) *The Nationalised Industries*, London: Penguin.

Robbins, S. P. (1988) *Management: Concepts and Applications*, Englewood Cliffs: Prentice-Hall.

Roberts, P. (1990) Still a Long Way to Go, *The Australian Financial Review*, 9 November: 50.

Robson, M. (1989) Quality of Management and The Management of Quality, *Journal of Quality and Participation*, 12(1):70–3.

Rogers, E. M. (1983) *Diffusion of Innovation*, (2nd edn) New York: Free Press.

Rumelt, R. P. (1974) *Strategy, Structure and Economic Performance*, Boston: Harvard University Press.

Safizadeh, M. H. (1991) The Case of Working Groups in Manufacturing Operations, *California Management Review*, 35(4):61–82.

Salzman, H. (1991) Engineering Perspectives and Technology Design in the United States, *AI & Society*, 5(4):339–56.

Sayer, A. (1986) New Developments in Manufacturing: The JIT System, *Capital & Class*, 30:43–72.

Scase, R. and Goffee, R. (1989) *Reluctant Managers. Their Work and Lifestyles*, London: Unwin Hyman.

Schein, E. H. (1985) *Organizational Culture and Leadership*, San Francisco: Jossey-Bass.

Schenk, H. (1982) Organizational Theory and the Analysis of Economic Crisis, in H. I. Ansoff, A. Bosman and P. M. Storm (eds.) *Understanding and Managing Strategic Change: Contributions to the Theory and Practice of General Management*, Amsterdam: North-Holland.

Schonberger, R. J. (1982) *Japanese Manufacturing Techniques: Nine Hidden Lessons in Simplicity*, New York: Free Press.

Schonberger, R. J. (1986) *World Class Manufacture: The Lessons of Simplicity Applied*, New York: Free Press.

Shtub, A. (1989) Estimating the Effect of Conversion to a Group Technology Layout on the Cost of Material Handling, *Engineering Costs and Production Economics*, 16(2):103–09.

Silverman, D. (1985) *Qualitative Methodology and Sociology*, Aldershot: Gower.

Smith S. (1989) Flexible Specialisation, Automation and Mass Production, *Work, Employment & Society*, 3(2):203–20.

Sohal, A. S., Keller, A. Z. and Fouad, R. H. (1989) A Review of the Literature Relating to JIT, *International Journal of Operations and Production Management*, (9)3:15–25.

Sprouster, J. (1984) *TQC The Australian Experience*, Horwitz: Grahame.

Steers, R. M. (1991) *Introduction to Organizational Behavior*, New York: HarperCollins.

Stewart, R. (1971) *How Computers Affect Management*, London: Macmillan.

Storey, J. (1983) *Managerial Prerogative and the Question of Control*, London: Routledge & Kegan Paul.

Storey, J. (ed.) (1994) *New Wave Manufacturing Strategies: Organizational and Human Resource Management Dimensions*, London: Paul Chapman.

Streeck, W. (1987) The Uncertainties of Management in the Management of Uncertainty: Employers, Labor Relations and Industrial Adjustment, *Work, Employment & Society*, 1(3):281–308.

Taylor, B., Elger, T. and Fairbrother, P. (1991) Work Relations in Electronics: What has become of Japanisation in Britain?, paper presented to the 9th ASTON/UMIST Annual Labour Process Conference. UMIST, Manchester.

Taylor-Gooby, P. (1985) Personal Consumption and Gender, *Sociology*, 19(2):273–84.

Taylor-Gooby, P. (1986) Women, Work, Money and Marriage: A Reply to McGlone and Pudney and Dale, *Sociology*, 20(1):93–4.

Tenner, A. and DeToro, I. (1992) *Total Quality Management: Three Steps to Continuous Improvement*, Reading, Mass: Addison-Wesley.

Thompson, J. D. (1967) *Organizations in Action*, New York: McGraw-Hill.

Thompson, P. (1983) *The Nature of Work. An Introduction to Debates on the Labour Process*, London: Macmillan.

Thompson, P. (1990) Crawling from the Wreckage. The Labour Process and the Politics of Production, in D. Knights and H. Wilmott (eds.) *Labour Process Theory*, London: Macmillan.

Tichy, N. M. (1983) *Managing Strategic Change: Technical, Political, and Cultural Dynamics*, New York: John Wiley.

Turnbull, P. (1988) The limits to Japanisation: 'Just-In-Time', Labour Relations and the UK Automotive Industry, *New Technology, Work and Employment*, 3(1):7–20.

Turner, B. A. (ed.) (1990) *Organizational Symbolism*, Berlin: Walter de Gruyter.

Tushman, M. and Romanelli, E. (1985) Organizational Evolution: A Metamorphosis Model of Convergency and Reorientation, in L. Cummings and B. Staw (eds.) *Research in Organizational Behaviour*, Greenwich: JAI Press.

Twiss, B. and Goodridge, M. (1989) *Managing Technology for Competitive Advantage*, London: Pitman.

Ulrich, D. and Lake, D. (1991) Organizational Capability: Creating Competitive Advantage, *Academy of Management Executive*, (5)1:77–92.

Vail, P. B. (1989) *Managing as a Performing Art*, San Francisco: Jossey-Bass.

Vecchio, R. P., Hearn, G. and Southey, G. (1992) *Organizational Behaviour: Life at Work in Australia*, Sydney: Harcourt Brace Jovanovich.

Vesey, J. T. (1991) The New Competitors: They Think in Terms of 'Speed-to-Market', *Academy of Management Executive*, (5)2:23–33.

Vries J. de, and Water, H. van de (1992) Quality Circles, the Production Function and Quality of Working Life: Results of a Study in Seven Large Companies, *International Journal of Quality & Reliability Management*, 9(4):30–45.

Waterman R. H. (1988) *The Renewal Factor: How the Best Get and Keep the Competitive Edge*, New York: Bantam.

Webb, J. and Dawson, P. (1991) Measure for measure: strategic change in an electronic instruments corporation, *Journal of Management Studies*, 28(2):191–206.

Webster, J. (1992) Chicken or Egg? The Interaction Between Manufacturing Technologies and Paradigms of Work Organization, in R. Badham, (ed.)

Systems, Networks and Configurations: Inside the Implementation Process, Special Edition of *International Journal of Human Factors in Manufacturing*.

Weir, M. and Mills S. (1973) The Supervisor as a Change Catalyst, *Industrial Relations Journal*, 4(4):1–69.

Weisbord, M. R. (1988) *Productive Workplaces: Organizing and Managing for Dignity, Meaning and Community*, San Francisco: Jossey-Bass.

Wemmerlov, U. and Hyer, N. L. (1989b) Cellular Manufacturing in the US Industry: A Survey of Users, *International Journal of Production Research*, 27(9):1511–30.

Whipp, R., Rosenfeld, R. and Pettigrew, A. (1987) Understanding Strategic Change Processes: Some Preliminary British Findings, in A. Pettigrew (ed.) *The Management of Strategic Change*, Oxford: Basil Blackwell.

Whisler, T. (1967) The Impact of Information Technology on Organizational Control, in C. Myers (ed.) *The Impact of Computers on Management*, Cambridge Mass: MIT Press.

Whisler, T. (1970) *The Impact of Computers on Organizations*, New York: Praeger.

Whittle, S. (1992) Total Quality Management: Redundant Approaches to Culture Change, *Quality of Working Life News & Abstracts*, 110:8–13.

Whyte, W. F. (1984) *Learning from the Field*, California: Sage.

Wickens, P. (1987) *The Road to Nissan: Flexibility, Quality, Teamwork*, Basingstoke: Macmillan

Wilkinson, B. (1983) *The Shop Floor Politics of New Technology*, London: Heinemann.

Wilson, D. C. and Rosenfeld R. H. (1990) *Managing Organizations: Texts, Readings and Cases*, London: McGraw-Hill.

Womack, J. P., Jones, D. T. and Roos, D. (1990) *The Machine that Changed the World*, New York: Rawson Associates.

Wood, S. (1979) A Reappraisal of the Contingency Approach to Organization, *Journal of Management Studies*, 16(3):334–354.

Wood, S. (1989a) New Wave Management?, *Work, Employment & Society*, 3(3):379–402.

Wood, S. (1989b) The Transformation of Work? in S. Wood (ed.) *The Transformation of Work?*, London: Unwin Hyman.

Wood, S. (1990) Japanization and/or Toyotaism, Working Paper, London: London School of Economics.

Woodward, J. (1980) *Industrial Organization: Theory and Practice*, (2nd edn), Oxford: Oxford University Press.

Zegveld, W. (1987) Technology and Change in Industrial Society: Implications for Public Policy, *Research Policy*, 15:175–86.

Zuboff, S. (1988) *In the Age of the Smart Machine*, New York: Heinemann.

INDEX